An Amish Miracle

Other Books by These Authors

OTHER AMISH NOVELLA COLLECTIONS

An Amish Christmas

An Amish Gathering

An Amish Love

An Amish Wedding

An Amish Kitchen

ALSO BY BETH WISEMAN

The Daughters of the Promise novels

Plain Perfect

Plain Pursuit

Plain Promise

Plain Paradise

Plain Proposal

Plain Peace

The Land of Canaan novels

Seek Me With All Your Heart

The Wonder of Your Love

His Love Endures Forever

Need You Now

The House That Love Built

ALSO BY RUTH REID

The Heaven on Earth novels

The Promise of an Angel

Brush of Angel's Wings

An Angel by Her Side

ALSO BY MARY ELLIS

The Miller Family series

A Widow's Hope

Never Far from Home

The Way to a Man's Heart

An Amish Family Reunion

The Wayne County series

Abigail's New Hope

A Marriage for Meghan

The New Beginnings series

Living in Harmony

Love Comes to Paradise

A Little Bit of Charm

An Amish Miracle

Mary Ellis

Ruth Reid

Beth Wiseman

THOMAS NELSON
Since 1798

NASHVILLE   DALLAS   MEXICO CITY   RIO DE JANEIRO

Published in Nashville, Tennessee, by Thomas Nelson. Thomas Nelson is a registered trademark of Thomas Nelson, Inc.

Scripture quatations are taken from THE NEW KING JAMES VERSION © 1982 by Thomas Nelson, Inc. Used by permission. All rights reserved. And from the Holy Bible, New International Version®, NIV®. Copyright © 1973, 1978, 1984, 2011, by Biblica, Inc.™ Used by permission of Zondervan. All rights reserved worldwide. www.zondervan.com

Thomas Nelson, Inc., titles may be purchased in bulk for educational, business, fund-raising, or sales promotional use. For information, please e-mail SpecialMarkets@ThomasNelson.com.

Publisher's Note: This novel is a work of fiction. Names, characters, places, and incidents are either products of the author's imagination or used fictitiously. All characters are fictional, and any similarity to people living or dead is purely coincidental.

Library of Congress Cataloging-in-Publication Data

Ellis, Mary, 1951-
  An Amish Miracle / Mary Ellis, Ruth Reid, Beth Wiseman.
      pages cm
  ISBN 978-1-4016-8870-7 (trade paper)
  1. Amish—Fiction. 2. Christian fiction. I. Reid, Ruth, 1963– II. Wiseman, Beth, 1962–
III. Title.
  PS3626.E36A88 2013
  813'.6—dc23   2013025298

Printed in the United States of America

13 14 15 16 17 18 RRD 6 5 4 3 2 1

Mary: This story in dedicated to my parents who adopted me from the Berea Children's Home (originally called the German Methodist Orphan Asylum) through Cuyahoga County Children's Services in Ohio. Thanks for all your guidance and love . . . and thanks especially for picking me.

Ruth: For their unconditional love and godly guidance, I dedicate Always His Provision to Paul and Kathy Droste. I love you, Dad. Kathy, you've been so helpful and influential in my writing. Thank you so much.

Beth: To Danny Kaspar

Contents

Glossary

ab im kopp: off in the head, crazy

ach: oh

aenti: aunt

appeditlich: delicious

Ausbund: Amish hymnal

ausleger: undertaker

bauch: stomach

boppli, bopplin: baby, babies

bruder: brother

daadi, grossdaadi: grandfather

daed: dad

danki: thank you

Das Loblied: Amish hymn of praise, sung in every Amish worship
 service

Derr Herr: God

dochder: daughter

dumm: dumb

Glossary

dummkopp: dunce

ehemann: husband

Englisch, Englischer: non-Amish

fater: father

fraa: wife

freind: friend

freinden: friends

fremm: strange

froh: happy

gegisch: silly

gern gschehne: you're welcome

Gott: God

grank: sick

grossvader: grandfather

guder mariye: good morning

gut: good

gut nacht: good night

hatt: hard

haus: house

hiya: hello

Ich liebe dich: I love you

kaffi: coffee

kalt: cold

kapp: prayer cap worn by all Amish women

kichlin: cookies

kind, kinner: child, children

kinskind, kinskinner: grandchild, grandchildren

kumm: come

lieb: love

maed: young women, girls

maedel: girl

mamm: mom, mama

mammi, grossmammi: grandmother

mei: my

mudder: mother

narrisch: crazy

nau: now

nee: no

net: not

Ordnung: the written and unwritten rules of the Amish; the understood behavior by which the Amish are expected to live, passed down from generation to generation. Most Amish know the rules by heart.

rumschpringe: running around period when a teenager turns sixteen years old

schee: pretty

schtupp: family room

schul: school

schweschder: sister

schwester/schwestern: sister/sisters

Sei se gut: please

The Budget: a weekly newspaper serving Amish and Mennonite communities everywhere

Was iss letz?: What's wrong?

wedder: weather

welcum: welcome

Glossary

Wie bischt?: How are you?

Wie geht's: How do you do? or Good day!

willkumm: welcome

wunderbaar: wonderful

ya: yes

yummasetti: a classic Amish hot dish made with spaghetti, cheese, and hamburger

Always in My Heart

Mary Ellis

Chapter One

Paradise, Pennsylvania

Stephen Bowman switched off the generator, swiped his brow with a handkerchief, and straightened his spine. Not even nine o'clock and the July day was already sweltering.

Since dawn he had milked, fed, and watered the animals and turned them out to pasture. The milk was now stored in the cooling room, awaiting pickup, and he was ready for breakfast.

He headed for the house, his stomach rumbling. What might his *fraa* have made this morning? Buttermilk pancakes swimming in maple syrup? A mushroom omelet covered with melted cheddar? Maybe a thick slab of ham with an over-easy egg on the side?

He entered the kitchen to find a box of cornflakes on the table, along with a banana. The pot of coffee had grown cold on the stove.

After thirteen years, he knew his *fraa* well. Hope usually only served a cold breakfast when pressed for time or when—

Stephen bolted toward the front room. "Hope?"

His wife sat in the rocking chair with her sewing basket at her feet. Sweat beaded at her hairline. The tiny white *kapp* she'd been crocheting lay abandoned in her lap.

"When did the contractions start?" He tried to keep his voice calm so as not to frighten his daughters. The three girls sat on the couch staring at their mother and holding hands.

Hope said nothing for at least half a minute. Then she spoke through gritted teeth. "A few . . . hours ago."

"Why didn't you send Josie to the milking parlor for me?" His glance flickered to his eldest *dochder*, who peered up at him through thick lashes.

"Thought I had plenty of time to finish this *kapp* and pair of booties." Her speech improved as the contraction loosened.

"You know what the doctor said. Things move along faster with each new bundle of Bowman joy." Stephen chucked his youngest child under the chin. Little Greta's green eyes sparkled as she giggled.

"True enough, but I still thought I had enough time. No sense dragging Jane Beachy out too soon." Hope's voice returned to normal, and her fingers released their grip on the chair. "She has her own family to tend."

"Midwives are accustomed to being called out at all hours of the day or night. At least she's not sleeping at this hour. I'll leave now to fetch her."

"May I ride with you, *Daed*?" asked Josie. She scrambled from her position on the couch to land on the floor near Hope's feet. "I could help Jane carry in things."

"*Nee.*" Stephen gave her *kapp* ribbon a pull. "You stay and help *mamm* get things ready." He felt himself blush. Discussing babies-on-the-way was not a proper topic between father and daughter. "You understand God is bringing us another *boppli*?" He peered at one pair of rounded eyes after another.

"Of course I do," she said, as though mildly insulted.

"*Ya*," replied the younger two, heads nodding. "*Mamm* said so. *Bruder* this time?" asked seven-year-old Emily.

"We'll soon find out." He buzzed a kiss across his wife's *kapp*. "I'm off. Put down your sewing, *fraa*. I believe you should start moving in the direction of our bedroom. But don't pick up a paintbrush to give the kitchen a fresh coat."

Stephen smiled at the memory of a woman in their district who decided to paint a room during labor. Things happened so fast she gave birth in their bathtub, assisted solely by her eldest daughter. By the time the midwife arrived, the mother had been bathed and was resting comfortably with her new son sleeping in the crook of her arm.

Suddenly, Hope grabbed his sleeve, her brown eyes huge. "I've prayed all morning for this one to be a boy." She turned her face up to him.

Stephen patted her hand. "We shall be grateful for another healthy child, whether boy or girl." He gazed at his family, then strode from the room. Within minutes Stephen hitched his fastest gelding to the buggy and raced down their lane. Not much traffic crowded the country roads, no speeding cars that could panic a skittish horse. And so far, no buses with tourists leaning out of windows snapping pictures.

He used the time to say his prayers and count his blessings. God had smiled upon the Bowman family. His wife and daughters were healthy; he'd inherited a fertile, productive farm from his father, and his large herd of Holstein cows supplied an abundance of milk. Even the new bulls had drawn decent prices from the veal producers, providing necessary cash to pay taxes, and medical bills, and to buy diesel fuel.

At thirty-five, Stephen Bowman was content.

But a son would be nice.

It would be good to have help with the harder farm chores. Although Josie could already plant a straight row of corn and pick more than her weight in beans in a day, he didn't want women riding dangerous equipment. Some chores like plowing, harrowing, and harvesting remained men's work. Growing up, he'd witnessed firsthand his father's challenge of having only one son. His sisters eventually married and moved to other parts of Lancaster County or to different states altogether. Stephen remained on the farm helping his *daed* until a heart attack took him to the gates of heaven.

Would an early death be his destiny? Only God knew the future, and whether this coming child would be another girl. He didn't feel comfortable praying for one over the other.

"Still, a son would be nice, Lord."

He whispered the words against his better judgment and added a hasty, "But Thy will be done."

Turning into the Beachy yard, a red-cheeked Nathan Beachy hurried to greet him. "Come for Jane, *ya?*" Nathan shielded his eyes from the glare of a hot July sun.

"We'd be obliged if Jane could lend a hand, if she's not too busy." Both men spoke in even tones as they marched quickly toward the house.

"Fraa?" called Nathan. "Stephen Bowman has come." They waited less than a minute before the experienced midwife bustled down the stairs into the kitchen.

She carried her black satchel, a diaper bag, and a sleeping infant. "Time has come, then." Jane issued a statement rather than asked a question. "Our *kinner* are dressed and fed," she said to Nathan. "They should be fine while you're in the fields since the oldest aren't back to school yet." A shy teenager peeked around her *mamm*. "No telling when I'll be home." Jane kissed his cheek, then hurried out the door with Stephen at her heels. Flanked by his brood, Nathan remained on the porch, waving.

"Might be home sooner than you think," murmured Stephen once they'd climbed into his buggy. With another man within earshot, it would have been embarrassing, but he didn't mind discussing the delicate topic with a professional midwife.

Jane pivoted toward him. "Why? How far along is she?"

Stephen shook the reins and released the brake. "Can't say in terms of minutes between pains, but from what I could gather, I should have fetched you at first light, if not sooner."

The midwife picked up the seldom-used crop and slapped it lightly on the horse's broad back. "Git up, there," she commanded. "Save the meandering for the trip back. We've got a *boppli* on the way!"

Stephen Bowman felt his excitement ratchet up a notch to match her enthusiasm. Another one of God's miracles was about to take place, right in his own family.

~

Hope experienced a moment of panic when the door closed behind Stephen. She was alone with three little ones with a fourth about to make a grand entrance.

I will never leave you or forsake you.

God's promise gave her strength as she struggled to her feet and dropped her crocheting into the basket.

"Come, Josie, we must prepare. Emily, Greta, I want you to stay in your room. You may play or read, but do not come downstairs until Josie calls you." Hope touched each of their cheeks tenderly. "*Mamm* will be fine."

Emily hugged her around the waist, then took Greta's hand and scampered up the steps. Greta glanced back at Hope but left obediently with her sister.

"What should I do?" asked Josie. Her dark eyes glowed with the eagerness of new responsibility. At twelve, the girl was ready for all but the most delicate portion of childbirth.

"Fill both kettles and the soup pot with water. Then bring them to a low boil. Jane will need plenty of warm water to bathe the *boppli* and me." She walked gingerly toward their ground-floor bedroom, her belly feeling impossibly heavy. "First, help me put the rubber sheet on the bed and set out the towels. And we'll need blankets to keep the baby warm. Jane will bring whatever else is needed."

By the time the next contraction stole her breath, the birthing room was ready. Josie went to prepare the kitchen while Hope climbed into bed, covering herself with their oldest sheet. "Won't be long now, Lord," she whispered.

Hope squeezed her eyes shut and concentrated on not screaming as a contraction hit. Just when she was about to call Josie to help, Jane Beachy bustled into the room, her sleeves rolled up and her hands still wet from scrubbing. A grin stretched across her face.

"Did you figure to pull this off alone to save yourself my fee?" Jane said. "Nothing doing, Hope Bowman. Nathan and I plan to use that money to visit Paris, France, in the springtime." She pulled long gloves up to her elbows.

The joke distracted Hope from counting breaths. "Please don't make me laugh until this is said and done." Josie retreated from the room, and Hope positioned herself for examination.

"From the looks of things, you won't have to wait long to appreciate my sense of humor." Jane rushed to prepare for the final stage. "You cut this one a bit close to the wire. Did you think that I charged by the hour?"

Her quip almost sent Hope over the edge. She had to wait several minutes to retort. "Remind me to come to the birth of your next baby. Between now and then I will save up a bag of jokes."

And so, together the two longtime friends brought a life into the world. The newest little girl to the Lancaster Amish community.

Hope swallowed down an initial pang of disappointment when Jane announced, "Looks like we have a fourth daughter for the Bowman family. All ten fingers and toes with plenty of hair—she looks perfect to me." A loud wail signaled a strong pair of lungs as well. "I'll get her cleaned up and warm and be back in a jiffy."

Jane disappeared from the bedroom, leaving Hope alone. "Thank You, Lord," she whispered, "for the smooth delivery and another healthy child." She didn't put words to her dissatisfaction and hoped God would overlook her discontent.

This is nobody's fault but mine.

Jane bathed Hope and helped her into a fresh nightgown, then she took the baby into the kitchen to examine, weigh, and bundle into a warm quilt. Hope could hear Jane instructing Stephen and Josie on their tasks for the next few days. When she returned to the bedroom, Hope reached for her hand, forcing a smile. "*Danki* for all you've done."

"All in a good day's work." Jane pushed damp hair off the new mother's forehead. "You've been blessed, Hope Bowman."

"*Ya*, but not as much as you and Nathan, with three sons." The words escaped Hope's mouth before she could stop herself. She felt a hot flush rise up her neck into her face.

Jane bundled the laundry and tidied the bedroom. "*Ya*, sons are helpful, but who's to say what your next one will be? The next dozen or so might be boys." She winked and plumped an extra pillow behind Hope's back.

Hope pressed a palm on her still-swollen belly. "Let's not talk about the next dozen quite so soon."

"I'll be back tomorrow to check on you. The paperwork has been filled out except for the baby's name." In a rare display of affection, Jane leaned over and kissed Hope's cheek. "You and Stephen put your heads together and come up with something *gut*." Then she bustled from the room.

But Hope had no chance to wallow in self-pity. Just as she finished feeding her infant, her best friend, Rosa Hostetler, marched into the room with a broad smile stretched across her face. "I heard from Jane Beachy on her way home you might have someone new to show off."

"Goodness, word travels fast." Hope pulled back the coverlet to reveal a pink face. "Meet the youngest Bowman *dochder*." She lifted the baby for inspection.

"May I hold her? Oh, she's just perfect. I'll bet she'll be a cheerful *boppli* too." She took the infant in her arms and strolled around the room explaining doors, windows, and vases of flowers as though the newborn were ready for language instruction.

"Let that *boppli* sleep. You can start the lessons next week." Throughout Rosa's fussing, the littlest Bowman slumbered peacefully.

"What do you suppose you'll call her?"

Hope's smile faded. "I'd selected David or Joseph—names of strength and fortitude. I was so sure this one would be a boy." Unbidden, tears streamed down her face.

"*Ach*, the next one will be." Rosa kissed the infant before settling her into the crook of Hope's arm.

As Hope tucked the blanket beneath the tiny chin, her tears fell unchecked. "You don't understand," she whispered. "There'll be no boys for me—not after what I have done." The words strangled in her throat. "God is punishing me just as He punishes all who disobey Him."

Rosa perched on the edge of the bed. "I doubt He would punish a sixteen-year-old girl. You had no choice." She slipped an arm around her friend's shoulder.

Hope shook her head violently. "We always have a choice. I could have refused. I could have run away. Now, because of my shame, I'll never give Stephen a son."

"Hush," Rosa demanded. "Stop those tears. You don't know what God has planned. No more worrying. You must have faith."

Faith. Hope looked into Rosa's eyes. The woman had lost so

much. She had been married for five years without the blessing of a child. And then, two years ago her husband, Uriah, had died and left her alone. Alone and struggling, both financially and emotionally.

And yet here she was talking to her best friend about faith. About trusting God, no matter what the circumstances. If Rosa could have faith, Hope certainly could.

She nodded and swallowed hard. "You're right. There's no place for wallowing in self-pity. You've given me the perfect name for our new little one—Faith." She brushed a kiss across the downy head. "And faith is what I shall have."

Chapter Two

Within two days Hope returned to most of her housewife duties. Stephen would still carry heavy cases of canning jars up from the cellar, and Josie did most of the weeding and harvesting in the garden, but Hope resumed cooking, cleaning, and ironing for her family. Rosa offered to come over each laundry day for the next month, and Hope's sister Rebecca volunteered to stay for several weeks—an offer Hope declined.

Baby Faith was thriving. Stephen loved the name, so when the midwife returned the next day, she completed the birth certificate. One week later, on a morning sunny and mild, Hope fixed a plate of sandwiches for Stephen's lunch, packed her four daughters into the buggy, and drove to her *mamm's* farm, a dozen miles away.

Hope spotted her mother near the barn. *"Guder mariye,"* she called. "I brought the newest Bowman to see you."

Mamm shifted the basket of tomatoes to her other hand and hobbled toward the buggy as fast as her bad knees would allow. "Good morning to you. I wondered when I'd see my new *kinskind*." She paused with a hand on her hip as the Bowman daughters sprang from the buggy. "If you didn't show up by noon, I would have told Silas to hitch the team to go to you. I started to worry something was wrong." Martha handed the basket to Emily and took hold of Josie's arm for support. Together they moved slowly toward the house.

"Everything went smoothly, no problems. And here is little Faith." Hope shifted the baby closer and peeled back the cover.

Martha chuckled. "Look at those eyelashes. This one will be a beauty like the other three." She patted the top of Greta's head. "Faith is a *gut* name too—none in the family yet and we're up to fourteen *kinskinner*."

A grimace pinched her features "Let's go inside. I'm ready for a cup of coffee."

Hope prodded Emily and Greta down the path. "Your knees acting up again?"

Martha waited until they were in the kitchen to reply. "*Ya*, I knelt in the garden yesterday. Even though I used that foam pad you bought, it still was a mistake. When I couldn't get up, your *daed* had to pull me to my feet. But I couldn't bear to leave plump, ripe vegetables hanging on the ground."

"Folks drop by often to visit. Send somebody young out to finish the rows." Hope placed the coffeepot on the burner to reheat while Josie set out cups, milk, sugar, and a plate of chocolate chip cookies.

"Suppose that's what I should do, but I hate not keeping up with my own chores." She angled a grin at Josie. "*Danki*, dear heart. Now let me hold that *boppli*; I've waited long enough."

Martha performed her own inspection of Faith, making sure all appendages were accounted for. "I'm your *Grossmammi* Klobentz," she whispered into the baby's ear. "And it will be my pleasure to spoil you terribly." She turned back to Hope. "She's on the thin side, but as long as she nurses well, that should take care of itself. God bless you, Faith Bowman." She kissed the tiny nose lightly, then settled her in the baby carrier they'd brought in. "How did Stephen take the news?" Martha asked as Faith drifted back to sleep.

Hope shifted on her feet. "What news?"

Martha frowned. "That he's got another girl and no sons yet." She held her cup with gnarled fingers.

Hope's spine stiffened. "He was thrilled that God graced us with another healthy child. Besides, Josie helps with chores as well as any *boy*." She winked at her, which brought a smile to the twelve-year-old's face.

"Of course she does. You've got *gut kinner*, no doubt about it." Martha sipped her coffee, not taking her focus off her daughter.

"Josie, why don't you empty that basket into the sink? I'll wash those tomatoes later. Then take your *schwestern* to the garden and finish picking any tomatoes that I might have missed. Be sure to check the low stems where the sweet ones hide."

Hope smiled and nodded to her girls, then listened to the clock *tick-tock* until they left the house. Turning to face her mother, her pleasant expression vanished. "What *can* Stephen say? Of course he wants sons, but there's nothing we can do." She inhaled deeply and exhaled with a gush. "After what I did, God will never bring us a boy." Hope clenched her teeth.

"What do you mean?" Martha's forehead furrowed.

"You know very well what I mean. God gave me a son and I

gave him away." Hope spoke with surprising vehemence. "Now even if I have twenty *kinner*, every one of them will be a girl."

Martha stirred a heaping spoonful of sugar into her coffee. "*Ach,* you don't know that. Adoption was the best solution for the situation. You were only sixteen years old and in no way able to care for a child." The crimson stain on her cheeks indicated the topic shamed her *mamm*, even after all these years.

Hope splayed her palms flat on the table. "Unable according to whom—*Daed*?"

"*Ya,* according to him. A husband is the head of the family. Scripture says so. Silas did what he thought best." A shaky hand lifted the mug to her lips.

"Best for him and best for the district. He was ashamed of me and wanted to bury the matter." Hope replaced the cookie on the plate, her appetite gone. "He never thought once about the guilt I would carry for the rest of my life." Against her will, tears flooded her eyes.

Martha shook her head. "No, *dochder*. Your father was considering you too. What if no man would marry you? Stephen might not have wanted someone unchaste. Then you never would have had your family."

Hope felt her face turn ugly. "Instead, I have lived a lie and broken a commandment with my deception."

Martha Klobentz paled. "You did not lie. No one knew, so no one asked questions."

"You should know better than to pick and choose interpretations, playing with words as though we can fool God."

Her mother shuddered at the statement. "Hush now. Don't say

such things." Martha glanced at the doors and windows. "What's done is done. Nothing can be gained by rehashing the past. You will only torment yourself."

"Maybe so, but I can't see how torment can be avoided." Hope rose to her feet with as much dignity as possible. "I'd better wash the tomatoes before the next load arrives."

For several minutes the two women remained silent, each lost in their own memories. "Should I boil water to blanche these? Why don't we can spaghetti sauce with today's pickings?"

Martha pushed herself up from the table. "Sounds *gut*. I'll fetch the new blanket I knitted for Faith, plus the two dozen muslin cloths I hemmed into diapers."

As she shuffled from the room, a wave of sorrow filled Hope's heart. She hated arguing with her *mamm*.

Besides, she was right: nothing could be done about the past.

Rolling over in bed, Hope briefly buried her face beneath the damp pillow. The July heat and humidity made a good night's rest impossible. Their small battery fan did little to move the air. Stephen had already risen for morning chores, allowing her a few extra minutes of sleep. Baby Faith, however, was not so indulgent. She alerted the household with a piercing wail that her diaper needed changing and she was hungry.

Throwing back the covers, Hope checked the clock. "Goodness," she exclaimed, "I'd better get a move on."

This was sisters' day—a tradition in their district. Women—young and old, married and single—gathered to help a family by sewing, quilting, canning, or cleaning to lighten the family's burden. Today they were coming to the Bowmans'.

Although Hope felt fully recovered, the women insisted on cleaning her house from top to bottom, washing and ironing her clothes, and cooking a few meals. Most had already dropped off pots of soup or casseroles for the first days after Faith's arrival. Now she would have an opportunity to return pots and bowls and show off her new *boppli*.

Lifting her squalling infant from the bedside cradle, she set to work changing a sodden diaper, then settled Faith comfortably to nurse.

Hope loved this time of morning. Rocking in a chair handmade by Stephen's *grossdaadi*, she prayed and thanked God for her blessings. Then she asked for guidance, along with a healthy dose of patience. During these moments of quiet introspection, her thoughts usually drifted to her firstborn. *Please, Lord, guide and protect my son, wherever he is. Draw him close and keep him safe from harm; help him find the peace that can only come from knowing You.*

Not that she knew much about peace. Seldom a day went by that Hope didn't regret giving her firstborn child up for adoption. But a daughter cannot defy her father, especially not a father like Silas Klobentz. If the boy had remained Amish, he would be finished with school and learning a craft or trade by now, or helping Stephen with their herd of Holsteins. He would almost be a man.

Hope squeezed her eyes shut to fight back tears. *Given away like old boots in the charity collection bin at the IGA.* Her last prayer that morning was for the *Englischers* who'd welcomed her baby into their home, providing the love Hope hadn't been able to give. "Be patient, be strong, and know that I am forever grateful." She whispered the familiar words while stroking Faith's head.

While the infant nursed, Hope tried to turn her thoughts to other things. Lingering too long in the past hurt too much.

Still, the memories would not leave her. Memories of a dark night when she'd chosen to walk home from a singing instead of riding with one of her *bruders*. Both Paul and Daniel had been courting young women. She knew neither relished the idea of a young *schwester* tagging along, eavesdropping on conversations, or watching for stolen kisses in the moonlight. Her sister had already accepted a ride with a beau.

And so Hope had set out on a lonely road by herself, a road without streetlights or porch lights to discourage those with wicked intent.

The pickup truck's headlights had blinded her when she turned to see who was approaching so slowly.

He had told her he was sick and needed assistance with calling for help.

He'd smiled and spoken in a soft voice.

He'd waved her closer to the truck, indicating she could use his cell phone to call his family. Too late Hope had smelled alcohol on his breath and noticed his glassy eyes. Too late her mind had registered danger from his slurred speech and clumsy movements.

"Aren't you a pretty lit'l Amish gal? How 'bout you climb up here and get to know a real man for a change. Not one of them sissy Amish boys with the stupid haircut."

He had laughed, grabbed her by the wrists, and dragged her into the truck cab. He hadn't listened to her pleas for mercy. He cared nothing for her tears. In the darkness he barely looked at her face, yet managed to change her life forever. Now shame and sorrow would stare back whenever she looked into a mirror.

Struggling to her feet, Hope laid Faith in the cradle. The memories might not leave her, but she had three other daughters to look after and work to do.

Within the hour, Josie, Emily, and Greta were bathed, dressed, and finished with breakfast. With his milking finished until evening, Stephen had bolted down his scrambled eggs and toast and headed to the fields. When the first buggy rolled up the Bowman driveway, Hope was standing on the porch waiting, her nightmare banished to the far corners of her mind.

"Welcum," she called, opening the door wide.

Three women scrambled down. While two hurried toward her carrying cloth shopping bags, one stayed behind to water the horse and turn him into the paddock. "I hope you haven't cleaned house in anticipation of sisters' day," called Rosa. "That's what we're here for."

Rosa's face showed more enthusiasm than usual. "Where's that *boppli?*" Dropping her sacks on the kitchen table, Rosa marched through the house until she found Faith in the crib near the front room window.

Hope trailed after her best friend. How Rosa loved *bopplin!* A widow at thirty with no children of her own, unless she remarried, she would never know the joy of motherhood.

"Are you going to sleep all day?" Rosa lifted Faith free from her summer blanket. "We need to get busy with our lessons. I see you've already discovered the delicious mystery of one's own thumb."

The crunch of gravel signaled the arrival of more buggies, so Hope left Rosa to bond with baby Faith.

"There you are!" said Ida May, the oldest woman in their district. "For a moment we feared you'd gone to the movies, leaving us to do your work without supervision."

Everyone laughed, including Hope. "And miss the delicious lunch you'll fix, Ida May? Not in a million years."

"Don't puff me up with your flattery." The old woman's face broke into a smile. "Why don't I tackle your ironing basket and leave the scrubbing and window washing to the younger gals? Look at those streaks," she teased, pointing to a nearly faultless pane of glass.

"I'll clean the windows, Hope," piped up a voice from the corner. It was Becky Byler, a shy girl who never ate anything but rabbit food and yet seemed heavier every time Hope saw her.

Hope approached her and gave her shoulders a quick squeeze. "Becky, so *gut* to see you. Thanks for coming."

"I'll use vinegar and water on the windows, then dry them with newspapers," Becky said. "And I brought a tray of sliced veggies for our lunch."

"Raw vegetables sound wonderful on a hot day. *Danki.*"

Hope watched as Becky headed to the stairwell for the bucket. She sent up a quick prayer for the girl and made a mental note to pay particular attention to Becky today.

Chapter Three

While waiting for the women to leave, Stephen cleaned every piece of milking equipment, scrubbed all the feed and water buckets, and swept the barn floor. Now he stood watching the last buggy roll down the driveway. He appreciated their help today, but spending thirty minutes at lunchtime discussing who had the best recipe for stuffed cabbage leaves didn't interest him.

Hope probably felt the same regarding alfalfa prices whenever she accompanied him to the grain elevator in Paradise. But there were benefits to the visit: Ida May's potato-bacon soup was excellent, and she had brought so much there was bound to be a big pot left over.

Peeking around the corner to make sure no *fraa* had doubled back, Stephen sprinted for the house. Lunch had been hours ago, and he was starved for supper.

"Hope," he called. "Is the coast clear?" He set his straw hat on a peg, but before he could roll up his sleeves to wash, two speeding figures shot through the kitchen.

"*Daed!*" Greta and Emily hugged him around the waist and knees as though he'd been gone for days instead of hours.

"Did you miss me? The barn's not that far from the house." He patted each of their *kapps*.

"*Mamm* needed me in the house today," said Josie from the doorway. "Or I would have come to help you."

He smiled at his shy *dochder*. "I know you would have, but your place was in here with all the noisy hens."

"Hens? What hens?" Hope entered from the living room, pulling a clean apron from the drawer along the way. "I noticed no chickens in my kitchen, only sweet ladies who ironed your shirts and cooked plenty of your favorites." She smiled wryly over the *kinners'* heads.

"I'm not sure why the chicken coop came to mind when I came in for lunch, but I refer to good-natured hens, of course." He kissed his wife's cheek while she set the table.

"Best change your shirt. That one smells like your horse." Hope pinched her nostrils.

"I might as well grab one of those freshly ironed ones, since someone went to all that trouble."

On his way to their bedroom, Stephen paused at the crib. Baby Faith slumbered peacefully under the open window. Her dark lashes fanned across her round cheeks while her mouth formed a perfect bow. Faith's bright pink coloring at birth had faded to a pale shade of cream. He bent close to kiss her forehead, careful not to wake her. Each time he gazed on a *boppli*, he felt huge and clumsy as an ox. When he returned, his wife and daughters were waiting patiently at the table. He slipped into his chair and bowed his head.

After their silent prayer, Hope was first to speak. "One of those *hens* you referred to made meat loaf just the way you like it—with plenty of onions and mushroom gravy." She handed him a heaping platter.

"*Danki.*" Stephen placed a slice on Greta's and Emily's plates, three on his own, then passed the platter to Josie. He might have preferred not to have so many women in his house today, but he couldn't deny that the supper they'd provided was a feast: sweet potato casserole, green beans with ham, pickled vegetables, and a heap of corn bread drizzled with melted butter.

He attacked the meat loaf with knife and fork. "You might have to let out a seam or two after this week's vittles," he said around a mouthful of sweet potatoes.

During the meal, his girls entertained him with amusing tales from sisters' day. "I'm glad no mishaps occurred today with that many women hard at work. That many cooks might not spoil the broth, but more than a ladleful usually gets spilled."

Hope studied him over the rim of her coffee cup. "Everyone managed to work without treading on each other's toes."

While he wiped up the last of his gravy, Josie scrambled to her feet. "Shall I slice the pies?" she asked.

"Just the rhubarb," said Hope. "We'll leave the rest. Emily, you start clearing the table. Fill the sink with suds and set the plates to soak. Josie and I will wash them later. Then sit down to eat your dessert and finish your milk. I want a private word with your *daed* after supper."

Stephen accepted a slice of pie from Josie and held up his mug for a refill. "Hear some choice gossip that can't wait another moment longer?"

Hope's dimples deepened as she fought back a smile. "Of course not. Our district doesn't gossip since Scripture forbids it. We simply share the news of those unable to attend."

Josie giggled, as did her siblings, even though they had no idea why they were laughing.

"Everybody wanted to hold little Faith," she told her father.

"For a short while our baby will be the newest kid in town." Stephen devoured his slice of pie. "But knowing our district, someone will soon bump her off the pedestal. Josie, bring me another slice of pie if there's a small one."

"While Emily and Josie clear the table and Greta dawdles over her dessert, why don't you tell me what the ladies accomplished?"

"They washed all the windows, weeded my garden, blanched and canned the green beans, and filled our propane refrigerators with plenty of cooked meals." She glanced between him and their *dochdern* while she spoke. "All right, girls. Go into the front room to read until I call you. You too, Greta, since you're obviously no longer hungry."

The moment they were alone, Hope drew a folded paper from her apron pocket. "This article appeared in a German Baptist magazine. *Mamm* spotted it at the chiropractor's office. Her doctor said she could take it home." Hope carefully unfolded several sheets stapled together.

"I don't have my reading glasses, *fraa*. Why don't you tell me the gist of it?" He took smaller bites of the second slice to make the pie last longer. Rhubarb was one of his favorites.

"A group of homeopathic physicians wrote the article, people who know every herb, spice, and natural compound. Did you know the poison ivy toxin actually improves certain arthritis symptoms? The relief can last for days or even weeks."

"Fascinating, I'll keep that in mind for the future." He drained the last of his coffee.

"I'll keep the whole article for reference, but the part I liked best was written by a fertility specialist. She provided a list of herbs and spices that increase a woman's chances of conceiving a boy." Hope lowered her voice to a whisper. "I can order special tea bags from this catalog. No guarantees, but if I drink several cups per day starting next month, I might have a better chance of birthing a son."

Stephen stared at her. "Your *mamm* gave you this article?"

Hope nodded, pulling the sheets back when he made no move to pick them up. *"Ya."*

"I'd bet your *daed* knows nothing about this hocus-pocus nonsense."

Her eyes began to water. "Lots of Plain folks use natural remedies."

"True enough, but a natural remedy is staving off a cold with echinacea and cider vinegar or applying a cabbage leaf poultice to reduce swollen knees. Not drinking some kind of weird tea to pre-determine our baby's gender. Would *Gott* approve of that?"

"Are you forbidding me to order these tea bags?"

Stephen selected his words carefully. "No, but I would greatly prefer you didn't. Let's leave the matter of our *kinner* up to God."

~

The showers that would assure abundant hay and soybean crops arrived the next morning, along with a cooler breeze from the north.

With her laundry and ironing caught up, Hope would have an easy day. She had enough prepared meals in the refrigerator to feel like an English working wife for some time to come. After so much attention, baby Faith had slept through the night, giving Hope some much-needed rest. Her child grew more alert and active by the day. The Bowman garden was yielding plenty to can, dry, or freeze for the coming winter months. And her girls never failed to make her smile with their inquisitive questions.

Still Hope's heart remained troubled. Picking up her *mamm's* magazine article, she reread the promises from the homeopaths. *No guarantees, but a much better chance of . . .*

She looked again at the prices and mailing address at the end of the story. Stephen hadn't forbidden ordering the tea, yet he'd made his stance clear. From the day they'd married, her husband refused to run his household like some older men who made all the decisions themselves. Men like Hope's father. Stephen talked matters over with her, even including the girls in their discussions when it was appropriate.

This would not be one of those times.

Clearly, he would be upset if she ordered the tea bags over his objection. But wasn't he the one who so yearned for a son? What would it hurt to drink some tea for a few months and see what happened?

Hope pulled out a pen, a postage stamp, and her checkbook. Stephen might not notice an extra box of tea on the shelf. And if they did the trick, he might change his opinion from "hocus-pocus" to "miracle cure."

She put the envelope in her mailbox and lifted the signal flag, then returned to the house, laughing at her own gullibility. Once in a doctor's office she'd watched a TV commercial for a new diet pill. *Take this capsule every day and lose twenty pounds within one month—no diet or exercise required.* Distressed by the weight she'd gained with Greta, Hope contemplated calling the 800 number from the payphone as she munched on her second glazed donut that morning. Instead, she'd thrown the rest of the donut into the trash and began walking daily with her *dochders*. They gathered wildflowers or kindling or just enjoyed a beautiful sunset high in the hills. The baby weight came off without depleting her wallet.

So why was she falling for a similar solution now?

And a better question was: why wasn't her faith as strong as her husband's?

Stephen was content to wait and see what the Lord had in store for the Bowmans. But she wanted to *do* something.

Without warning, a tear ran down her face.

"What's wrong, *Mamm*?" Josie appeared in the doorway with Emily at her side, carrying a full basket of lettuce, carrots, and radishes for supper. "Why are you crying?"

"*Ach*, no reason." Hope opened her arms to her daughters. They set down the basket and fled to her embrace. "Sometimes a woman gets sad after having a *boppli*, but it's nothing to worry about. I feel better knowing we'll have a big salad tonight. I've had such a taste for one." Hope kissed their foreheads.

"Betsy told me *Englischers* call that baby-depression. She read about it in a library health book." Josie, a voracious reader, nodded with authority.

Hope rose to her feet to start washing the produce. "Such a

thing for a young woman to read about. You should stick to stories about horses."

"I usually do, but Betsy said *mamms* need to spend time alone when they feel short-tempered and unhappy. They should take a bubble bath or a long walk on the beach." Josie took out the paring knife, peeler, and cutting board.

"Considering I take a bath every day and the closest beach to Lancaster County is a couple hundred miles away, I'll have to ignore Betsy's sage advice. I don't think our horse would appreciate that long a trip."

"But you could take a walk up to your favorite place. And enjoy some peace and quiet."

Hope stared at her oldest child. Her favorite place was the highest point on the Bowman land—a rocky outcropping at the top of their pasture. Beyond the fence line stood a dense woodlot that supplied firewood and an occasional deer for venison meat. She hadn't walked up there in at least a year. Once she discovered she was carrying Faith, she chose to take it easy. "What made you think about that spot?"

"You said you felt close to God there. Surrounded by His handiwork, it was hard not to count your blessings." Josie repeated her words verbatim. "I love it there too. I always see plenty of hawks and turkey vultures circling above the treetops."

Hope smiled, remembering the day they spotted a bald eagle. "Maybe tomorrow we'll rig up a sling to carry Faith and hike to the top. We could even pack sandwiches for a picnic lunch." She peeled and trimmed a carrot with practiced dexterity.

"No, *Mamm*. We'll do that another time. You need to go by yourself." Josie pulled the carrot from Hope's fingers.

"Seems like you and Betsy are determined to mend something that's not broken." Hope arched an eyebrow. "I've got supper to fix and a newborn to tend, young lady."

Josie glanced at the wall clock. "Didn't you just feed her? Faith should sleep for another two hours. Where's Greta?"

"Napping on the couch, next to the day-crib, but——"

"I'm a big girl. I can heat the chicken casserole that Ida May made and finish the salad. Emily will set the table." Emily nodded, her brown eyes very round. "Why don't you go to your favorite place now?" Josie's voice turned downright pleading. "I don't want you to be sad anymore."

Hope's tears returned, but this time they were for the blessing of sensitive, compassionate daughters. "All right, I'll go tell your *daed*, then take a quick hike before we eat. *Danki*, Josie and Emily, for your help."

Josie clutched her arm. "I'll tell him when he comes in. Go before you think of another reason not to."

"Goodness, this isn't like a gash on your finger that needs stitches in the emergency room. I'm *fine*, Josie."

Both girls giggled. "I know, but by supper you'll be even finer."

For a brief moment, mother and daughter looked at one another. Josie had become so grown-up since Greta's birth. *"Danki,"* she whispered. On her way out the front door, she checked on Faith. Josie had been right—the baby slept soundly.

Walking up the well-trodden cattle path, Hope felt like a child sneaking out after dark to catch fireflies. But once beyond sight of the house, she relaxed. She needed this. Time to pray and surrender her will to God.

Hope picked up her skirt and ran, suddenly eager to reach the summit. As she neared the outcropping, breathless and sweaty, she found the air cooler, the breeze refreshing, and her heart lighter. True to Josie's prediction, hawks soared high overhead while butterflies trailed behind, moving from flower to flower.

But she hadn't come here to bird-watch or gather bouquets. She came to welcome the Holy Spirit into her heart. Dropping onto a large rock, Hope turned her face skyward and prayed, first for forgiveness and then for guidance and direction. At last she spoke the words closest to her heart—she prayed for a miracle: "Please, God, I'm grateful for four healthy daughters. But please bring us a son to help Stephen and to carry on after we're gone."

Hope sat in silence then, and as she waited, a sense of well-being settled over her. She was filled with a sense of purpose, and she knew what she had to do.

If she wanted God to grant her heart's desire, she must first unburden her soul.

Chapter Four

When Hope opened the kitchen door, she was greeted by four smiling faces and the pungent scent of herb chicken. The table had been set for supper, and Stephen was already at his place, sipping a cup of coffee. The moment she hung up her cloak and bonnet, Josie sprang into action. She carried the casserole to the center trivet, added ranch dressing to the salad, and then tossed. Bread, butter, and honey were already on the table.

"All better, *fraa?*" he asked, winking. "Emily said you went to the high pasture to get un-sad."

"Truly, I am. That walk did me a world of good." Hope brushed a kiss across Josie's cheek on her way to wash her hands. *"Danki,"* she murmured.

"Happy to hear it," he said after prayers. "I feared you might have taken off bareback on the old mare, leaving me alone to raise four wildcats." Stephen leaned forward to scoop a hearty portion of chicken and rice.

"What's a wildcat?" Emily frowned, unsure whether or not to be flattered.

"Something you are not, my sweet girl." Hope divided the salad among the five bowls, giving herself a huge amount. The walk had piqued her appetite.

Stephen studied her while he ate. "Something bothering you?"

"Nothing to worry about. I needed to clear my head. Why don't we talk after the girls go to bed?" She tried to ease his mind with a smile.

Stephen's brows connected over the bridge of his nose. "Did one of the ladies say something to rile you yesterday?"

"Goodness, no. Josie simply reminded me the high pasture was a good spot to pray—something I've neglected lately."

With a grunt of approval, Stephen concentrated on the delicious meal, taking two helpings of both chicken and salad. "Say, you should ask Ida May for this recipe. It's mighty tasty."

"I have, dear heart, many times. Ida said she'll leave it behind like a last will and testament."

All throughout dinner, kitchen cleanup, Faith's final feeding, and putting her daughters to bed, Hope felt no anxiety about what lay ahead, only peace. She was doing the right thing. Finally.

With a light step, she entered the living room where Stephen sat reading Scripture.

"Everyone asleep?" he asked, closing his Bible. "If so, it's time to speak your mind." He reached for her hand.

Hope clutched his calloused fingers, then with little preamble she told the sorrowful tale of a summer night almost twenty years ago—the night she had been raped by a man full of hatred. She spoke of her parents' shame and how her father insisted she keep silent, even when the loathsome act led to a pregnancy. No one had found out—not her brothers who should have taken her home, not her sisters who might have become more cautious, not even the district brethren who might have offered consolation . . . or a solution other than giving her child away to English strangers.

Stephen listened without interrupting. When she paused, he asked, "You left town expecting a child and then returned to the district without one?" His voice sounded skeptical.

"*Ya*, my father sent me away before I was showing. He made the arrangements without telling even the bishop."

"Where did you go if you were only sixteen?"

Hope's confidence slipped a notch. "He sent me to Harrisburg to stay at a special center equipped to handle . . . these situations. There was no cost as long as the child was given up for adoption. A lawyer at the center handled the paperwork, and my son was placed with an English college professor and his wife."

"*Your son?*" Stephen's voice rose.

Hope glanced toward the stairs. "The child was a boy. They allowed me to hold him for a few minutes before taking him away."

Every drop of color drained from his face. "You birthed an Amish child and gave him to *Englischers*?"

"I didn't want to!" Hope's courage vanished, and her stomach cramped into knots. "I argued with my father, but he wouldn't permit the *boppli* in his *haus*."

"Why?"

It was the question she had wrestled with for years.

"He said the child had been spawned by an evildoer, and nothing but evil would follow him and me. He said the boy would have a better chance to thrive in the English world."

Hope couldn't speak for several moments, then she whispered hoarsely, *"Daed* was ashamed of me. He treated me as though I'd done something wrong. He said the district would never accept the boy. What I was too young to realize at the time was that *he* couldn't accept the boy. He lied to everyone in Paradise about sending me to a dying relative—a shunned cousin who had no one to care for her—rather than accept the truth."

Stephen covered his face with his hands and remained quiet. When he lifted his chin, his eyes were red-rimmed and watery. "You told no one for all these years?" His voice had hardened.

Hope stared at the wall clock. "I told my friend Rosa, and of course *Mamm* knew. That's all."

Stephen blinked. His lips thinned into a line. "You told a girl-friend but you never told me—the man you pledged to honor and love for as long as you lived?" He slapped his palm on the arm of the sofa.

She couldn't swallow; she could barely breathe. "By the time we started courting, I had kept my secret for so long. *Mamm* said no man would have me if he knew the truth."

"She taught you to *deceive,* and you went along like a mindless sheep?" He shook his head with disgust.

She couldn't look him in the eye. "I know I shouldn't have, but I was weak."

"Thirteen years we've been married. You could have told me

at any point. You are a complete stranger to me, and I to you, if you thought you couldn't trust me." He struggled to his feet, all six feet three inches of him, set his Bible on the table, and stomped out of the house, letting the screen door slam behind him.

Hope remained frozen in her chair. This wasn't what she expected. She thought he'd be sympathetic, understanding. She thought he'd *care*.

At first she sobbed. Then she prayed. Finally, she realized, *It is done. Whatever his response, I'm no longer keeping a secret from my husband.*

A knock on the back door drew her out of her reverie. She heard the screen creak open and a halting step approach through the kitchen.

"Hope?" Rosa's voice called. "I knocked but no one answered. I knew you hadn't gone anywhere at this hour."

She came into the living room, looked Hope up and down, and frowned. "What happened? Are you all right?"

Hope nodded. "I told him, Rosa. I told him the truth about the baby."

Rosa lowered herself to the sofa. "Where is he?"

"He left. But I know he loves me." Hope pronounced the words like some sort of revelation. "He will come back. And if necessary I'll spend the rest of my life making amends for my sins."

"It wasn't your fault."

"Not the rape, no. But I am responsible for my deception. I made a grievous mistake. Still, all will be well. I've prayed on the matter too many times to count; at last I feel peace in my heart, unburdened, as though I've finally turned this over to God."

"All will be well," Rosa whispered. She stayed, silently holding her friend's hand, and after a while left through the front door without another word.

~

When Stephen marched out the front door and down the porch steps, he didn't know where he would go. He crossed the lawn waiting to be mowed, passed the barn where horses nickered as they settled down for the night, and circumvented the cow pasture. The last thing he needed was to step in a flop or two in his present state of mind.

Pausing in a thin circle of moonlight, he gazed skyward. A fleeting cloud scuttled across the surface, but otherwise the night was clear. A million stars shone down on him. Suddenly, the sound of a nightjar broke the stillness—the bird's shriek seemed to be mocking Stephen's ignorance. "Scat!" he called to his unseen tormentor. Then he stomped off toward the cornfield. Maybe he could lose himself in the maze of cornstalks and wander until he spent every ounce of energy.

How could the love of his life keep a secret for thirteen years?

How could she neglect to tell him something so important? More to the point, what other secrets was Hope keeping from him?

On he walked, lengthening his strides and quickening his pace. Stephen kept his head down and gritted his teeth. Tough, brittle cornstalks scratched his face and arms, while mosquitoes feasted on his bare arms. He stumbled over a hidden rut, nearly falling facedown between the straight rows of corn. Yet he didn't stop until he'd crossed the field and reached the fence line.

Hot, itchy, and exhausted, Stephen fell to his knees under the sole tree along the property line. His heart slammed against his ribcage; beads of sweat slid down the sides of his face. But his anger had started to dissipate. He'd ground it into dust along with the chaff from dead stalks.

"What should I do, Lord?" he asked, turning up his face. But he knew the answer. He needed no parting of the clouds or trumpet-heralding messenger to give him direction.

Forgive. Not seven times, but seventy times seven.

His wife had done nothing unforgivable. She had been victimized as a girl. And then her own father had shown not one shred of compassion. Instead of comforting and helping her deal with the trauma, he had made her feel ashamed and culpable. And as if that weren't enough, Silas Klobentz committed the unthinkable: he forced his child to surrender her baby.

The person he needed to forgive was his father-in-law, not his wife. But Stephen sensed he would have to spend much time in prayer before facing Hope's father.

He rose to his feet, brushed off his knees, and started home with a heavier step but a lighter spirit. He opened the door on an empty kitchen where a sole kerosene lamp burned on the table. But as he washed his hands and face at the sink, he sensed someone enter the room.

"You're back," Hope said, her hands folded behind her back.

Reaching for the towel, he turned to face her. "I am. You discovered the high pasture to be a *gut* thinking spot. It took the length of our cornfield to bring me to a few conclusions."

Tentatively, she reached for him. "You're bleeding."

Stephen welcomed her touch. "It's nothing—don't fret." He

took her hand and drew her to the table. Her hand felt small in his palm. "Sit with me awhile." He pulled her into his lap.

"What conclusions did you come to?" Her voice quivered.

"You've carried a heavy burden for a long while. I wish I could have lightened it for you. But what's done is done." Stephen tipped up her face with one finger. "You're not to blame for what happened to you, or for giving your baby up for adoption. A young girl with an eighth-grade education and no job has few options. Had we been courting then, we might have married earlier. I would have raised the boy as my own."

Hope buried her face against his shirt, and her tears seeped through the cotton.

He stroked her back to soothe her. "Your father wronged you and the district with his lies, but all that is past. After today I won't bring this up again, unless you wish to talk about it. Then I'll listen for as long as you like. Don't ever think you need to keep something from me. There is no truth involving you I cannot bear."

"I love you," she said against his chest.

"And I you." He held her until she had exhausted her tears. When she lifted her face, her lips formed the tiniest of smiles. "*Danki*, Stephen. Your forgiveness is a cherished gift. My deception separated me from God, but He has been waiting for me to seek Him with my troubles. He will grant us our desire once I finish what I started." She wiped her eyes with her apron.

"What do you mean?" he asked, puzzled. "God's forgiveness should be sufficient."

"It is, I assure you, but God's not finished with the Bowman family. I just know He will bring us a boy-*boppli*." Hope sprang off his lap as Faith's cries reached their ears. "There's one more thing I need to do."

"Don't associate the past with our current situation," he warned. "One has nothing to do with the other."

At the doorway she turned back to him. "Oh, but it does. One has everything to do with the other. Tomorrow I will face my *daed* and truly put the past behind us."

Chapter Five

That night after Faith's last nursing, Hope slept soundly and awoke refreshed. No bad dreams with evil phantoms following her down dark country roads. When she raised the shade with a snap of her wrist, a pink-tinged dawn greeted her with the promise of fine weather. She hummed a hymn as she fed and bathed the baby and cooked breakfast for her family. Oatmeal with sliced peaches had never looked so appealing in her bowl.

"What's wrong, *Mamm?*" Josie said. "Why are you so happy? Did our chickens lay two eggs instead of only one?"

Emily burst into giggles, and Greta laughed too.

Hope carried the jug of milk to the table along with three glasses. "I'm joyous about having such *gut dochders.*" She winked at Josie.

A twelve-year-old wasn't so easily fooled. "What's the real reason?"

Hope sipped her coffee, leaning against the stove. "After morning chores we're driving to *Grossmammi's haus.*"

"Again? We just went a couple of days ago."

"Again. Days as pretty as this call for a buggy ride. Eat up and see to your chores." Eager to put an onerous task behind her, Hope turned back to the skillet where a ham slice sizzled.

As if the man could smell ham and eggs all the way from the barn, Stephen entered the kitchen just as Hope slipped his over-easy eggs onto a plate. "*Ach*, you're just in time. I didn't have to send out Emily." Hope placed his breakfast on the table, then began filling her sink with warm water and suds.

"In a big hurry today?" he asked, sitting down with his favorite mug.

"*Ya*, we're going to *Mamm* and *Daed's*." She filled his cup to the rim.

"Still got *that* on the mind, I see."

"Time to clear the air with him. I've waited too long already." Hope didn't turn around, knowing Stephen wouldn't pursue the conversation with the girls in the room.

He ate in silence and then filled a travel mug with coffee. "I'll be cutting hay today in the south fields," he whispered close to her ear. "Think long and hard before you overturn this particular rock. You know what your *daed* is like."

Hope kissed his cheek. "I do indeed, *ehemann*. I am doing this for my sake more than his."

He exhaled heavily. "Then I wish you the results you seek."

All the way to her parents' farm, Hope mulled over how to best broach the subject. But she received no great intuition on how to crack the thick shell of Silas Klobentz. When she arrived, Hope found her *mamm* canning green beans. Her face was flushed from the heat at the stove. Hope set her daughters to work trimming and washing the beans, which sat in bushel baskets against the wall, then placed Faith down for a nap in the substantially cooler front room near the window.

"I'll pitch in later, but there's something I must do first. Where's *Daed*?" she asked.

Her mother immediately raised an eyebrow. "He's out scrubbing the henhouse. Why?"

"I need to talk to him." Hope made sure Greta could reach a supply of beans to snap.

"You intend to talk to your father?" asked Martha. Only a family member would understand: nobody sought out Father's company unless it was absolutely necessary.

"I do." Hope placed her hands on her hips. "Girls, stay here with *Grossmammi*. I will come back soon, so there's no need to hunt for me if Faith starts to cry."

"Maybe you should wait until—"

"No, *Mamm*," Hope interrupted. "This conversation has waited too long already."

Hope fled the *haus* before Martha could dissuade her. Inside the henhouse, she found her father washing the floors with bleach. He did not look up when she entered. "It's me, *Daed*, Hope."

"I know who it is. I saw your buggy pull up the driveway from the window." Silas continued to dunk and wring his mop.

"Then why do you ignore me like I'm not in the room?" Her voice lifted a notch.

Silas's head snapped up. "*Me?* You're the one who shut your father out years ago, refusing to pay me the respect I deserve."

She reflected for a moment. "True, I did shut you out. I was angry because of the way you treated me after . . . everything that happened."

The blood drained from his pale, deeply lined face. "Must we rehash that night? Nothing *gut* can come from it." He resumed scrubbing the floor.

"*Ya*, we must. You accused me of not struggling hard enough, of not fighting off my attacker because of weakness or fear."

Silas froze, his knuckles whitening on the wooden mop handle. Finally, he spoke. "I never should have said that. I lost my temper and spoke harshly." He released his grip one finger at a time.

Hope waited for an apology. After half a minute she realized that none would come. But her forgiveness did not depend on his apology. "And I was angry about what you forced me to do." She enunciated her words carefully.

This time Silas met her gaze with eyes cold as January. "I did what was best."

"Best for you." She forced herself not to look away.

"*Nein*, best for all of us, including the boy. He never would have fit in."

"I disagree. But I've not come to argue with you. All of that is water under the bridge. We can only pray the child has found love and happiness with his English family." Hope swallowed hard and drew in a calming breath. "I've come to say I forgive you for forcing me to give away my son. The Lord has forgiven me, and I hold nothing against you." She wiped perspiring palms down her apron before extending her hand in Christian love.

Silas stared as though he no longer recognized her. "You forgive *me*? You wish to shake *my* hand?" The incredulity in his voice stung like a slap in the face. "How *dare* you place yourself above me? You're in no position to offer forgiveness to anyone, *dochder.*" He glared at her outstretched hand as if it were a rattlesnake poised to strike. "Go into the *haus* and help your *mamm.* Leave me to my chores."

Slowly, she drew back her arm. "I will go, but I wanted to clear the air with you." Hope forced herself to smile. "I pray that the Lord blesses and keeps you, *Daed,* and extends His grace in every way."

Hope turned and left the chicken coop. She headed toward the kitchen where a full afternoon of labor awaited. But no matter how hot the kitchen or how her back would ache by day's end, nothing could dampen her good spirits. A weight had been lifted.

When she arrived home, Hope found the box of fertility tea bags in the mailbox. Before entering the house she tossed the package into the trash. "Forgive me, Lord," she said, "for being wasteful, and for putting my faith in a foolish potion instead of You."

~

Stephen placed the pot of chili into the oven on low heat before heading into the shower. Hope had left a list of specific directions regarding their supper that night. After all these years she still spelled things out for him. Amish husbands typically did very little in the kitchen, considering it a woman's duty. But he didn't object to helping out when necessary, since the sooner the meal was ready, the sooner they would eat. And after a long day of raking and baling hay, he was hungry.

Tonight the Bowman family would dine on beef and bean chili, pickled vegetables—the last of last year's—and sliced tomatoes.

Tomatoes, like houseflies and mosquitoes, seemed limitless during late summer. The chili was one of the many contributions from sisters' day. He silently thanked the ladies, especially whoever came up with the original idea of cooking for new *mamms* and shut-ins. A meal ready to reheat came in handy because it would be eight o'clock by the time his family returned from the Klobentz farm. Hope would feed the girls at her *mamm's* but she would wait to eat with him.

As he stepped under the shower spray, the hot water relieved his sore back and shoulder muscles. Too bad warm water couldn't soothe his troubled soul so easily. Each time he thought about Silas Klobentz his mind filled with rather un-Christian thoughts. How dare he force his will on Hope in such a fashion? Stephen lifted his face into the direct spray, hoping to wash away his anger with the dust from the fields.

A son. His wife had given birth to a boy. A son he could be raising now, along with their four daughters. Hope knew that the lack of common blood would mean little to him. He could have adopted the child, making him legally a Bowman. Who knew what kind of family the boy ended up with?

Later, as he nursed a cup of coffee, waiting for Hope to return, he couldn't get the boy out of his mind. She had held him in her arms for a few minutes, then he'd been taken away like a toy from a naughty child. Stephen ground his teeth. *Lord, help me forgive Silas, because right now I'm having trouble with that.* The sound of buggy wheels in the driveway distracted him from his uncharitable thoughts. Stephen opened the door in time to greet his family. Even at this hour, after a full day at *Grossmammi's haus,* his daughters were still fireballs of energy.

"*Daed!*" they cried in unison.

"Did you miss us?" Josie asked.

"I could barely stand it another minute." He enfolded them in a group hug as Hope climbed the steps, carrying the youngest Bowman.

"I'll bet you're starving." She brushed his cheek with a kiss on her way inside.

"Oh, I'll definitely put a dent in that pot of chili. Why don't I tend to your horse while you put the *kinner* to bed?"

"*Gut, danki.* Supper will be on the table by the time you're finished." Hope smiled. This was their routine whenever she'd been gone all day—he would rub down, feed, and water the horse while she put the girls to bed.

And Hope was true to her promise. When Stephen reentered the kitchen twenty minutes later, his *dochders* were nowhere to be seen, two places had been set at the table, and the steaming pot of chili waited on the center trivet.

"How is your *mamm*?" he asked, hanging his hat on a peg.

"Tired from all the canning. Her garden produced a bumper crop of everything this year. I hope my sister comes tomorrow to help."

"Surely Rebecca will since she lives next door."

"Probably so, but today she had a doctor's appointment." Hope lowered herself to the chair slowly, moving like an old woman from fatigue.

"Long day?" Stephen scooped chili into two bowls.

"*Ya*, I will be seeing green beans in my sleep. But everything went well with my father. At least from my perspective. I took care of what I needed to." She dished a portion of vegetables onto small plates.

"Silas accepted your olive branch?" He made no effort to hide his shock.

Hope chose her words carefully. "He admitted regret over accusing me of not fighting hard enough."

"But no regrets regarding the baby?"

She tried a mouthful of chili and then set down her spoon. "None whatsoever. He still believes it was the best course of action." Hope popped a pickled carrot into her mouth.

"I expected as much from him."

Hope patted his arm. "It doesn't matter—that's between *Daed* and the Lord now. I have shed the resentment I held for so long. It did me far more harm than it did him."

Stephen rubbed his neck as the stiffness spread across his shoulders. "I'm glad your heart has been unburdened," he said. "But what about the boy? Isn't there some way we could contact him? Or at least determine if he's being well cared for?"

"No, *ehemann*," Hope said. "We must both put the matter from our minds. I tried to find out if he's happy and properly taken care of. I contacted several agencies in Harrisburg, seeking those who might ease my conscience. But the records are sealed. I signed away my rights during the adoption. The child and his new parents are protected from those with second thoughts." Hope's spoon halted midway to her mouth. "If I understand correctly, when he's an adult he will have the option to track me down, but it must be his choice."

"So there's nothing we can do?" Stephen pushed away his bowl and plate.

Hope met his gaze. "You can do what I do each night—pray

that the Lord protects him and our *dochders*, keeping them safe within His grace throughout their lives." She rose and began clearing the table.

Stephen sat for several minutes digesting the new information so he could be as supportive as possible. If only he could find the same mercy for Silas. Finally, he wrapped his arms around Hope's waist while she stood washing dishes at the sink. "Today you've forgiven your father, and I know you forgave that *Englischer* long ago. Now you must release any guilt you still harbor. The chains on your heart are gone. We are washed clean of the past."

Hope turned within his embrace. *"Danki, ehemann."*

"If you've been praying for the boy for years, it's time to surrender him to the Lord. Our future is in His capable hands."

Chapter Six

"You have reached your destination."

The British voice from the GPS announced the impossible. James Webb leaned over the backseat toward the taxi driver. "That thing must be broken. How can we be at the address I gave you?" he asked. "We're in the middle of nowhere."

The driver pulled off the highway into the mouth of a gravel driveway. "It's not broken, young man. This is it. There's the address on the mailbox." He pointed to a dented rural box sitting crookedly on a wooden post.

True enough, the address of the Bowman family of Paradise, Pennsylvania, was stenciled in block letters in black paint.

"But there's not a light on anywhere." James hesitated. Every bad horror movie about ax murderers luring teenagers to decrepit farmhouses came to mind. And it was close to midnight—the witching hour.

The driver shifted to face him on the seat. "This is farm country, son—people go to bed early and get up before dawn. Whoever you're visiting has probably been asleep for hours. Want me to take you back to town? You could come back tomorrow." The driver grinned, revealing a gold cap on a back tooth.

James did a quick mental accounting of his finances. The bus trip from Philadelphia to Harrisburg to Paradise, along with a few fast-food meals, had taken most of his savings. After he paid for this cab ride, he didn't have enough left for a motel room, no matter how budget-minded the chain.

"No, thanks. If you're sure this is the place, I could always sleep on their porch until they wake up. Don't country folks usually have one of those rope hammocks hanging from a tree?" He gave a forced laugh as the car jostled up the rutted lane.

"Okay, in that case, here you are." The cab driver pulled to a stop and punched the button on the meter. "That will be forty-two dollars."

While the cabbie retrieved his duffel bag from the trunk, James nervously counted out his remaining cash. He had just enough, including a two-dollar, thirty-cent tip. "Here ya go. Sorry the tip's not bigger." He handed over the wad of bills and coins.

The cabbie set his bag on the bottom porch step. "Don't worry 'bout it. I was young once." He craned his neck to gaze at a row of dark windows. "You're sure you want me to just leave you here? Maybe I should wait to see what kind of welcome you get." He sounded genuinely worried.

"Nah, that's okay." James picked up his bag and fortified his courage. "I'll be fine. The lady who lives here is . . . *my mother.*" He locked gazes with the cab driver, daring him to dispute the claim.

But the man merely shrugged. "Sounds like you haven't seen her in a while."

"It's been quite some time." James focused on a potted geranium in full bloom.

"Okay then, call the dispatcher when you need a ride back to the station." He hopped into the car and left in a cloud of dust.

Right after I win the lottery, James thought. For several minutes, he stood completely still until his eyes adjusted to the darkness. When the moon crept from behind a bank of clouds, a white three-story house with a wrap-around porch emerged. The house was plain but well maintained. There wasn't anything eerie or haunted about it.

James dragged himself up the steps and looked around for a hammock or glider. Nothing. Just one hard wooden bench and two rocking chairs. Not a single comfy pillow anywhere.

Something flitted past his head in the darkness. James shuddered. He wasn't a country boy, and the idea of spiders crawling under his shirt collar or mosquitoes feasting on his arms gave him the heebie-jeebies.

Without considering the consequences, he raised his fist and pounded on the door, loud enough to wake the dead. Then he stepped back and waited for the house to flood with light.

Nothing happened. He knocked again. Still nothing.

Then, through the front window next to the door, James saw a flickering light move through the house until it stopped in the room before him. At last the porch door creaked open.

In the doorway stood a tall man with a flashlight trained on James's chest and a tiny woman holding a lit candle. Both wore long dark robes and had bare feet.

The woman said nothing, just stared at him. She reminded him of a tour guide at one of those historical villages. The man blinked like an owl and frowned at him.

"Can we help you, young man? Did your car break down?"

James looked up at the man and tried to sound more confident than he felt. "I'm not old enough to drive. I've come to see Hope Klobentz—guess her name is Bowman now, if this is the right house. It's so dark on your road, nobody can see the addresses." James dug his hands deep into his pockets and shifted from one foot to the other.

"This is the Bowman household. Who might you be?"

"My name is James Webb. I used to be James Klobentz."

"Oh my, it's a—" The white-faced lady spoke, but her legs gave way before she finished the sentence. If the big man hadn't been quick, she would have collapsed into a heap on the floor.

If James had heard correctly, she'd tried to say, "It's a miracle." She thought he was a miracle?

The man half carried, half walked her to a kitchen chair and then patted her cheeks with his fingers. "Come in; have a seat," he said to James. "Hope, are you all right?"

For the next ten minutes, Hope Bowman—if it really was her—cried as though somebody had died, while her husband played nursemaid and polite host to him.

"Are you hungry? Is that all the luggage you brought?" The man pointed toward his forgotten duffel bag by the door. "Did you come by yourself?" One by one he fired off questions while trying to get his wife to stop crying. Finally, his might-be-mom wiped her face on a dish towel and sucked in deep gulps of air.

James supposed she was pretty, even though she didn't wear a bit of makeup and her hair was pulled back into a tight braid. "So, I take it you're my mother?" he asked. His voice sounded weak and childish, not at all the way he had intended.

Hope Bowman cleared her throat. "If you were born in Harrisburg fifteen and a half years ago, I believe I am. I'm so glad you found me." After calming considerably, she smiled. "Praise the Lord! He is infinite in His mercy and grace."

"Welcome, James," said the man. He placed a glass of milk and some type of muffin in front of him. "I'm Hope's husband, Stephen Bowman. Hope tried to locate you but wasn't able." He gestured toward the muffin. "Go ahead, eat. Then tell how you found us."

James didn't know much about God's grace. Only a couple foster families had bothered to take him to church, and then only once or twice. But one nice foster mom enrolled him in vacation Bible school for half days for a week one summer. That church served the best snacks at refreshment time. Glancing around the huge kitchen, James shook off a nervous twinge. Everything looked spooky in the flickering candlelight. "Could we turn on some lights, folks? Sitting in the dark seems a little weird to me." He laughed, hoping he didn't sound disrespectful.

But Stephen Bowman laughed too as he jumped to his feet. "Yeah, I'll bet it does." He lit three glass-globed kerosene lamps. They filled the room with plenty of yellow light. "This is the best we can do—we're Amish."

James stared at one and then the other, and everything fell into place like pieces in a jigsaw puzzle.

"You're *Amish*?" The tone in his voice made *Amish* sound like a substitute for *Martian*. They didn't seem to notice—or if they did, they were polite enough to ignore it.

"We are," said Hope. "I was only sixteen when I had you." Her voice had grown stronger.

"I'm almost that old now." James held the woman's gaze for a moment and then launched onward, apparently unable to stop himself from talking.

"I've always been good with computers. In the last two foster homes I lived in, they let me spend all the time I wanted on the Internet. Guess I stayed out of their hair that way." He giggled ridiculously while the Amish couple sat watching and listening. "I got curious about breaking into databases. I kind of made it a game. It didn't matter how secure the server or how protected their firewall . . ."

Neither seemed to have a clue what he was talking about.

"That means I was able to *unseal* the records of my sealed adoption. I found out you came to Harrisburg from a town called Paradise in Lancaster County. According to the website, tons of Amish people live here, but I didn't think you would turn out to be one. I didn't think the Amish gave their kids up for adoption."

Hope Bowman's eyes filled with more tears. "Soon I will tell you why, and anything else you wish to know," she said in a shaky voice. "But first, what are your adoptive parents like? Is your new mom good to you? Does she show you plenty of love?" Her voice squeaked like a wheel in need of grease. "I have prayed for years that you found a happy home."

James glared. "My *new mom*? Do you mean the couple who took me home for a one-year test drive? I guess it was a nice place, since the guy was a big-bucks Philadelphia lawyer. But I don't remember anything about my first twelve months of life. Before the court could finalize the adoption, the couple gave me back to Children's Services. Turned out I had a congenital heart murmur. I outgrew it, but apparently my adoptive parents didn't want to take a chance with a kid with a bad ticker. What if I didn't make the guy proud on the peewee football field? Or worse, ended up costing them a bundle in medical bills? They threw this defective fish back into the pond and went on the waiting list."

"Then who *did* adopt you?" Stephen asked while Hope sniffled in her handkerchief.

James looked at the two befuddled people in their tattered bathrobes and felt a surge of pity. "Nobody," he answered. "I'm a ward of the county. I've lived in one foster or group home after another—some good, some bad, mostly mediocre. But don't worry; the current folks who are paid to take care of me are really nice. They'll wait three days before reporting me as a runaway. That will give us a chance to get caught up." James realized that he sounded sarcastic and mean-tempered, but he couldn't help it.

The woman's head reared back as if she'd been slapped. Hope Bowman—his mom for the first few minutes of his life—dissolved into a sea of tears. She laid her face down on the table and sobbed. And this time nothing her husband said or did could stop the hysteria.

~

When Hope raised her head, she found her son and her husband watching her. One looking young and shocked, the other far older than his thirty-five years.

"Are you all right?" they asked simultaneously.

Nodding, Hope turned toward James Webb. "They told me you had been adopted by a childless couple desperate to have a baby. You were going to a good family, rich enough to send you to any college you wanted." She straightened her spine as Stephen pressed a glass of water into her hand.

"College? No university in the country would ever accept me. I'll be lucky to get into a two-year community college." James gulped half the glass of milk, then wiped his mouth with his sleeve. "Of course, I'd have to pass the GED."

Hope swallowed several gulps of water. "But you said you're good with computers, that you were able to break down the barriers on the adoption paperwork."

"That's called 'hacking,'" James interrupted.

"Hacking into government records," Stephen said. "Anybody able to do that can't be stupid." Her husband tugged on the frayed cuffs of his robe.

James appeared to find something Stephen said amusing. "I didn't say I was stupid. I'm good in math and science and with computers, like I told you. But I don't see a need for English grammar—all those rules and exceptions to the rules. Why can't people write stuff down like they talk? And what is the point of English Lit? Why read Shakespeare or Charles Dickens or William Faulkner? Those dogs are long dead and buried."

"Those *dogs*?" asked Stephen, retrieving another fresh blueberry muffin for the boy.

"It means dudes or guys—just a slang term for men." James sounded delighted to help with vernacular. "And it ain't just English classes that tick me off. Health is stupid, so is American history, and don't even get me started on political science. Considering my grades in those subjects, it'll be a miracle if I graduate high school, let alone get into college." He lifted the muffin from the paper napkin and devoured it in four bites.

"The miracle is that you found us," Hope murmured.

"The Amish schools here only go to eighth grade," said Stephen. "Most students graduate at fourteen, then start work."

"Yeah, I'd be done with books and homework if you had kept me, but I guess I wasn't part of your master plan."

When James Webb focused his clear blue eyes on her, Hope thought she might melt onto the floor. She swallowed hard but with a throat so dry, her gasp was audible. "I'm so sorry."

"There's much you don't know, young man," said Stephen. "Your mother didn't have a choice at the time—she was sixteen with no money to support you. You can't raise a child on good intentions." He picked up her glass of water and finished it. "You're welcome to stay as long as you wish. But I won't have you criticizing my wife for something she couldn't control then and has deeply regretted ever since." Stephen's message came through loud and clear without raising his voice.

James shifted on the kitchen chair and looked directly at her. "Sorry," he murmured. "That didn't come out right."

An uncomfortable silence stretched between them. "It's okay," she said at last. "It's hard to know the right thing to say."

Stephen grabbed a muffin for himself. "So you make good grades in math and science?"

"Yeah, I get straight As in both of those." The boy bent his fingers back to crack his knuckles. "Don't know how schools work here, but an A is the best grade you can earn."

Stephen nodded. "The marking system is the same in Amish classrooms. We've got two girls in school who would love to get an A in any subject. Do you want more milk or muffins?"

"No, thank you. *Girls*—you mean I have two half sisters?" The boy's eyes went wide.

"You have four sisters," Hope said. "Josie is twelve, Emily is seven, Greta is four, and we have a newborn named Faith."

"Will I get to meet them? I never had any real brothers or sisters."

"Of course," Stephen and Hope answered together. "But right now you need to get some sleep. Tomorrow you'll meet everyone and take the grand tour of our farm." Hope smiled, feeling stronger by the minute.

"Sounds good." James Webb stood and walked toward his bag. "Gotta admit, I could use some z's."

Stephen rolled his eyes, grinning. "Too bad you hate English class. I could use a few lessons from you. Follow me. I'll show you the guest room. It's on the third floor; hope you don't mind steps."

"Nah, a guy's gotta stay in shape to keep the bullies at bay." He glanced back at her. "Good night . . . ah, Mrs. Bowman."

"You can call me Hope."

James nodded and followed Stephen from the room.

Hope remained seated at the kitchen table, lost in wonder and thankfulness. Her tiredness had vanished with the knock on the door. God had answered her prayers. She'd been expecting another pregnancy within the year—one that might turn out to be a boy.

But God had something else in mind; He had given her back her only son.

She had a second chance with her firstborn. And she would do everything in her power to make things right this time.

Chapter Seven

Despite his exhaustion, James tossed for hours in the narrow twin bed, wide-awake and restless. Amish. He had been born—of all crazy things—Amish.

He couldn't wrap his mind around it. Not having electricity. Using a flashlight to find the bathroom in the middle of the night. Driving a horse and buggy instead of a car.

Well, at least he wouldn't have to worry about getting his license in six months.

He racked his mind for the little he knew—mostly from television and movies—about the Amish. They grew most of their own food, he was pretty sure. Raised chickens, gathered eggs, raised and slaughtered their own beef and pork. Plowed with horses instead of tractors. Made their own clothes. Pumped water into the house with windmills or gas generators.

Would he be learning to farm now that his schooling was finished, or maybe training to be a carpenter, or roofer, or woodworker? Surely they had no need of computer geeks in their short list of job opportunities. No computers or video games or Xboxes. No e-mail or Facebook or Twitter. No DVDs or music downloads or web browsing.

Would he have to give all that up if they asked him to stay?

Would he go back to reading paper books instead of his e-reader, looking up numbers in phone books, and writing letters on stationery like during the colonial days? Surely the Amish used telephones, but come to think of it, he didn't see one on the table or sitting in a charger, or even hanging on the wall with one of those old-fashioned hand cranks.

"Good grief," James said aloud in the dark room. He laughed at his own foolishness. Nobody was inviting him to move down on the farm. No matter what circumstances had forced Hope to give him up, he was fifteen, not five. He didn't need a mommy to wipe his nose or bandage his cuts and scrapes.

And even if he did stick around, he didn't have to turn Amish just because the Bowmans were. He could keep his jeans and T-shirts, along with his laptop. There had to be somewhere he could charge it.

Closing his eyes, he tried to turn off the what-ifs and how-comes that crowded his brain. Yet he couldn't shake the image of the group of Amish girls he'd seen in the Lancaster City bus station. In their pink and green and blue dresses with little white caps, they reminded him of dolls on a toy store shelf. Would his new sisters look like that?

And what would they think of him?

He'd probably better watch his language and stay on his best behavior. In foster care he had learned a lot about getting by, but he sensed that sarcasm and attitude probably wouldn't fly among the Amish.

In the system you had to be tough—or at least talk tough and act tough. It was survival of the fittest: eat or be eaten; the best defense is a good offense. He'd heard it all, seen it all, and one thing was true: you had to do unto others before they did unto you.

And so James Webb had spent a lifetime maintaining distance from boys his own age. Once you let down your guard, the stash of cash in your sock drawer disappeared. If you let someone in on your secrets, they would soon find a way to use that information to their own advantage. And the girls were no better. They would lie, steal, or bat their eyelashes to get their way.

James turned over and punched his pillow. He shouldn't have made that crack about not being part of Hope's master plan. Despite what she should or shouldn't have done, he'd found no pleasure in hurting her feelings. After all, he knew all about being broke. Judging by the amount of money in his pocket, he couldn't support himself, let alone a tiny baby. Better to accomplish what he came for, then go back to the real world and leave these pioneers alone.

He didn't need to understand them. And he sure didn't have to become one of them. The past could not be changed. And his future didn't include suspenders, straw hats, or planting corn for a living.

Still, one question refused to let him rest: was this why he'd never fit in with guys his own age—because in his blood, he was Amish?

When boys picked teams on the playground for softball or basketball, he would always head in the other direction. He'd rather see what bugs lurked under rocks than whack at some ball until he was breathless and sweaty.

Even now when his foster siblings glued themselves to college or pro sports on TV, he only pretended to be interested. He forced himself to learn the terminology of baseball, basketball, and football to prevent shouting out something ignorant at the wrong moment. But records, standings, and point spreads left him bored to tears.

"You're a square peg trying to fit into a round hole, James Webb."

The words of his social worker, not spoken unkindly, rang in his ears until he finally drifted off to sleep. Then visions of riding a huge horse down a pitch-dark road in the middle of the night haunted his dreams until a loud bird jarred him awake. A rooster— just like in the movies. But James fell instantly back to sleep, *cock-a-doodle-do* or no.

Later he washed up in the second-floor bathroom and dressed in a clean shirt but the same pair of jeans. At least he didn't need to bathe in an icy creek behind the house. When he exited the bathroom, he nearly knocked over a little girl. "Sorry," he mumbled. "Did I take too long in there?"

"Nope," she replied. "I went downstairs. My name is Emily." With long lashes and a face spattered with freckles, she was awfully cute.

"Pleased to meet you. I'm James." He leaned against the door frame since she was blocking his path.

"I know. *Mamm* said you're our *bruder*, but we didn't know you 'cause people took you away and gave you to *Englischers* and we couldn't get you back." Her grin stretched from one ear to the other while she kept her hands clasped behind her back. "We don't have no *bruders*."

"If *bruder* means brother, I guess you do now, at least for the next few days." He couldn't keep from grinning too.

"It does. *Mamm* says we should talk only English, but I sometimes forget. You're not very tall for fifteen. Maybe that's because *Mamm's* not very tall."

"Maybe so. I'm surprised you heard the story already. I just showed up last night."

Emily wrinkled her nose. "We've been up for hours. *Mamm* had time to tell us three times while we were waiting for you to wake up. We finally gave up and went out to do chores. I rushed through mine to come stand watch. Josie said sooner or later you would have to go to the bathroom." She rocked back and forth on her heels. "Josie was right."

James grinned. "Smart girl, that Josie."

"Dad says that all the time. You're not going back to bed, are you? Will you come downstairs now?"

James tried not to laugh at her enthusiasm. "Sure, why not?"

Emily marched to the open window at the end of the hallway. "Josie, Greta—he finally woke up!" she yelled through the screen.

Downstairs in the kitchen, Hope was washing vegetables at the sink. She turned off the faucets when James and Emily walked in. Hope addressed the little squirt first. "I could hear you hollering for your sisters down here. Folks probably heard you in Mount Joy. Next time I prefer you walk outside to inform them."

"Yes, ma'am." Emily slumped onto a chair and folded her hands.

"Sorry, Hope," he said. "I'm late for breakfast."

She smiled. "Don't worry about it. We figured you were tired from traveling and needed rest." She nodded toward a chair. "I've kept your breakfast warm."

"Thanks." He sat down next to Emily.

Emily pointed at the opposite rows of chairs. "That's the boys' side of the table now that there are two of you!"

"It's okay, daughter. Let him sit where he likes for today."

"Nope, rules are rules." James walked around to sit across from his sister. Before Hope could carry the platter of food to the table, two girls came through the door. The taller one smiled and took the seat next to Emily, while a tiny puffball of energy raced toward him. She talked a mile a minute, yet he couldn't understand a single word she said.

Hope said something in *Deutsch*, which stopped the child from climbing into his lap. She reluctantly returned to the girls' side.

"This is Greta," Hope said. "She's only four, so she knows no English yet, but that won't stop her from talking your leg off."

"Just say *ya* every so often and nod your head," added Emily. "Greta will be happy."

"And this is our eldest, Josie." Hope placed her hands on the girl's shoulders. "She's three years younger than you."

James nodded at the thin, dark-haired girl. She had luminous brown eyes, but her complexion had turned bright red from her mother's attention. "How ya doing?" he asked. "Actually, I'm almost sixteen, but close enough."

"Welcome," murmured Josie while focused on her hands.

Hope shoved the platter directly in front of him. "Go ahead and eat. You must be famished."

"We ate *hours ago*." Emily passed the salt, pepper, and butter across the table.

James suddenly realized the entire plate was for him. "*All this*? I've never seen so much breakfast."

Hope smiled. "I didn't know what you would like, so I cooked bacon, eggs, sausage, and pancakes. Emily, fetch James another plate so he can take what he wants."

Emily scrambled to the cupboard. "I made the toast," she said, handing him a plate. "But you took so long it got cold and *Mamm* had to reheat it."

"Enough about that; let the boy eat." Hope slipped into a chair next to Greta.

"It looks great. I'll try some of everything." After scraping food onto his plate, James couldn't swallow a single bite. With four pairs of eyes watching, he felt like a specimen under a microscope.

Hope winked at him. "Okay, girls. You've met your brother and have certainly seen people eat before. Go wait on the porch, then you can give him the official tour of the Bowman farm."

The three girls stood, but Josie remained rooted to the floor. "By ourselves? Aren't you coming with us?"

"You'll be fine; you won't get lost." Hope patted her back. "I need to bathe Faith. Her diaper probably needs changing by now."

Josie exited the kitchen behind her sisters. Hope waited until the door closed behind them to explain. "She's a bit shy until she gets to know you."

"I know all about shyness. I'll do my best to put her at ease."

James concentrated on finishing every morsel of his breakfast quickly so as not to keep them waiting long. For reasons he didn't understand, he really wanted his sisters to like him.

Hope stood at the window watching four of her five children until they entered the barn. Josie stayed at James's side but a full yard away; Emily walked backward in front of him, talking endlessly. At some point during the tour she was bound to trip and land on her backside. Greta circled around the group like a hummingbird.

Once they disappeared from view, Hope realized she was shaking like a leaf. Her son was back—her little boy.

Unbelievably, she'd planned to name the baby Jamie if she'd kept him. His adoptive parents had somehow read her mind. Except they hadn't adopted him after all. They had returned him to the center like defective merchandise. He hadn't fit their plans because of a medical condition.

Yet how could she judge them harshly? He hadn't fit the plans of Silas Klobentz either. Her poor little boy had spent a lifetime moving from house to house, never quite part of any family.

But he is home now. "Thank You, Lord. I will prove myself worthy of this second chance."

⁓

Stephen led the troop of *kinner* into the *haus* at lunchtime. Hope was ready with Faith sleeping in her wind-up swing, her house tidy, and fixings for sandwiches on the table. She had baked a batch of chocolate chip cookies and opened a bag of potato chips she'd been saving.

"I would have been in sooner, but they roped me into joining the tour." Stephen winked and hung his hat on a peg near the door.

James hooked his Phillies ball cap on a peg too. "Man, I can't believe how much land you own," he said. "And horses and chickens and pigs and all those cows."

"That's because this is a *dairy* farm. You gotta have cows." Emily grabbed James's sleeve. "Come, we must wash up or we won't be allowed to eat." She dragged the boy toward the bathroom.

"No, young lady. A man needs privacy from little girls." Stephen caught Emily by the arm. "You wash at the kitchen sink with your sisters."

Five minutes later all were clean and seated. James's enthusiasm hadn't flagged one ounce. "You have acres of hay and corn and grazing pasture, plus three barns—four, if you count the chicken house." He grabbed two slices of bread and speared several pieces of ham.

"It's called a coop," corrected Emily. "And we can't eat till we pray."

"Sorry," he murmured, dropping his fork. Following suit, he immediately bowed his head. After a few moments, he opened one eye and peered around, blushing. "Isn't somebody gonna say grace?"

Stephen raised his hand to silence Emily. "Prayers are usually silent among the Amish. We thank God quietly for His gifts."

"Okay." James lowered his head again, then resumed spearing ham. "You've got quite a handy milking setup, using diesel-powered generators. Sure beats sitting on a three-legged stool milking by hand." He mimed the action of pulling on cow udders.

"Truly, it does." Stephen suppressed a laugh while Greta and Emily giggled. Greta duplicated his mimicry. "But our farm is by no means large in the English world. Farms in Lancaster County get broken up to create new homesteads for newlyweds."

"Well, it's a beauty in my book." James waited until everyone prepared a sandwich before taking a bite. He took a handful of chips and passed the bag to Josie.

Josie accepted the bag, her cheeks a deep crimson. "What book are you talking about?"

He thought for a moment. "Not a real book. It's just an expression like 'ducks in a row,' or 'run it up the flagpole,' or 'call the shots.' It means 'in my opinion.'"

Josie looked to her *mamm*. "We're just glad you like it here," Hope said.

"After lunch, we're taking James to the pond where *Daed* goes fishing and we ice skate." Emily almost levitated off her chair with anticipation. "Then down to the creek to where the tadpoles live."

"Fine, but don't neglect your chores." Stephen locked eyes with his middle daughter.

"Maybe I could help you," said James to Stephen.

He chewed thoughtfully for a moment. "When the girls come inside to help their *mamm*, you come find me in the hay field. You can ride along on the baler."

"Sounds good." The boy devoured his sandwich and then fixed another.

That night after supper, James stayed in the kitchen while the women washed and dried dishes. He appeared to be reading the Amish newspaper, but Hope knew he was listening to the girls' conversations. When Stephen came into the room for a cup of tea, James folded the paper and leaned back in his chair.

"Girls, go up to your room so we can talk to your brother," said Stephen. "He probably has some questions for us." Hope hung up her towel and sat down across from them.

James shrugged his shoulders. "I've always been curious about my natural mother. After I hacked into the records, I decided spur-of-the-moment to find you. What if I should need a kidney down the road, or part of a liver? Having no medical background can be tough. So, yes, I have a lot of questions."

"I owe you the whole truth," said Hope softly. "I was raped, and my father sent me to live at an adoption center until you were born. I have long forgiven the man responsible—now I seek only your forgiveness." She forced herself to look him in the eye.

"Guess you didn't have much choice at sixteen." He met her gaze but glanced away quickly.

"I can't change the past, but I can change your future if you want."

"Let's not get too far ahead of ourselves. I'm pretty much past needing somebody to tell me what to do. Thanks just the same." He rose to his feet and walked toward the sink with a swagger. "I'd better turn in if I gotta get up at the crack of dawn." He headed upstairs without a backward glance.

But Hope had heard something in his voice—something small and young and still in desperate need of love.

Chapter Eight

James slept soundly that night. Maybe it was all the walking he'd done with his sisters. Or maybe it was the fresh air while riding around on that bizarre piece of farm equipment pulled by two gigantic horses with feet as large as an elephant's. Or it might have been the security of knowing no one would steal his iPod or laptop while he slept. He hadn't taken either one out of his duffel bag since he arrived.

Besides, anybody who didn't have electricity wasn't going to have wireless Internet service either. But it didn't matter. He couldn't think of a single person he wanted to e-mail.

James showered and dressed in the oldest clothes he'd brought, per Stephen's instructions. When he left the bathroom, he half expected Emily to be standing guard, but she was nowhere to be seen.

He rather liked the little squirt. She had followed him around the farm all day yesterday, explaining everything as if he just arrived in an escape pod from an alien planet. And in some ways, he had. Even though he'd lived in at least eight different foster homes, none of them had been farms.

For instance, he had no idea that you cut hay like mowing the lawn. Then within a few weeks hay grew back, ready to be cut, raked, baled, and stored until needed.

And he had no clue so many kinds of horses existed—some for hauling heavy plows, some for pulling buggies, some for riding the back trails to visit a friend. He'd been a little spooked by the horse's big teeth until Emily taught him the safe way to approach a horse.

Emily had charmed him almost at "hello." And little Greta—did that little girl ever stop smiling? She would rattle on for ten minutes straight and then grin like a beauty pageant winner. No matter how many times people explained he didn't know *Deutsch*, Greta continued to chatter away.

James had peered into baby Faith's cradle a few times, amazed by how much infants slept. Once when he'd been watching, she opened her huge brown eyes. He half expected Faith to start chattering like Greta, but she merely burped and stuck her thumb in her mouth.

Only Josie perplexed him. He caught her studying him several times, but quickly glanced away before they made eye contact. She said little during their tour, preferring to prompt Emily into any necessary explanations. He felt sorry for her; girls that quiet faded into the wallpaper in the English world.

The English world—only his second full day, and he was picking up the vernacular.

When James arrived in the kitchen, Hope and the girls were already seated. Surprisingly, so was Stephen.

"I hope I didn't keep anybody waiting," he said. "I got out of bed the first time that rooster crowed." He padded to the same chair he occupied yesterday.

Hope handed him a glass of milk. "Not at all. I just finished the oatmeal. Josie sliced fruit and Emily made toast."

"It's still warm." Emily clapped her hands, ecstatic.

"Settle yourself, daughter. Let the world wake up before you fire up your chatter." Stephen sipped a cup of coffee as Hope placed a full bowl of hot cereal before him. "I trust you have a cell phone, *ya*? Did you call your foster parents to let them know where you are?"

"Ah, no," James stammered. "My phone's dead. No place to charge it."

It was a lie—his phone still held a charge. He just wasn't ready to call home. He needed more time with Hope.

Stephen ate several spoonfuls of oatmeal before speaking. "Right after breakfast you and I will walk next door. They've got a phone line that neighbors are welcome to use. We need to call those who care for you so they don't worry or call the police to report you missing." His tone brooked no debate.

"Okay, but like I said, foster parents usually give it a day or two before sounding the alarm." James dug into the cinnamon sugar oatmeal, amazed at how much better it was than the stuff in little pouches.

"Can we come too?" Emily said while Josie also looked hopeful.

"No, you get to picking the garden. Your mother wants to can corn and succotash today."

This was another difference from most households James had lived in. He knew foster kids who would argue that the moon was blue just to be heard. But no one argued when Stephen Bowman issued an order. During the entire meal Hope kept glancing between him and her husband. She said nothing and barely ate two spoonfuls of food.

After breakfast James tried not to worry as he and Stephen walked toward the neighbor's house. What was there to worry about? He was here checking out his once-upon-a-time mother, never with the intention of staying.

"Okay, the phone is in there," Stephen announced after a long meander down the country road. "You can explain the situation first, but I wish to talk to those in charge of you, so don't hang up."

"*In there?*" he asked, pointing at a small shed. "It looks like an outhouse."

Hope's husband did not laugh. "I assure you, it's not. Go on in."

James entered the hut with trepidation but found it clean and free of spiderwebs. It had a small window in the back wall for ventilation, a wooden stool, and a shelf of phone books. A black phone hung on the wall while a tablet and pen rested atop the directories.

"I'll mark on the pad the date and time of your call so the district member who gets the bill will know who to collect money from."

"I'm kind of tapped out at the moment. Can I owe you for the call?"

Stephen's eyes crinkled into deep lines. "Nope, this is on Hope and me. Now, make the call." He stepped back from the shed.

James had no choice but to do as he was told. His foster mother answered on the second ring. In four succinct sentences he explained where he was, what he'd done, and why he had done it. Then he held his breath and waited.

"Thank goodness you're all right, James Webb! You had us worried. We called your caseworker immediately and they alerted the police. You were reported as a runaway instead of a possible abduction, so there was no Amber alert."

"Sorry," he mumbled halfheartedly. "Sure don't want to see my face plastered on milk cartons."

After some additional browbeating, Mrs. Hyde asked, "You say you're with an Amish family?"

"Yeah, my birth mother is Amish. Didn't see that one coming. I'd like to stay a few more days if it's okay with you. I'm kinda curious about them, but don't worry, I'm not turning Amish anytime soon." He whispered the last sentence, then allowed his foster mom to whine more about his lack of respect for authority and sense of responsibility. After a while James handed the phone to Stephen. "She wants to talk to you."

Stephen switched places but closed the door to speak privately. James tried to eavesdrop but could hear nothing through the thick wood. When Stephen exited the phone shed, he was smiling. "Mrs. Hyde agreed you can stay for a few days but wants you home by Sunday and back in school on Monday. You'll have to make up your homework when you return, but she'll notify the school, the police, and your social worker. She said I should expect the county sheriff to pay us a call to make sure you're not being held against your will."

James laughed. "Tied up and gagged?"

Hope's husband frowned. "Creating a ruckus isn't a joke. I said the sheriff could come anytime. In the meantime, you must help with chores if you expect to eat and allow Hope to wash your clothing."

"These are different from yesterday's." He pointed at his jeans. "They just look the same. I'll bring the dirty clothes downstairs."

"You agree with doing chores?"

James nodded. "Sure. I liked yesterday, and the idea of no school."

"You do realize we don't have a TV or a computer." A twinkle in Stephen's eye gave away his improving mood.

"Yeah. It'll be like a camping trip I once took, with way better eats at suppertime."

And so the two men walked back to the Bowman farm with James looking forward to some physical labor for the first time in his life.

~

Hope couldn't stop humming that evening. Everything had gone well. Sweet Becky Byler had stopped by for a few hours to watch Greta and baby Faith so that she could take Josie to the dentist in town and stop at the drugstore for a few necessities. The dentist easily fixed Josie's one cavity. Hope found the items she wanted on sale. And very little traffic troubled her ride home. Most of all James Webb had settled nicely into the family routine, which brought her boundless joy.

The boy rose each morning with the rooster. He dressed quickly, remembering to deliver his clothes for her to wash instead of leaving them strewn on the guest room floor. He cleaned his plate at every meal, never once complaining about their simple Amish fare. Plus, he got along with all his sisters. Greta and Emily adored him and would follow him around like puppies if Stephen hadn't specifically forbidden it. Even Josie was emerging from her shell. She'd been spotted making eye contact and initiating conversation with James. Maybe that wasn't another Bowman family miracle, but Hope was pleased. Her second oldest was conquering shyness while her eldest was forming positive sibling relationships.

What had his life been like in the variety of foster homes? Had he been tormented or bullied, as children often did to those who were even slightly different? James mentioned to Stephen one evening that he cared little for sports. That alone put him at odds with most of the English male population.

Hope struggled to force away a mental picture of boys mocking her son. Even in the Amish community, children could be mean to each other. Poor Becky Byler was often taunted for her obesity. Being heavy was unusual among Plain folk, and even adults were often thoughtless with their questions and comments:

"Did you gain more weight since the last time I saw you, Becky Byler?"

"How much fabric must you buy to make a dress these days?"

"Here, take this jar of pickled cauliflower home to eat. That should have fewer calories than potatoes or sweet corn."

Hope was fond of Becky, so she was happy to find the young woman with James when she returned from town. The two were at the kitchen table drinking iced tea and talking, while Becky rocked Faith's swing and Greta and Emily napped. From what Hope overheard of their conversation, Becky was explaining some of the reasons behind Amish life.

If James was bothered by Becky's size, he didn't show it. And Becky asked no uncomfortable details about his life in the city. After Hope paid Becky for babysitting, the girl said to James, "Welcome to Paradise. I hope you enjoy your stay with the Bowmans and come back often."

When James went out to help milk cows, Hope started thinking. *Come back often? Why should he travel back and forth from Philadelphia to*

Paradise? He needed to remain with his family. She couldn't wait until her kitchen was clean that evening to discuss the matter with Stephen. The moment her husband came in after his final livestock check, she ambushed him. "I don't want James to leave tomorrow."

Stephen stared at her, then headed to the stove to heat water for tea. "You're not talking sense, *fraa.* I've already arranged a hired van to drive him back to the bus station. And I reserved tickets to take him to Harrisburg and then on to Philadelphia." He pulled two mugs from the shelf.

"But why should he leave? His foster mother has several other boys. They don't need this one. I am his *mamm*—we are his family. This is where he belongs." It took all her reserve to not stomp her foot.

Stephen arched one dark eyebrow. "It's not a question of them not *needing* this one. That is where he lives—they have legal papers."

"But I want this to be his permanent home. I prayed to God for a miracle—to be given a son—and God gave us my firstborn. Not another baby down the road, but an almost-grown young man who needs love and acceptance. If James is willing, you should call those folks again to say he's staying."

Stephen placed tea bags in mugs as he waited for the water to boil. "We are Amish and he is not."

Hope paced back and forth. "James could become Amish. And if he doesn't want to, he could live with us as an *Englischer* until he leaves for college or marries and finds a place of his own. The two of you can build a cabin on our property near the road so the driveway wouldn't be too long when he eventually buys a car."

Stephen held up his hand. "You're talking crazy. We are Amish and therefore subject to the *Ordnung* and rules made by the bishop. Decisions regarding James's future aren't ours to make. They're up to James and his caseworker and our bishop, along with the ministerial brethren." The whistle from the teakettle added a harsh punctuation mark to his words. "Have you thought about what your *daed* or other elders would say about a fifteen-year-old *Englischer's* influence on a houseful of impressionable girls? They would never permit it."

This time Hope did stomp her foot. "I don't care what my father has to say about this. He made an evil mistake years ago, and I won't let him make another one now."

Stephen dunked tea bags into the steeping cups of water. "Don't throw the word *evil* around casually. Silas's decisions were misguided, but I doubt he had evil intent."

"Fine, but I still won't seek his counsel with anything concerning James."

"What about the bishop or the other elders? Will you disregard their advice as well?" Folding his arms across his chest, Stephen lifted his chin.

Hope shrank back a little. "No. I'm Amish and always will be, but I want my son in my . . . our lives."

Stephen stared for a long moment. "Don't get ahead of yourself, Hope. It's up to the boy. He might decide one farm visit is enough." He blew across the surface of his mug. "Come get your tea. It might help you think clearer."

"I've lost my taste for the stuff tonight. And there's not a thing wrong with my thinking." In a rare show of temper, Hope strode from the room and headed upstairs without waiting for her *ehemann*.

Chapter Nine

Stephen's jaw dropped and his stomach churned. Before he could form a thought, his *fraa* stomped out of the room like a stubborn child. His first inclination was to follow after Hope to demand she discuss the matter like an adult. To show him the respect he deserved as her husband and head of the household. To place her family before herself as instructed in New Testament scripture and follow the *Ordnung* of her district.

But as soon as he formed the thought, it disintegrated like fireplace ash along with his anger. She was right, pure and simple. Silas had done her a grave injustice by forcing his will on her—an injustice to the entire family. James Webb wasn't the only one who'd been enlightened these past few days. That boy was a Klobentz through and through and therefore now a Bowman.

Stephen saw Hope in so many of James's features and mannerisms: in the tilt of his head and the way he laughed, in his fondness for any fruit but disdain for turnips and squash. At first his Englishness set him apart from his natural *mamm* and half siblings, but as the week progressed resemblances grew more apparent. Not just to Hope but to Josie, Emily, and Greta as well.

Yesterday while they walked the fence line checking for breaks or any weak spots, James had shared the story of one of his foster mothers who, when he was five, decided to break him of a bad habit. While he slept, she carefully withdrew his thumb from his mouth without waking him. Then she coated it with butter and cayenne pepper. When James reinserted the thumb, he awoke to a mouth on fire and a lifelong distaste for pepper—black, white, or red.

Thumb sucking he had in common with baby Faith. Yet he and Hope would allow Faith to outgrow the habit on her own, just as his other three daughters had.

By the light of a nearly full moon, Stephen headed up the lane in between the cow pasture and hay fields. No mad dashes through dry cornstalks tonight. His anger at Hope's willful outburst was gone. Instead, Stephen realized he agreed with her.

After all, the adoptive mother had changed her mind once she discovered an imperfect baby. James said he'd lived at his present foster home for less than a year. Although James liked Mr. and Mrs. Hyde, the couple had taken in four hard-to-place boys in addition to their three natural sons. James hadn't had enough time to grow too fond of Mrs. Hyde or she of him.

Seven sons, he mused. *Just think how much an Amish farmer could accomplish with seven sons.* Halting on the path, he turned his face skyward. "Forgive me, Lord. That was a self-centered thought. I should be thinking about the welfare of the boy, not how much help he'd be with chores."

But the fact remained that James seemed to enjoy working the land, milking cows, and helping his sisters in the garden. He hadn't even complained when the two of them washed the chicken coop floor. He kept saying, "This sure beats school."

Stephen knew it was more than just avoiding homework, boring lectures, and school-yard bullies. He had watched as James stood on the highest point of the Bowman land—Hope's favorite spot to think and pray—and beat on his chest with his fists, declaring, "I'm king of the world!"

Stephen assured him he was not. They were merely two of God's millions of creatures, none more special than any other.

Last night James had rocked on the porch for hours, listening to night sounds and studying the stars. After Hope and the girls had gone to bed, Stephen watched from the screen door, contemplating whether or not to join the boy. He heard his cell phone ring twice—the phone with a supposed dead battery—but James had ignored it. In the end Stephen had left him alone. Sometimes a man—young or old—needed time to think things through. And James Webb had plenty to ponder.

How odd they must appear to him with their accents, occasional lapses into *Deutsch*, and avoidance of technology and the electrical grid. How he must miss the pastimes that had taken the place of strong family bonds. Yet deep inside his heart, Stephen knew the Bowman family had much to offer James.

He could offer James much. He'd set out merely to be a supportive host, providing a Christian home to a weary traveler who'd lost his way, literally and figuratively. But instead, he'd grown protective and fond of Hope's son. And if pressed for the truth, that fondness could easily grow into love. Hope's son—his son—the one the Lord in His infinite mercy had returned to them. At that moment he had never felt so sure about anything . . . and so much in love with his wife.

Stephen turned and ran all the way to the house. By the time he reached the steps, the house was dark. Hope was probably in their first-floor room, unable to rest until he returned. Faith's cradle would be at arm's length. Josie, Emily, and Greta would be asleep in their second-floor bedrooms, dreaming of school or some last-minute summer outing. And James, up in the attic? What thoughts occupied a fifteen-year-old *Englischer's* mind in the night? Was he eager to return to civilization tomorrow or sad that his fate had been radically changed many years ago?

Toeing off his boots, Stephen crept through the silent house to their bedroom. He undressed and slipped under the cool top sheet. "Are you still awake?"

"Of course I am." Hope was facing his side of the bed. "I'm sorry about stomping my foot and not listening to reason. If Emily had behaved that way, she would get no candy for a month."

Chuckling, he reached for her hand in the dark. When he found it, he brought it to his lips for a tender kiss. "You might have acted rashly, but you're not wrong to want the boy in our lives. I'm willing to do everything in my power to convince the bishop and ministerial brethren of the soundness of reuniting James with us. I'll speak to his foster mother and caseworker, even fight for him in an English courtroom if necessary."

"You would go up against my father?" Her words floated on the humid night air.

"Silas Klobentz doesn't intimidate me. This is our family and the boy is part of it, if he wishes to be." Silence spun out between them for several minutes. A light breeze stirred the curtains, bringing welcome relief to his overheated skin.

Then she spoke in a choked voice. "Thank you, *ehemann*."

Stephen kissed her fingers a second time. "But please remember the choice must be his. James may not want to stay, whether he remains English or not. We can't force him or make him feel obligated. We must not add to his burdens."

"I understand. I'll try not to get my hopes up, and let's not say anything to the girls for now. But I will pray—that's one thing I can do."

"I will too. God needs to hear how grateful we are for this blessing."

~

Hope had never known two weeks to pass so slowly in her entire life. Stephen was busy harvesting corn from sunup to sundown with the help of some district members. Emily and Josie started a new school year, while poor Greta moped around the house without her sisters or her new brother.

Because James Webb was gone—back with his foster family in Philadelphia.

Following Stephen's advice, Hope said nothing about their desire for him to live permanently with them. If they were unsuccessful, it would only be one more setback in a long line of disappointments. She had tried to convey how glad she was he came to visit. She encouraged him to return as often as his caseworker permitted. Stephen thanked him profusely for his help with the hay harvest, echoing her sentiments. And the girls? Shy Josie kissed his cheek and Emily hugged him around the waist, refusing to let go, and little Greta had cried inconsolably.

James had blushed from all the attention. He had returned his sisters' hugs and shaken Stephen's hand vigorously. Only with Hope was the boy reticent. He didn't approach her until the taxicab blew its horn. Then he extended his hand and shook it briefly, thanking her for her hospitality as though she were a hostess at a garden party. And he had called her Hope.

What had she expected? *Mamm, I love it here and wish I could stay forever?* He threw his duffel bag into the trunk along with her bag of snacks, declined her offer of several apple pies, and didn't glance through the rearview window as the cab drove away. After he arrived home, he had neither called nor written.

After several nights of crying herself to sleep, Hope contacted his caseworker, Carolyn Webster, from the neighbor's phone shed. The woman was willing to see her in Harrisburg, but a full two weeks elapsed before the meeting could be arranged. Hope left the house before dawn to make their afternoon appointment, traveling solely with Faith. The minute Hope entered the office, Faith started squalling.

Miss Webster peered over her reading glasses and frowned. "You were unable to find a sitter, Mrs. Bowman?"

Hope shifted Faith to her other arm and rubbed the baby's back. "A sitter? No, I can't leave her for this long since I'm nursing." Faith let out another wail while Miss Webster blinked, then focused on papers on her desk.

"Do you have someplace I can change her diaper? I believe she'll settle down once she's dry."

The woman stared blankly at her. "Yes, there's a restroom down the hall with one of those drop-down tables. I'll wait for you here."

When Hope returned, her daughter quickly fell back asleep. The discussion with Miss Webster was by no means as successful.

"From your message, I understand you wish to pursue custody of James Webb." Miss Webster looked up from the open folder.

"Yes, I do, since I'm his mother."

The woman's brows knitted together. "You were his birth mother, but you surrendered all parental rights upon signing the adoption papers."

"I understand. But that couple didn't keep him. They gave him back, and the agency never bothered to contact me. I would have found a way to raise the boy myself had I known."

Miss Webster's frown deepened. "After his initial unsuccessful adoption, we continued to seek permanent placement for James. But the decision by his adoptive parents didn't change your situation regarding legal custody. You severed ties, Mrs. Bowman. All this was explained to you at the center."

"Well, it *should* have changed things." Hope kneaded her hands in her lap.

"I'm sorry you feel that way. How does James feel about this? Has he asked to live with you and your family?"

"Well, no, but he came looking for us."

"Teenagers often become curious at his age and seek their natural mothers. The end result is often not what either party expects." Miss Webster softened her tone.

"I'm sure that's true, but James liked staying with us. He got along with his sisters, helped with chores, and ate everything I cooked without turning up his nose." She hoped that didn't sound as pathetic to Miss Webster as it did to her own ears.

"I'm glad James enjoyed his visit to your farm, but there're many things to take into consideration. When he turns eighteen, he'll be able to choose for himself where he lives, since he'll no longer be under Children's Services' care."

"Like what things?"

"The fact that your family is Amish and James isn't makes a difference. We want him to finish high school and will insist he not leave before he's eighteen."

"There are English high schools in Lancaster County."

Miss Webster rolled her chair back from the desk. "I'm sorry you traveled all this way, but you must understand that changing a child's custody is no simple matter. Foster homes must be screened by social workers and regularly inspected. James must stay where he is, but try not to worry—the Hydes are a good family." She stood, smiling. "May I drive you and your daughter back to the bus station?"

"No, thank you. I'm used to walking." Hope rose to her feet, suddenly weak-kneed and mildly sick to her stomach. "But you'll ask him?"

"Ask him what?" The caseworker was halfway to her office door.

"Ask James if he wants to live with his birth *mamm*?"

Carolyn Webster gazed at Hope with a pitying expression. "I will ask how his visit to Lancaster went and if he wishes to maintain contact with you. But please don't get your hopes up. Boys are rather set in their ways by age fifteen."

Hope trudged through the doorway and out of the glass-and-steel building. She and Faith reached the station, boarded her bus, and returned to Paradise. But during the entire trip her gut churned as it never had before.

That evening Stephen accepted the news with his usual complacency. His only comment was, "We'll continue to remember him in our prayers."

Rosa, unlike Stephen, had plenty to say on the matter. "I can't believe your being Amish would make a difference. Sounds to me like the boy could benefit from people with strong faith." Rosa paced the room.

"She's worried he won't graduate high school." Hope lifted Faith from her carrier for feeding.

"Your word that he'll stay in school should be sufficient. After all, you are his *mamm*."

"Not legally." Desperation crept into her voice.

"Then you need to talk to a lawyer, Hope."

"That's not our way, you know that."

"Your father started this years ago. Sometimes traditions need to change, or at least exceptions should be made." Rosa halted in front of Hope's chair. "You need to become one of those foster parents. If that's the only way to get your boy back, then that's what you should do."

Hope pressed her fist to her chest. "I'm so lucky to have a smart best friend."

Rosa patted her shoulder. "Sometimes you have to join them instead of trying to fight them."

"I don't want to beat anybody; I just want my boy back." Hope's mind whirred with plans and possibilities. While Faith nursed and Rosa fixed mint tea, the seeds of hope began to grow inside her heart.

Chapter Ten

Hope adjusted her reading glasses and scanned through the sheaf of papers Rosa had provided for her. Apparently Rosa read much more than recipes in the magazines at the doctor's office. And since her husband's death, she spent a lot of time at the public library. Lately she had expanded her reading to include the adoption laws in the state of Pennsylvania and the requirements to become foster parents in Lancaster County.

If Hope lived to be a hundred and five, she would never be able to repay Rosa for her help.

November brought cooler weather, brisk winds, and more rain to Lancaster County. In the months since Hope's trip to Harrisburg, activity around the farm had accelerated. Stephen was grinding the last of the corn into silage, along with spreading composted fertilizer on the fields to prepare for winter. Dairy cows had to be milked twice a day, along with the other barn and field chores. Stephen would love to hire someone, but for now they relied on occasional help from neighbors and district members.

Josie and Emily were thriving in school under the guidance of a young single woman by the name of Charity Yoder. Amish schools often had frequent turnovers, as young women took the position and then married. Marriage usually meant *bopplin* would soon follow and the teacher would retire to stay home. But for now, Charity seemed settled, and the girls adored her.

Everything was going well, except for the fact that James was missing from the household.

But Hope intended to change that, as soon as possible.

~

"How goes it, *fraa*?"

Stephen's simple question startled Hope. "Goodness, *ehemann*, must you sneak up on a gal?" She peered over her reading glasses.

He buzzed a kiss across her *kapp*. "I come for lunch around noon every day. Sorry if today I took you by surprise." Rolling up his sleeves, he washed his hands and arms at the sink.

"Lunch? Goodness, I lost track of time while filling out the latest batch of government paperwork." Hope jumped to her feet. "Roast beef sandwiches okay, with horseradish and tomatoes? I have a chilled jar of pickled beets too."

"I'd been hoping for roast turkey with corn bread dressing and cranberries. But I guess a sandwich will do." Stephen grinned at his own joke and settled into his usual chair.

"I'll stuff and roast a bird on Saturday. Then we can eat cold leftovers on the Sabbath." Hope placed the platter of meat, a loaf of fresh bread, and pitcher of milk on the table. "Greta, come eat," she called in *Deutsch*. They waited for the child to join them before bowing their heads.

"Problems with us getting a foster home license?" Stephen built a sandwich around two thick slices of beef.

"Not really a problem, but I must detail in writing how I plan to accommodate an English student in our home. We must enroll him in high school, arrange for his transportation, and explain how he can keep his computer and cell phone charged up. They insist he maintain phone contact with his caseworker at all times. And he must be able to use his laptop for classes with access to the Internet."

Stephen scowled over his sandwich. "They require us to provide an Internet connection? What else—a television and one of those movie-recording machines? The bishop would never approve of such things, Hope."

"No, no, don't upset yourself. He only needs a place to charge them up. We can run our diesel generator in the barn to accomplish that. And he could use the computer after school or at the library on the weekends. If James chooses to live with us, he must accept the fact we don't listen to radio or watch TV."

Stephen chewed silently while Hope cut Greta's meat into small pieces. "And what have you heard from the boy?" He met Hope's gaze.

"Still not a word. I have written twice to say we're getting a foster home license in case he wants to try living with our family, but he hasn't written back. I gave him the number of the phone shed. He could always leave a message on their machine. I've heard that many *Englischers* aren't good letter writers."

"Maybe he's thinking the matter over or waiting to see if we're successful getting approved."

"I hope that's it." Hope stared at her untouched sandwich. "But I won't relax until I hear that he's willing to give us a chance."

Stephen reached across the table, his palm open. "What does Scripture tell us to do?"

She stretched her hand to meet his. "Be patient and wait on the Lord. His timetable is perfect."

He smiled. "You've got the gist of the passage." He speared a pickled beet. "Now, what are your plans for the afternoon?"

"I will pick more cabbage and put up sauerkraut for the cold months. When the girls come home, they can help me." Hope started eating in earnest, but the crunch of buggy wheels on gravel distracted her attention. "Who can that be? I wasn't expecting anyone."

Stephen walked to the window, his lunch finished. "Looks like your father's buggy." Hope dropped the sandwich on the plate. "I wonder what would take *Mamm* and *Daed* away from chores?"

She asked the question, but in her heart, she knew.

Father marched toward the *haus*, followed by Mother, who was limping along the flagstones.

Hope swung the kitchen door wide. "*Welcum*, I didn't expect to see you two until preaching on Sunday." She felt Stephen move to stand behind her.

Silas stepped across the threshold, pulling off his hat. "That's what I had planned, *dochder*, but the bishop mentioned some troubling news to me." He braced his hand on the table but didn't sit down. "Don't you think we could have discussed this before you pursued this nonsense?"

Hope crossed her arms. "If you're referring to my son as 'nonsense,' then no, I don't think I need to discuss it with you first."

Silas's lips thinned, his face pale. "You're making a mistake. That boy doesn't belong here. He should stay with his own kind."

Faith's cries pierced the tension in the room, but Silas reacted before Hope. "Martha, you tend the *boppli* while I finish with our *dochder*. She needs to come to her senses."

"I'm James's *mamm*, so that makes me his kind, same as Josie, Emily, Greta, and Faith."

Stephen slipped his arm around her waist. "I've spent time with James—I seem to be his kind too."

Silas peered at one, then the other. "You will be disgraced in the district, Hope Bowman." He snarled rather than spoke the words.

"No, any who judge me are wrong to do so."

Her father frowned. "What did the bishop tell you?"

"He isn't against fostering James, providing our family keeps the *Ordnung*. His English activities must stay at school and not influence our *dochders*. But the bishop will welcome him to our community and hopes the boy will take up a Christian path."

"I doubt the bishop prefers the situation as such," Silas said.

"But this is our choice," said Stephen quietly.

Faith's cries hadn't abated under Martha's care. "Excuse me, *Daed*. Faith is hungry, so I need to tend her myself. *Danki* for dropping by, and I shall continue to pray the Lord will guide me on this matter." She strode from the room with composure and assurance she didn't feel. But she had held her temper and hadn't dishonored her father.

~

James Webb stepped off the school bus into a two-inch puddle. His younger housemates giggled. A wet foot just iced the cake on his bad day. His English Lit teacher sprang a quiz on this week's assignments—the ones he hadn't read. He'd forgotten his lunch on the kitchen counter along with his wallet in his room. With no desire to borrow money from anyone, he'd gone hungry. A late-afternoon headache had been his reward for forgetfulness. At least Mrs. Hyde always had fruit and cookies for snacks after school. And providing the kids still ate their supper, she allowed them to eat enough to take the edge off.

The cookies were store-bought, not homemade like Hope's, but at least Mrs. Hyde didn't fill his head with a pack of lies. She presented life like it was—he could live here until he finished high school, even after he turned eighteen, providing he didn't pick fights with the other boys and didn't flunk out. After that he was on his own to find a job or move into a cardboard box under the freeway overpass.

"Hey, Mrs. Hyde," James said, dumping his backpack on the floor. Kevin and Larry ran for the pantry, while the three boys who rode an earlier bus were already seated at the table.

"Wash your hands before you dig in." Mrs. Hyde set a pitcher of generic fruit punch on the table.

James ran cold water over his fingers for a few seconds and dried his hands on his jeans. He'd barely swallowed his first choco-late chip cookie when Mrs. Hyde paused next to his chair.

"She called again today," said Mrs. Hyde.

"Who?" James shoved another into his mouth, not looking at her.

"You know who—Mrs. Bowman." She rested a hand on her hip. "This is the third time she's called. And I know she wrote at least twice because I noticed the Paradise postmark. Isn't that a couple hours from Philadelphia?"

Reaching for another cookie, James lifted both eyebrows. Usually his foster mom butted out of their personal business.

"I think you should call her. See what she wants."

He shoved the entire cookie in his mouth and chewed thoroughly. "I know what she wants—she wants me to come to their farm to get to know my *family* better." He spat the word like a watermelon seed.

Mrs. Hyde's forehead furrowed. "I thought you had enjoyed yourself. Why don't you spend your break there—sort of like a getaway."

"Thanks, but no thanks. Hope had her chance with me. We both know how *that* ended up." He rose to his feet, drained his fruit punch, and took three more sweets. "Excuse me, but I should do my homework before supper."

She blocked his exit. "One of my jobs as your foster mother is to teach you manners. And polite people return phone calls. Rudeness will get you nowhere in life. It's your decision whether or not to see the Bowmans again, but you should call her back."

He smirked and rolled his eyes. Polite people? What next—they had to sip tea from tiny cups with raised pinkies? But since Mrs. Hyde seldom asked anything from him, he shrugged. "Fine, I'll call her on my cell phone."

"Right now?"

"Right now." He forced a smile.

"Thanks, James." She patted his shoulder in a rare demonstration of affection, then handed him a slip of paper.

He polished off the rest of his snack on the way upstairs. Luckily his roommate wasn't home from football practice yet. Slinging his backpack onto the bed, James punched in the number from the paper. To his astonishment, someone picked up the other end. He'd expected an answering machine.

"Hello?" said a woman's voice.

"Hope?" he asked ridiculously. Why would she be hanging out at the phone shed?

"No, this is her neighbor, Donna Miller."

"Could you tell her I called, please? She's been calling me."

He was ready to hang up when the voice said, "I'd be happy to, but who are you?"

What should he say—her son? No, Hope didn't deserve that distinction as far as he was concerned. "This is James Webb, an acquaintance from a long time ago. Thanks." With a surge of hostility, he clicked the phone shut.

James stood in his small bedroom with his fists clenched, breathing hard and sweating. Finally, he picked up his books to return to the kitchen, but before he could reach the doorway, his cell phone rang. James lifted the phone to his ear, yet his mouth refused to form words.

"James?" asked a familiar voice. "Is that you? It's Hope Bowman."

"Yeah, it's me. Mrs. Hyde said you'd been phoning a lot, and she made me call you back." He heard a sharp intake of air and then a pause.

"Yes, I've called and written twice. I wanted you to know we completed the paperwork to become a licensed foster home in this state. We're just waiting on final inspection. So if you'd like to live with us—for a short time or a long while—it would be allowable." She sounded weak and whiny—two traits he despised.

"I get three square meals here, my clothes washed, and nobody fills my head with trash. Why would I want to come live on your farm?"

"Because you have four sisters here and I am your mom." Her last words were barely recognizable as Hope's voice faltered.

"My mom, really? I don't think so. If you wanted to be my mother, you never would have sold me to the highest bidder."

She gasped. "Who said such a thing? I never sold you. I didn't receive a dime. And they never told me the adoption didn't go through."

"But your expenses were paid the entire time at the center. So you took a sweet little vacation while preserving your precious reputation among the Amish. I cost your family nothing in medical bills."

"I explained that my father left me no other option."

"You implied that I'd been taken away from you by Children's Services because you couldn't afford to keep me, but I thought you at least *tried*. I did a little more snooping into my past. According to my records, you came to Harrisburg alone and signed all the papers willingly after I was born. Nobody took me away—you gave me up without blinking an eye." He heard mewing on the other end as though from a kitten.

"I'm sorry you got the wrong idea. I did give you away—something I've regretted ever since. Please forgive me, James. If I could change the past I would, but I can't."

"Nope, and neither can I. Seems to me you've got four Amish kids already, and I'm not Amish. I don't think milking cows in the summertime will help me get into college. Thanks anyway, Hope. Have a nice life."

He snapped the phone shut before she could reply.

Chapter Eleven

Stephen Bowman had spent all day spreading manure over harvested fields. He swept off his hat and ran a calloused hand through his hair, then went into the kitchen to wash up.

Inside the kitchen he found Josie stirring a pot of something at the stove. "Where are your mother and sisters?" he asked.

"Greta and Emily are in the front room playing. *Mamm* took baby Faith and the diaper bag and hiked to her special place." Josie glanced at him over her shoulder. "I made her go. She's been so sad lately."

Stephen sighed. "I know that, *dochder*, but I don't know how to help. If you're *gut* in here, I'll hike up there to join her." He turned toward the door, then caught a whiff of his clothes. "First, maybe I'll take a quick shower."

Ten minutes later Stephen was headed to the high ground with an extra blanket for Faith and Hope's heavier coat. She seldom dressed warm enough in late fall. And he carried a flashlight and thermos of hot chocolate, courtesy of his eldest daughter.

That Josie—always a thoughtful child, now a responsible young woman.

Dead leaves swirled around his boots as he made his way up the hill with long strides. He found his *fraa* on her favorite rock, humming and playing with Faith in her lap. She'd taken off the harness used for carrying and bundled the infant warmly. While Hope hummed a hymn, the baby grasped for a rattle just beyond her reach.

"I thought I would find you here," he said.

She peered up, her face streaked and red. "I've cried myself out; guess it's time to come home."

"*Nein.* It's time for us to talk." He opened the thermos and filled the lid to the top. "Drink some of this."

Hope sipped the hot chocolate and sighed. "I can't stop thinking about the way James sounded on the phone. Like he hated me, that I had purposely deceived him with the particulars of his birth." She clutched the cup in both hands. "But I've prayed that he finds happiness in life wherever he lives, wherever he goes."

"I know you're upset by his reaction," Stephen said, "but don't give up too easily. Praying for the boy is *gut,* but sometimes action is required. God didn't pave the way for His early believers in the Bible. Remember the stories of Ezekiel, Ruth, and Moses? He made them fight for what they wanted."

Hope stared at him. "Fighting isn't the Amish way. You know that, Stephen Bowman. We are to surrender our will to God."

He paused to collect his thoughts. "I don't mean take up a sword or even make someone your adversary. But you shouldn't give up too soon if you believe your desires are just and in the best interests of all."

"I truly do believe that." In her eyes shone a glimmer of hope. "What can I do?"

"Go talk to that social worker again. Apparently she has great influence on James. Something she said turned him against us. You need to win her to our side."

"How on earth could I do that? That woman with her high heels and fancy suit didn't like that I had brought an infant to her office. She doesn't think an Amish family has anything to offer an English teenager. After all, we don't embrace modern *conveniences*."

Stephen slapped his palms down on his knees. Hope's flare of temper was a step in the right direction. "There's the woman I know and love! Pour me some of that cocoa. Are you going to hog it all yourself?" As Hope refilled the cup to the brim, he continued, "Now, did Miss Webster actually *say* those things?"

She shook her head. "No, but I could . . . read between the lines."

"Sounds to me like you got off on the wrong foot with her. It happens sometimes, even when two people aren't of different cultures. Why should the woman help a thorn in her foot?"

"You're right," Hope said. "Tell me what to do, *ehemann*. You're seeing this clearer than I am."

"No matter how brusque Miss Webster appeared, I'm sure she has James's best interests at heart. You need to convince her that our family offers the boy value, that we can somehow help him grow up."

Hope tucked the blanket tighter beneath Faith's chin. The baby had fallen asleep again. "James never wants to set foot in Paradise again."

"Then you go to Philadelphia once a month on the bus. And keep writing letters to inquire how his English class is going. Maybe ask if he's hacked into any interesting places lately."

"Databases," she interjected. "That's what he called the places he hacks into."

"Perfect. Josie would be happy to help write letters. She could include messages from Emily and Greta. I'm sure Emily has stored up plenty of things to say to James."

Jumping to her feet, Hope shrugged into her wool coat that was lying on the ground. "Emily colored him a stack of pictures and drew some of our cows. Now I know what to do with them." She screwed the lid on the thermos and reached for Faith's carrier. "I need to call Miss Webster today for an appointment. I know how her calendar fills up." She stared down at Stephen. "Are you planning to sit here all night chewing the fat? I've got supper to fix and *kinner* to bathe. Look at that sky. It's almost dark. Good thing you brought a flashlight or we'd be picking our way home in the dark." She was already starting down the path toward the house.

Stephen grinned and brushed leaves from his trousers. "Thank You, Lord," he murmured under his breath. His *fraa* had some of her fight back.

⁓

Hope wiped her palms down her coat for the third time and concentrated on not losing her breakfast. Miss Webster flew down the highway, zipping past trucks left and right. Too fast, Hope thought. At least from the perspective of someone who travels by horse and buggy.

"You're sure Mrs. Hyde said today would be a good day to visit?"

"She said this morning would be perfect," said the caseworker. "James usually spends a few hours Saturday afternoons with his friends at the mall. They play Wii in the video parlor." She turned and smiled. "Mrs. Hyde is one hundred percent behind this, so she'll help the visit go smoothly. I'm glad you made another appointment, Hope. This could be just what the boy needs." Carolyn patted Hope's clenched fingers. "Relax. The first time for anything is the hardest."

Relax? How could she relax? What would she talk about with her son? Hope had no idea what a Wii was and only a vague idea about video parlors. Would James care that Emily had drawn him pictures all week? Or that Josie had baked him both chocolate chip and snickerdoodle cookies—two dozen of each? Or that Becky Byler asked several times when he would return for a visit?

She took in a gulp of air and tried to focus. Better concentrate on not throwing up in the car, or James's caseworker might not be so cooperative in the future.

Finally, they exited the freeway, went through four lights, and entered a community of two-story houses. All had concrete driveways, closely clipped lawns, and shrubbery in their flower beds. This was where her son lived—his neighborhood. Hope studied the details for clues to James's foster family.

"We're here," announced Carolyn, turning into the drive of a large, older home. It looked to be the original homestead, owned by the farmer who'd sold his land to a housing developer. That was common in Lancaster County.

"James lives here?" She gazed up at a rooster weathervane attached to the roof's eave with a dish contraption clamped to one side of the chimney. "It's a very nice home," she murmured.

"Six bedrooms, four baths, finished attic and basement. The Hydes have seven boys altogether, both natural and foster. Nancy Hyde has a cleaning lady, but the boys do the yard work."

"She has a maid?" Hope's jaw dropped.

"No, no, just a twice-a-month service to help her keep up."

Hope's apprehension must have registered on her face. "You live in a fine house too, Hope, very comfortable for your family," Carolyn said. "And believe me, houses and furniture don't matter a bit to teenaged boys."

"Thank you." Hope breathed deeply, trying to rally the courage she'd shown Stephen. She followed Carolyn up the walkway, clutching her totebag with both hands.

Mrs. Hyde opened the door before they had a chance to knock. "Welcome, Carolyn, Mrs. Bowman. Come in." She ushered them into a cozy living room where two small boys sat cross-legged in front of the television, past the kitchen where a candle burned atop the refrigerator, and into a den where a fire blazed in the hearth. "This is my husband's office. You can visit comfortably in here. I set out a plate of Oreos, and I'll bring hot chocolate later." Mrs. Hyde pointed at three chairs flanking the fire.

"But you have no spark screen. Don't you fear igniting the carpet?" Hope asked.

"It's a natural gas fireplace, which we have regularly inspected. Don't worry, Mrs. Bowman. We try to keep James and the other boys safe."

"Call me Hope. Thank you for letting me come."

"Call me Nancy, and you're more than welcome. I think you're approaching this correctly by giving him a chance to know you in a familiar environment. This can't be easy for you—traveling so far, staying overnight in a hotel, plus dealing with our legal system. It's a confusing maze to me at times, and I'm not Amish." Nancy Hyde clasped Hope's hand.

The gesture nearly brought Hope to tears—not a good way to start the meeting. The social worker had instructed her to keep things unemotional and nonconfrontational. "Thank you again," she whispered.

"I'll stay for the first few minutes since James is only expecting Miss Webster." Then Mrs. Hyde vanished through the doorway.

Hope's heart pounded as they sat down, leaving the chair facing them vacant. *Help me, Lord,* she silently prayed. *I need Your guidance more than ever.*

Within a few minutes, James Webb sauntered into the room wearing a Penn State sweatshirt. When he saw Hope, his eyes went large. "What are *you* doing here?" he asked.

"Sit down, James." Mrs. Hyde pointed at the empty chair. "Since Hope cares about your welfare, she asked Miss Webster if she could see you. The court has approved her request for once-a-month visitation, here in your home." Nancy smiled, nodding amicably at all three. "Miss Webster agreed to combine this with her regular assessment. Why don't I bring in some hot cocoa? I hope everybody likes mini-marshmallows." She closed the door on Hope's only means of escape.

James looked trapped too. "I thought I made myself clear on the phone. I don't intend to turn Amish," he said.

Hope cleared her throat. "I understand, but that's not why I'm here."

"Then suppose you tell me why you traveled halfway across the state." His words lost a bit of their bite.

"I came because you're important to me, and I'm interested in your life. And Josie wanted me to ask you about Wii. She heard some kids talking about it at McDonald's and couldn't make heads or tails of what they were saying." Hope took a breath and rushed on. "Emily and Greta miss you. As does Stephen. As for me, I'm curious how your grades were in English since midterm reports. Did that tutor they assigned help at all?"

Nancy Hyde bustled back into the room. She carried a tray of mugs and a carafe she must have kept on a warmer. "This should hit the spot on a day like today. If it gets much colder the rain will turn to snow." She left the room wearing the same pleasant smile.

James stared at the plate of sandwich cookies with a grim face, then reached for one. With his mouth full of Oreo, he finally answered Hope's question. "I got a C+ on my last essay and a B on the grammar quiz. So I guess the tutor is helping." He jammed another cookie into his mouth.

With a shaky hand Hope picked up the carafe and filled three mugs. "I'm glad it's working. Josie is learning the difference between theme and topic of a paragraph. I'm afraid I can't help her, but Becky Byler said she would sit down with her tomorrow. Oh, by the way, Becky said to tell you hi when I saw you again." She passed around the mugs and then blew gingerly across the surface of hers.

"Tell her I said hey right back." James gulped his drink and yowled, "Wow, that's hot!"

Everyone laughed, including James, as ice in the air began to melt. "Did you really stay overnight yesterday? Where's Faith? What if she gets hungry?"

"She is with my friend Rosa in the motel room. Carolyn will take me back before her next feeding. Faith will be fine." Hope sipped her drink.

Wiping his mouth on a napkin, James trained his eyes on Hope. "You've gone to a lot of trouble to see me. I want to know exactly why." The hard edge returned to his voice.

Hope set her mug on the table. "I know you're happy being English, and I know you can never forgive me for abandoning you after you were born. But now that you have found us, we can't help but want to stay in touch. Emily colored you another batch of pictures." She withdrew a packet from her totebag and laid it on Mr. Hyde's desk. "And Josie baked you four dozen cookies. I told her that was too many, but she said you could share with the others. Plus, Stephen wanted you to know our mare had a little filly last week. That's what he'd been hoping for." Hope clamped her mouth shut or she would ramble for the entire hour.

Tick-tock. For a long moment the mantel clock produced the only sound in the room. "What kind of cookies?" he asked.

"Walnut chocolate chip and snickerdoodles."

James nodded. "Good choice. Tell Josie thanks." He picked up the envelope and withdrew the top piece of artwork. "Say, this looks better than the ones you sent with your letter. Tell Emily good job."

Hope leaned forward. "That one is her favorite."

Tick-tock. Miss Webster shifted in her chair but remained silent.

"Okay, Hope, you can visit me, but next time bring Faith. What if she wakes up crying? I won't have her getting hungry on my account. Might be nice seeing the little squirt anyway."

"Josie and Emily want to come too. I'm afraid if I say no, they might sneak away and buy bus tickets going east."

"Sounds like somebody taught them a sneaky trick." James Webb settled back in his chair with a broad smile.

Carolyn Webster chuckled while Hope exhaled. "You'll have to talk sense into their heads next month. I wish you luck with that."

Chapter Twelve

"Okay, your cell phone and laptop are fully charged, right?"

"Yeah, don't worry. Stephen said he could charge them in the barn with the diesel generator." James wiped window condensation away with his sleeve as his caseworker drove slowly up the Bowman lane.

"Stop smearing my windows. Now, do you have plenty of coins to call me from next door if you change your mind about staying and your phone isn't charged? Two weeks can be a long time. You might get bored, especially in the winter." Miss Webster slowed the car to a crawl and gazed over fields covered with frost. Last night's light rain had crystallized over acres of pasture.

James looked too while anticipation built in his veins. "First of all, the neighbor's phone works on the honor system. You don't need quarters. Second, Stephen said there's always plenty to do on a dairy farm. They raise cows for milk, cheese, and butter, not steers for beef."

She cocked her head, laughing. "I know what a dairy farm is, young man. My, you do sound sure of yourself."

"I'm kind of glad to get away from the Hydes' for Christmas vacation. Christmas morning gets crazy with nine people opening gifts. Mrs. Hyde likes to wrap up lots of cheap stuff so we all have plenty to open. Not that I don't appreciate her effort, but I'd rather keep the holiday more low-key."

She stopped the car within sight of the frame farmhouse and pivoted on the seat. "The Amish do celebrate Christmas, but it will be definitely low-key and very religious."

James shrugged. "Christmas is a religious holiday. Who needs all the other stuff? Did you see that car commercial where this guy surprises his wife with a sixty-grand sedan? Who can really afford something like that?"

"Not many. I like your worldview, but I'm surprised you wanted to come back so soon." She craned her neck to watch a curl of smoke rise from the chimney into low-hanging clouds. "Hope Bowman meant what she said about traveling to Philly once a month to see you. And she's willing to bring your half sisters."

"I know, and she can for the rest of the school year. I think I'll try out for the cross-country team in the spring. That should be a sport I can handle. Running fast is one talent every computer geek should develop."

They laughed as she parked the car next to the Bowmans' side porch. "Sounds like a plan," she said. "Remember, James, if things become uncomfortable you can always call me. I'll come get you."

"Thanks, Miss Webster, but I'm not six years old. I can convince people to give me space without bloodshed. And I don't have a problem with their rules. That's life, isn't it?" He opened the door, then yanked his bag from the backseat. "Have a nice Christmas and try not to worry about me."

Just then Josie, Emily, and Greta came running out of the house. "James!" they shouted in unison.

James felt a tightening in his chest that left him breathless. Never before in his life had he been greeted with so much enthusiasm. Stephen and Hope stepped onto the porch with baby Faith. They grinned and waved.

"I will be fine," he repeated, and stepped out into a different world. She tooted the horn and drove away, leaving him surrounded by girls all talking fast—two in English and one in *Deutsch*. *"Ya, ya, gut,"* he said to Greta, patting the top of her head. He didn't have a clue what she said.

"Come inside." Emily grabbed his hand and dragged him toward the house. "I want to show you the gingerbread men I baked."

Josie took the position at his side. "I'd like to read you my part in the Christmas skit," she said. "I need to practice my lines. Maybe you can teach me how to project my voice. The teacher said nobody can hear me past the front row."

Little blond Greta danced around them, chattering away in her native language. Distracted and eager for attention, she tripped over the bottom step. With one hand, James lifted her to her feet. Greta's dialogue barely faltered as she climbed the stairs, this time facing forward. James glanced at the elder Bowmans to his left.

"We'll say our hellos inside," said Hope as Stephen pulled the bag from his hand.

In the kitchen the wood burner had turned the room cozy,

while a simmering pot of herbs scented the air like potpourri. "I smell cinnamon and cloves. Has someone been baking?" James winked at Josie.

"It's cookies." Emily clapped her hands. "Josie can't seem to stop herself—three different kinds, plus the gingerbread men I helped *Mamm* with."

Josie reached for his coat to hang on a peg. "You're probably smelling stuffed chicken and sweet potato casserole. I hope you're hungry, since *Mamm* roasted three."

"I'm starved, actually. I haven't eaten anything since cereal at breakfast."

"Come look at the gingerbread." Emily dragged him to the counter where frosted men cooled on baking trays. "The faceless ones are for us; the ones with faces are for you. Look at that one—he's frowning because he'll be eaten." She burst into giggles.

Doing a quick addition, James calculated that he would have plenty of cookie eating to do. "He's my favorite," he said. An odd tremor of emotion clogged his throat.

"All right, girls," said Hope. "Go to the upstairs bathroom and wash for supper. Take Greta with you. Your *daed* and I would like to squeeze a word in edgewise." Frowning but without argument, the three filed from the room as though separation would be unbearable.

Stephen dropped James's duffel on the floor and took a step toward him. "Welcome back. Maybe after we eat I'll show you the new filly."

"I would like that." James found it hard to focus as Stephen stretched out his hand for a clumsy shake. Then he disappeared up the steps with his bag. James was alone in the room with the woman who'd given birth to him.

"I hope you enjoy spending Christmas here," Hope said. "But don't be afraid to tell your sisters to leave you alone. And regarding things between you and me? We'll take life slow, with you calling the bullets."

Hope's incorrect slang took him a moment to decipher. "I believe you mean calling the *shots*." When he met her gaze she was smiling. "And I think we'll do just fine."

~

Hope drew the quilt tighter around the baby. Stephen checked the road ahead and behind. It was Christmas Eve—the holiest night of the year. Their buggy rolled down the two-lane road at a brisk pace since the gelding was eager to get to the barn and his bucket of oats. Hope was equally eager to get her family home, safe and warm.

Her whole family.

James Webb had settled easily into the Bowman routine. He stayed in touch with the Hydes and his friends with his cell phone or e-mail whenever near the McDonald's in town. He said they had free WiFi, which apparently meant he could send e-mail. In the backseat Josie, James, and Emily talked endlessly about the school pageant and the caroling afterward.

"I heard you just fine, Josie. And I was sitting in the second to the last row." James had been trying to build Josie's confidence since they left the school.

Josie sighed. "But I stuttered several times and lost my place. If the teacher hadn't prompted my lines, we'd all still be sitting there."

"Plus you mispronounced the word *myrrh*. It sounded like you said 'murf,'" Emily added.

"Only a minor slipup," said James. "Everyone makes those. Basically your performance was top-notch. Your voice contained the most emotion."

"Thanks, James. I'm glad it's over." Josie sounded more than relieved; she sounded self-assured.

And Hope? She wished his two-week vacation would never end.

When they arrived home everyone changed clothes and went to do their chores. Even on Christmas Eve, animals still needed to be fed, watered, and milked. Hope served a light supper of beef vegetable soup with homemade bread so they had room for the popcorn, sugar cookies, and cocoa. Later they gathered in the living room around the fireplace—James on the ladderback chair; the girls lined up on the couch, Hope in the rocker with Faith in her arms.

Stephen took his well-worn Bible down from the mantel, settled into the recliner, and cleared his throat. "On Christmas Eve, we like to read the three gospel accounts of Jesus' birth. I'll read the first story in the book of Matthew."

Josie raised her hand. "I'll take Mark. I won't be nervous with family like I was in school."

Hope, the usual reader of the third account, hesitated just a few seconds. Her patience was rewarded.

James lifted and dropped his shoulders. "I'm not great with American novelists or poetry, but I can read pretty well."

"Then let's begin." Stephen began the account in his baritone voice. Greta, with the typical attention span of a four-year-old, dozed off during Josie's recitation. Bible reading was a new experience for

James, and he stumbled over unfamiliar names. But everyone had to start somewhere on their spiritual path.

And between the cookies and snacks and toasted marshmallows, Hope could barely contain her joy.

⁓

On Christmas morning, Hope rose at first light to say her morning prayers before excitement made concentration difficult. Stephen had kissed her brow and gone to his chores thinking she still slept. But soon after he left she got up and dressed, set out gifts on the kitchen table, and started breakfast. She had barely filled her skillet with strips of bacon when James padded into the room. He wore dark slacks and a solid, long-sleeved shirt.

"Good morning," he said, but stopped in his tracks before reaching the fridge. "Presents? I thought Amish people didn't get into the commercialization of Christmas." He pointed at the array of wrapped packages.

Hope sliced a loaf of bread. "We don't decorate the house or put up a tree, but we exchange presents—everyone usually gets one. After all, didn't the wise men come to Bethlehem bearing gifts?"

"But I didn't get anybody anything."

Hope shook her head. "Trust me—having you here is all we wanted."

James opened the cupboard for a glass. "I guess it'll take awhile to learn the ropes."

"The Bowmans are nothing if not patient."

He poured a glass of milk and drank half, then cleared his

throat. "While it's just the two of us, I've got something to ask. A favor, kind of."

Hope turned. "A favor?"

"Yeah, well." He hesitated. "I've been thinking—that is, if it's all right with you—I thought, well, maybe I could spend next summer on the farm."

Hope blinked back tears and for a moment couldn't speak.

"Did I say something stupid?"

She shook her head. "You're wrong, you know, about not getting us a Christmas gift. This is the best gift ever. Nothing could make me happier."

James ducked and grinned and gave her a one-armed hug. "It's settled then."

Yes, it was settled. Her son was back—her family restored. And no one would separate them again.

"So what's on the agenda for today?" he asked.

Hope turned the burner to low, then wiped her hands on her apron. "We'll drive to my parents' for dinner. My sisters and their families will be there. Everyone brings food to share. I'm taking potato and macaroni salads."

"So I'll meet your dad—the one who wouldn't let you bring me home." James met her gaze and held it.

"Only if you wish to. Otherwise, you could stay here and read or go to Lancaster in a cab. The McDonald's on Lincoln Highway will be open." The words stuck in her throat. "Tomorrow will be the second day of Christmas. We'll head to my brother's house. Half the district will be there, including Becky Byler and plenty of young people. If the pond freezes, everyone will be ice skating. If we get more snow, there will be sledding, sleigh rides, and a bonfire. I think you'll enjoy yourself."

"I don't own ice skates."

Hope nodded toward the stacked boxes. "You do now. I believe they'll fit."

"Thanks. So you have two days of visiting folks? I think I'll go to both, if that's all right. I'm not afraid of your dad. It's water under the bridge."

Hope turned back to the stove, exhaling her pent-up breath. "He's only one man. His opinion cannot hurt us."

~

The Klobentz farm was a frenzy of activity when the Bowmans arrived. All the nephews and nieces were building snowmen and snow forts in the front yard, while adults congregated on the porch as if it were a warm summer day.

"Those are our cousins," announced Emily. "I'll introduce you to everybody, James, but don't worry if you can't remember folks' names."

James leaned forward between her and Stephen. "Will everyone speak English?"

"Yes, everyone older than six. Don't worry." Hope smiled as young people ran toward their buggy.

"Looks like they found out you were coming." Josie grasped his hand as they stepped out to a dozen smiling faces . . . and one with an expression like sour milk.

Silas Klobentz marched toward them bundled in his heavy wool coat. He waited until his grandchildren finished introductions, then stepped forward like Pharaoh about to address his subjects. Most of the *kinner* took a step back.

Except for James Webb. He stood straight and tall, his shoulders back, and met the older man's eye. "Hi, I'm James Webb. I'm Hope's son."

Hope held her breath.

After a moment Silas nodded his graying head. "In that case, I'm your *grossvader. Welcum.* Come inside to eat before you involve yourself in any snowball fights. You'll need your strength with your new cousins."

Side by side, the two headed toward the house, while Hope remained rooted in place.

She had just witnessed another miracle . . . on Christmas Day, no less.

Always His Provision

RUTH REID

Chapter One

Rosa Hostetler rolled to the other side of the mattress and gazed out the window next to her bed. In the clear October sky, a faint halo of light surrounded the full moon and cast a soft glow over the rolling pasture.

Since Uriah's death two years ago, and more recently, since discovering he had let the property taxes default, sleep came intermittently at best. Tonight was no exception. She couldn't stop thinking about the future, about the looming threat of the tax sale.

Rosa yanked the wool blanket over her head. She missed Uriah's comfort, the reassuring warmth of him beside her. Now whenever her foot drifted over to his side of the bed, she felt only the chill of loneliness.

But tossing all night accomplished nothing. Rosa pushed the covers aside and crawled out of bed. She padded barefoot down the squeaky wooden stairs and into the kitchen, and struck a match against the cast-iron stove. She lit the lamp, and a soft yellow glow filled the empty kitchen.

Sometime during the night, the fire in the stove had gone out. Rosa wadded a few pages of newspaper, laid on the kindling, and touched a match to the crumpled paper. Occasionally she wished she had one of the fancy propane ovens like her friend Hope had. But as it was, Rosa had only herself to cook for, and it seemed pointless to want something so extravagant.

Coveting material items wasn't a problem for Rosa. She struggled with more basic issues: the battle she had fought throughout five years of marriage to accept her childless state and, more recently, the loss of her husband. Now widowed at age thirty, it seemed she would never experience the fulfillment of motherhood.

Rosa set the glass jar of cookies on the table, plopped down on one of the ten empty chairs, and waited for the water in the kettle to boil. The *tick-tick-tick* of the clock on the wall broke the silence. One a.m. Gorging on cookies in the middle of the night had become a routine.

Propped against the saltshaker, the latest letter from the Tax Claim Bureau caught her attention. Marked DELINQUENT in a bold red stamp, the property taxes listed not only the current tax lien but the amount due from unpaid taxes and accrued late fees from the previous years.

She scanned the document. *Notice is hereby given that the Lancaster County Tax Claim Bureau will hold a continued tax upset sale on . . .* The November date and time blurred as tears welled. She had less than a month to settle the lien. On her egg money that would be impossible.

Boiling water erupted from the kettle's spout and sizzled on the cast-iron stovetop. She dropped the letter on the table, grabbed the hissing kettle with a potholder, and poured water over the herbal tea bag. The wafting lemony scent soothed her senses.

Somewhere outside a dog barked, then others joined the chorus. She lowered the kettle and leaned over the sink to peer out the window. But even with a full moon, she couldn't see into the darkness.

The barking grew louder. Rosa jerked her cape from the hook and opened the door. The hens had gone wild, clucking and flapping frantically. She bolted back inside and grabbed her husband's shotgun.

~

Adam Bontrager slowly opened his eyes. His mind vaguely registered the sound of dogs barking, but he closed his eyes and slid back toward sleep.

Moments later the racket roused him again. This time he shot out of bed and went to the window that faced the Hostetler house. Light illuminated the kitchen window. The same disturbance must have awakened Rosa too.

A small shadowy figure stepped onto Rosa's porch. He couldn't understand the muffled words, but the angry tone carried through the night.

Adam pulled on his clothes and rushed out of the house without tying his boots or grabbing his hat. On his way across the yard, he snagged the heavy metal rake leaning against the utility shed. Above the panic of flapping wings and the fierce growl of an animal, he could hear Rosa shouting—something about leaving her chickens alone.

"Rosa?" he called. He didn't mean to startle her, but he also didn't want to be clubbed in the head with whatever it was she had in her hand.

"It's after *mei* chickens!" He heard a mechanism click and a half sentence about hoping the shell was loaded right.

"Don't shoot!" he yelled.

She lowered the gun. He crossed in front of her and struck the large dog with the rake. A hen thudded to the ground, and the yelping dog bolted for the corral, where it crawled under the fence and slipped into darkness.

He bent a knee next to the motionless chicken.

Rosa leaned over his shoulder. "Is she dead?"

Probably, Adam thought. It was difficult to tell if the bird was dead or in shock because of the large oak blocking the moonlight. "I don't know. I can't see."

"I'll get a lantern." She turned and sprinted toward the house.

"Hey." Adam waited for her to look his way. "Don't run with a loaded gun in your hand."

Rosa slowed.

Once she disappeared behind the door, he resumed his inspection of the chicken. If it wasn't already dead, he had a notion to put it out of its misery before she returned with the light. The other hens kept their distance yet continued to cluck.

The screen door snapped. Unarmed, she trotted back with the lantern.

Rosa dangled the lamplight over the lifeless bird. "That rotten dog killed her."

Adam reached down and picked up the chicken by its neck. "I guess you'll be making dumplings to go with this."

"That's *nett* funny. That was Penny." Her voice cracked.

He wasn't sure why, but it surprised him that she named her

chickens. He cleared his throat. "At the risk of sounding insensitive, where do you want . . . Penny?"

She sighed. "In the *haus.*"

At least she wouldn't let the meat go bad. Carrying the mangled chicken, he followed her up the porch steps and into the house. He'd barely crossed the threshold when he heard a loud gasp.

"What's wrong?" Adam thought he might have trailed chicken blood on her floor. Then his eyes met hers, and he understood immediately.

She stood before him clutching the woolen cape closed at her neck. Adam's gaze traveled downward, over the hem of her night-dress, to her bare ankles and curled-under toes. Without waiting for direction from Rosa, he took the hen into the kitchen, crossed the room to the sink, and plunked it into the basin.

She snatched a folded paper from the table and shoved it into a nearby drawer.

"I'm sorry to get you out of bed at this hour," she said.

"That's all right. I wanted to make sure you were safe." He turned the tap on and rinsed his hands. "I didn't realize you knew how to shoot a gun."

She shrugged slightly, reached under the sink, and handed him a bar of soap. "I'm *nett* so sure I do. I've never shot one."

The woman was more dangerous than he thought.

"*Danki,*" he said, accepting the towel she offered. "Maybe I better unload the gun so you don't try to shoot something else in the middle of the night." He finished drying his hands and handed her back the towel. "Where is it?"

She led the way to the sitting room.

He spotted the shotgun propped up against the wall and groaned under his breath. She hadn't set the safety either. Clearly she had a lot to learn about firearms.

"It's best to unload it outside." If she joined him, he would demonstrate the proper technique, but she didn't. It was probably just as well; she didn't need a lecture tonight. One dead chicken to pluck was enough to deal with at this late hour. He opened the 12-gauge barrel and dislodged the shell. Adam flipped the safety lever to the locked position even though the gun was no longer loaded.

She wasn't in the sitting room when he reentered the house. He placed the gun on the rack and slipped the shell into his pocket. Pots and pans clanged in the kitchen. Adam ducked his head into the room. "Hopefully the dog won't bother your chickens again."

She looked up from filling a large pot with water. "I hope you hit him with the prongs of that rake."

He frowned. He had overheard her plenty of times talking lovingly to her animals. "Rosa, you don't mean that."

"*Ya*, I do." She placed the oversized pot on the stove to boil. "That dog's attacked *mei* chickens before. Penny laid the most eggs—the biggest too. I found several double yolks from her box. I can't afford to lose any egg sales."

"Don't worry about tomorrow, for—"

"For tomorrow will worry about its own things." She opened a drawer and removed a butcher knife. "It's after midnight. This *is* tomorrow—and I am worried."

She nudged the drawer closed with her hip. "And I will shoot that dog."

Chapter Two

Rosa's eyes burned from lack of sleep. She hadn't slept much before the commotion last night, and once she had plucked the feathers, cooked the chicken, and mourned over the loss of her best egg layer, sleep was a lost cause altogether.

Perhaps she could nap after she returned from her morning egg deliveries. But that wouldn't happen if she didn't get started. On a normal day, she would have already been to the bakery by this time. She donned her barn-mucking boots and grabbed the empty basket to collect the eggs.

Outside, she drew in a deep breath of the crisp morning air. Fall was always her favorite time of year.

"*Guder mariye*, girls," Rosa greeted the clucking hens. The flock clustered around her and followed her to the barn as they did every morning.

Rosa entered the barn humming "Das Loblied," one of her favorite praise hymns from the *Ausbund*. She crossed the concrete floor of the old milk parlor that now served as a storage room for the different drums of livestock feed. As she removed the lid and retrieved the coffee can at the bottom, she noticed with dismay how the melody echoed in the empty drum.

There wasn't much feed to collect. Certainly not enough to feed over forty chickens.

At least it hadn't snowed early this year. The chickens still had a few weeks to forage bugs, plants, and anything they could scratch up as their primary source of food. But in the morning, she liked to scatter corn for them to eat while she collected the eggs from the nesting boxes.

She leaned into the barrel and scooped up feed, unaware she had company until she heard someone singing along. She jerked upright, coffee can in hand, and turned toward the doorway of the milking parlor.

"Please continue," Adam said. "I've never heard you sing before."

She hadn't heard him sing before either, but it didn't mean she wanted to harmonize with him now, bent over a barrel with her backside facing him. "I usually just hum."

Why did she feel the need to explain herself to him? Next she'd be telling him how singing helped keep her mind focused on God instead of her looming tax problems.

"I see you're in a better mood this morning. You didn't shoot any dogs after I left, did you?"

"You ask, but I know you took the shell." What he didn't know was that she had more.

He smiled. "I wanted to get a *gut nacht's* sleep. I wouldn't have slept a wink if I thought you were out there trying to shoot something."

Rosa looked down at the meager amount of corn she'd collected in the can. "At least someone was able to sleep," she muttered.

She rarely ran into Adam in the mornings. Usually he tended the horses he kept in her barn while she was out making deliveries. "I'm sorry. Am I in your way?" She stepped away from the barrels. The oat bin for the horses was next to the chicken feed.

"*Nee.* I was heading to the tack room to get tools to mend the fence."

"Did the horses get out?"

"*Nee.* It's the part I sectioned off to do training."

She hadn't paid much attention to the changes he'd made to accommodate his horse-training business. After a fire destroyed Adam's barn, he needed a temporary place to keep his horses, and she agreed. It's what her late husband would have wanted. Uriah thought of Adam as his little brother and looked out for him—enough to lose his life to save Adam's.

"You have a nice voice."

Rosa wasn't sure how to respond. Since Uriah's death, Adam had pushed his way into her life like a sibling with his finger in the cake batter. In the beginning, he treated her as if it was his duty to look out for Uriah's widow. Adam's way of working out his guilt. And probably God's way of forcing her to face the bitter resentment she harbored.

"*Danki.* You're *nett* too off-key yourself," she said.

His sheepish grin gave him a youthful appearance. So did his shaven face, his long, dark lashes, and his cobalt-blue eyes. Rosa recalled what his mother, Eunice, had said at the widows' luncheon: "I don't understand why *mei sohn* hasn't proposed to Claire Milner yet. I don't even know if they've seen much of each other since the fire."

Eunice seemed to think it had something to do with the third-degree burns on Adam's neck, arm, and left hand. He'd also lost part of his earlobe. But his scars were not such an eyesore that they should chase away someone as sweet as Claire.

He looked around the building. "Ever thought about getting a few milk cows?"

"Nee."

"I know you had that bovine respiratory disease run through here, but I thought—"

She shook her head. "More than half our stock died." The cattle loss trickled down to the mess she was in today. The taxes wouldn't be two years past due if they hadn't had to pay vet bills and hire a company to sanitize the place according to commercial milking standards.

Rosa recalled the defeat in Uriah's eyes. The quarantine hadn't worked. Their dreams went up in smoke with the burnt carcasses.

She shook the grain can. *"Mei* girls are waiting for me."

Once outside, Rosa resumed singing. Her clucking hens met her at the barn door and chased after the corn she spread over the ground.

She fell silent as she approached the coop. Last night it had been too dark to see the damage the dog had done. The chicken yard was filled with feathers.

Perhaps now would be a good time to have a word with the *Englischer* about his dog. Two summers ago he had moved in next door, not the friendliest *Englischer* she'd known, but at least not some nosy neighbor who thought nothing of disrupting the Amish way of life by chasing them around with a camera.

She looked toward the *Englisch* neighbor's house, a hundred yards away. There seemed to be no activity. The man's truck wasn't in his driveway either.

Rosa entered the coop and gathered the few eggs from the nesting boxes. The count was down. Way down compared to yesterday. Chickens laid fewer eggs in the colder season, but this wasn't about the weather. It was the stress and fright of the dog attack. Another reason she needed to have a talk with the neighbor about controlling his animals.

Rosa took the eggs into the house and washed them. She separated them according to the delivery route, grateful she had enough to fill the existing orders. Then she took the basket out to the barn and prepared to harness Blossom to the buggy.

She had just removed the harness from the nail stud when the stall door creaked open behind her and Adam stepped out.

"I'll do that for you." He reached for the equipment in her hand.

"That isn't necessary. I'm more than capable."

He smiled. "I know."

After a brief hesitation, she released the harness and followed him to Blossom's stall. "I appreciate that you came over to check on me last *nacht*, but . . . well, eventually you're going to have to move on with your life." She held her tongue from adding that he could never make up for her losing Uriah.

Adam's jaw tightened, but he said nothing.

Rosa sighed. Lack of sleep had sparked these emotions. He'd only offered to harness her mare.

"I suppose I should share the chicken supper since you were kind enough to chase that dog away."

"That would be nice." He guided the straps through the proper metal rings. "What time should I *kumm* over?"

Ach! She hadn't meant for it to sound like an invitation to eat at her house. He must think she was forward, suggesting such an idea. "I'll bring it over to your *mudder's haus*."

He paused in buckling the girth belt.

"It's a *gut* size chicken," she said. "There will be plenty."

Adam continued to fasten the harness.

"What do you like, white meat or dark?" She fiddled with her apron. "Of course, I could bring over a helping of both."

Stop, she told herself. *Just stop talking*. Next she would be rambling on about vegetable side dishes and dessert.

"Dark." He led Blossom by her halter out to where the buggy sat under the lean-to.

Rosa followed.

He made the final attachments, and after she climbed up on the bench seat, he handed her the reins. "Drive safe."

"Danki." She clicked her tongue and Blossom lurched forward. Once off the gravel drive and onto the road, the mare perked up her ears and trotted faster. Blossom liked the cooler temperatures of fall too. Rosa didn't discourage the pace. She was already late.

It wasn't long before the bakery came into view. The enticing scent of cinnamon rolls filled her nostrils as Rosa entered the cozy storefront. She smiled at Becky Byler, the owner's daughter, who was busy arranging pastries in the glass display counter.

"Guder mariye, Becky." Rosa set the egg basket on the counter and unfolded the cloth covering.

"Hiya, Mrs. Hostetler." The girl wiped her hands, leaving a

spot of what appeared to be strawberry filling on the front of her apron.

Rosa tried not to stare for fear that Becky would think she was passing judgment on her figure. At eighteen, Becky Byler was the largest girl in the district. She seemed to take things in stride, but Rosa suspected that the girl's size was what kept her from smiling more.

Becky carefully transferred the eggs from Rosa's basket into one of the bakery's storage bins. The girl opened the cash register and counted out the payment for the eggs, then handed the cash to Rosa. She said little and appeared particularly dejected today.

"Did your *mamm* leave a note as to how many eggs she wants tomorrow?"

"I think so." Becky rifled through a stack of papers on a nearby counter, then handed Rosa the slip.

"Danki. I'll see you tomorrow?" Rosa gave her a beaming smile in hopes that Becky might return the favor.

She didn't. "I'll be here," she said. "I'm always here."

Rosa continued her route and completed the remaining deliveries before she reached Stephen and Hope Bowman's farm. She wanted to spend some time with Hope and of course dote on little Faith, who always brightened Rosa's spirit.

Hope opened the door and welcomed her into the house. "I figured you were too busy to stop for *kaffi* today."

"Running late is all." Rosa followed her into the kitchen. "Where are the *kinner*?" Even though she doted on the fifteen-month-old Faith, Rosa was close to Hope's other children too.

"Faith is napping. Josie, Emily, and Greta are in *schul*, and

James is outside with Stephen." Hope looked at Rosa and frowned. "You're *nett* sleeping, are you?"

"I had problems with the neighbor's dog last *nacht*. He attacked *mei* chickens. Killed *mei* best laying hen."

"That's awful."

"I plucked feathers until two in the morning." She yawned.

"*Kumm* sit." Hope tapped the wooden chair. "The *kaffi* is hot. I'll pour you a cup."

Rosa desperately needed a nap, but she also wanted to visit with her friend. So much had changed over the past several months. "James is doing well, *ya*?"

"He's adapting more and more every day to our ways." Hope set the cup before Rosa. "So tell me, was it Adam's dog that killed your chicken?"

Rosa shook her head. "Adam doesn't have a dog. He heard the vicious attack and came over to help me." She decided not to mention being outside, barefoot and in her nightdress, when he arrived. Still, Hope lifted her brows as though she suspected Rosa had left out important details. Rosa sipped her coffee before continuing. "It was the *Englischer's* dog. The man who bought the *haus* on the other side of me."

"What did the man say?" Hope offered a cookie from the jar.

Rosa shook her head. "Nothing yet. I plan to talk with him later today."

"Once a dog kills, it's difficult to change him."

Rosa set her cup on the table. "That's what I was thinking too. It might start nipping at the horses next and agitate them. That reminds me, is Stephen interested in buying *mei* plow team?

Bolt and Thunder are only going to get fat and lazy. I need to sell them."

"I don't know, but I'll ask him."

"If I can't sell them in a week or so, I think I'll make arrangements for them to go to auction."

"You're in that kind of a rush?"

Rosa avoided her friend's eyes by looking into her cup. "I don't want to feed them all winter just to sell them in the spring." That should be understandable. She lifted her head and smiled. "Tell me about your *sohn*. Are he and your *daed* still getting along?"

Hope smiled. "I'm still in awe of the miracle. God has been so *gut* to me."

"*Ya*," Rosa said with a sigh.

Dare she pray for a miracle too?

Chapter Three

Rosa drew a deep breath and knocked on the back door of the *Englischer's* house. Maybe she should have written a note this morning and dropped it into his mailbox. She knocked again, this time harder. No answer. She glanced over her shoulder toward the barn-style shed and debated if she should check there for him. The last owner worked on cars in the building. She wished an Amish family had bought the property when it went up for sale. But real estate prices in Paradise were such that even a small place with minimal acreage was overpriced.

The door opened, and a man in a navy T-shirt and faded jeans stepped onto the threshold. He looked to be in his thirties, maybe, with broad shoulders and longish brown hair. When he combed his fingers through his hair, she noticed a flash of silver at his temples. "Can I help you?"

"I hope so." She cleared her throat. "I'm Rosa Hostetler. I live next door." She pointed to her place on the right.

"It's nice to meet you. I'm Tate Wade." His smile was warm

enough to melt a slab of butter straight from the *icehaus*, but she wondered briefly if it was completely genuine.

"Mr. Wade, I'm not sure if you're aware of it, but your dog killed one of *mei* chickens." His expression went blank. She wanted to give him the benefit of doubt, but how could he have missed the commotion? Frown lines stretched across his forehead as she continued. "The ruckus late last night." She hesitated. "You do own a large dog, don't you?" She made a hand gesture a few inches above her knee to indicate the approximate size.

"I own several, but I don't allow them to roam free."

Was he implying her chickens shouldn't be allowed to roam? It would be different if her chickens had been on his property when the attack took place. She cleared her throat again. "One of your dogs attacked my chickens. In my barnyard."

He crossed his arms over his chest.

If only she had left a note in his mailbox instead of confronting him. "I'm not asking you to pay for the chicken," she said in a calm tone. "Only that you keep your dog out of my yard—out of my chicken coop."

"I told you. My dogs are in the kennels." He pointed toward the barn. "Even if they escaped the kennel, they wouldn't have escaped the barn. And on the off chance that one did, it's unlikely that he would break into a chicken coop. All of my dogs are highly trained."

"I leave the door to my coop open so my chickens can come and go."

"I wouldn't advise that or you'll have more trouble with wild animals."

She shook her head. "It wasn't a wild animal. It was a dog. I saw it with the chicken in it's mouth."

"Then it's probably a stray." He made a slight nod as if trying to coax her into agreeing. When she didn't, he shrugged. "I don't know what else to say."

"I've heard that once a dog has a taste for blood its disposition often changes. I just wanted to make you aware of the situation. Good day, Mr. Wade."

She turned and stepped off the porch. There was nothing more to do. No doubt he'd deny unleashing the dogs last weekend when they went off in the direction of the woods. Sure, the dogs responded to the man's whistle, but that didn't mean one wouldn't chase her chickens if its master wasn't around.

What would she have to do now, stand watch day and night?

Adam washed up and changed into his Sunday clothes before supper. He wet the comb with tap water, then slid it through his hair. But every time he flattened his hair down, the curls flipped back up, exposing his missing earlobe. He touched the grafted area on his neck where he'd been burned. Without a collar on his shirt, he couldn't even pull the material up to cover the scars. This was one time when he wished the *Ordung* didn't have such strict rules about the way they dressed.

He didn't consider it vanity, the wish to hide the scar from Rosa. Looking at him had to be a raw reminder of her losses. He foolishly went inside the blazing barn to free the horses, and there hadn't been a day since that Adam wasn't painfully aware of what that decision had cost. His best friend, Uriah Hostetler, died to save Adam. Guilt tore through him when he looked into Rosa's eyes and found restrained animosity. He didn't blame her. But Adam begged God to give her the desire to forgive.

He tossed the comb aside. Nothing he did could shield the scars. Nothing could hide the past. It would have to do.

Rosa hadn't arrived yet when he entered the kitchen.

His mother paused from pouring coffee, tilted her face up, and sniffed at the air. "What's that smell?"

"Soap. The same stuff I use every day."

"You must *nett* have rinsed it off." She continued filling the cups, then shot him a sideways glance as he reached into the cabinet for a water glass. "I'm glad you changed your clothes. We're having company."

Adam cocked his head sideways, but before he could remind his mother that he was the one who told her about Rosa planning to bring chicken tonight, someone knocked on the back door.

He opened the door expecting Rosa, but instead Claire Milner stood on the stoop. "Claire," was all he could muster for a greeting. They had only seen each other once outside of church meetings since the fire.

She smiled nervously. "I brought an apple pie."

He looked beyond her at the buggy leaving.

"*Mei bruder* dropped me off," she said.

Mamm darted around the corner. "I'm so glad you were able to *kumm* for supper." She took the pie so Claire could remove her cape. Then after nudging Adam to take the cloak from their guest, *Mamm* led Claire to the kitchen.

Just as Adam hung the garment on the hook, someone else knocked on the door. This time it was Rosa. "Hello." He swung the door open wider and stepped aside, but she didn't move from the threshold.

"I just wanted to drop this off." She extended the dish toward him.

"You're *nett* staying?"

His mother bounded out of the kitchen. "Is that Rosa?" She reached in front of him for Rosa's hand and led her inside. "I hope you don't mind. I had already invited Claire Milner for supper before Adam said you were bringing over a chicken."

"*Nee*. There's plenty of food. But—"

"I have the *kaffi* already poured," *Mamm* said, helping Rosa out of her cape. "I missed you at the last widows' get-together."

Rosa's jaw twitched.

His mother didn't seem to notice. She directed Rosa to the kitchen.

Adam followed behind them carrying the warm meal. He set the dish in the center of the table next to the bowl of pickled beets and plate of sliced bread.

"*Hiya*, Rosa," Claire said. "Do you take cream or sugar in your *kaffi*?"

"Just cream, please."

Adam craned his neck toward the dish. "So what did you make out of—?" *Penny*, he remembered. *The hen's name was Penny.* He stopped himself before finishing the sentence. *Don't be an insensitive fool*, he thought. "Did you make dumplings?"

"Chicken casserole with acorn squash."

Claire set a steaming mug of coffee in front of Adam as *Mamm* set one with cream in front of Rosa.

"Adam told me about the neighbor's dog," *Mamm* said once they were all seated and grace was given.

"The neighbor won't admit his dog did any harm."

"You talked with him?" Adam's jaw went slack.

Rosa nodded. "It didn't do any good."

The dog had only killed one chicken. Adam found it odd that Rosa didn't just let it go. Then again, she named her chickens. And last night she was angry enough to consider shooting the dog.

"Hopefully the dog won't bother you anymore," he said. "Then it won't matter if the neighbor admits to owning the dog or *nett,* right?" He spooned a large helping of casserole onto his plate and passed it to Claire.

"This was very kind of you to share with us tonight." *Mamm* sampled the food and smiled. "It's very tasty."

"It's a recipe passed down from *mei grossmammi* to *mei mamm,* and then down to me." Rosa's voice faded.

Mamm was too busy adding pickled beets to her plate to notice how Rosa's expression changed. Adam suspected it had nothing to do with the actual family recipes, and everything to do with not having children to pass them down to.

"I have a book saved with recipes to pass on to *mei kinskind* one day." *Mamm* shot an obvious glance at Claire and smiled.

Adam coughed and cleared his throat. After the fire, he and Claire had put their courtship on hold. He didn't want to get married until things were back on course with his horse-training business. That, and he had promised Uriah that he would look after Rosa.

Claire seemed to take the postponement well enough, although neither of them thought it would be this long.

"Did you hear about the get-together tomorrow at Katherine's *haus*?" *Mamm* asked Rosa.

Rosa shook her head.

"A few of us widows are getting together to sew." His mother droned on about the planned frolic, unaware she had lost her audience, except for Claire who must have felt it her duty to follow along.

Mamm seemed oblivious, but Adam noticed how Rosa winced every time the word *widow* was used.

"Why don't you plan on joining us, Rosa?"

"Oh, I don't think I can. I have plans." Rosa fiddled with the corner of her napkin.

His mother stared at Rosa for a moment, then gently shook her head and forked the casserole on her plate. "Did you put garlic in this?"

The conversation shifted to spices and cooking, with Claire chiming in about her favorite dishes. Adam ate silently but observed closely. Until today he hadn't compared Rosa with Claire. But watching them now, he could see that Rosa was reserved, while Claire giggled and shared lofty plans of cooking for a large family one day.

He supposed that was a normal dream for most women. Still, he wished Claire wouldn't talk so much. Didn't she see Rosa's downturned mouth? Couldn't she tell that Rosa was torn up?

"A slice of your pie sounds *gut*," he said to Claire.

Mamm stood. "I'll pour us more *kaffi* while Claire serves dessert."

It was late by the time they were finished. Rosa stood. "I'll help with dishes, Eunice."

"*Nee*, I need something to do."

Adam glanced at Claire. "I'll hitch up the buggy so I can take you home."

Rosa scooted to the door, slipped on her cape, and reached for the doorknob.

He snagged his hat from the hook, grabbed his coat, and followed her outside. "Would you like me to walk you home?"

"I'll be all right." She disappeared into the darkness before he could thank her for the meal.

Adam quickly readied the buggy and drove Claire home. Neither spoke on the ride other than to agree how chilly it had turned since the sun went down. He stopped the buggy next to her house, and Claire reached for his arm.

"You didn't know your *mamm* invited me tonight, did you?"

"*Nee*."

"When do you think you'll be ready to . . . ?" Her voice quivered.

"Claire, I told you before. I gave Uriah *mei* word that I would watch over Rosa."

"What does that mean exactly? It's been two years. Surely you're ready to move—" She paused a moment before continuing. "I don't want to wait any longer, Adam. *Mei* friends are all getting married, and I'm watching *mei* life pass me by."

"I'm sorry."

"You don't share the same feelings for me anymore, do you?"

He wanted to be truthful. The fire had changed him. It seemed more and more he wanted Rosa's approval. He wanted her forgiveness.

"I don't know how I feel." He reached for Claire's hand and gave it a gentle squeeze. "But I don't want you to feel like your life is passing you by either."

"Mark Raber has asked me to go for a ride in his buggy next Sunday afternoon."

"He's a *gut* man."

"Then you think I should say yes?"

He understood the ultimatum. "I want you to be happy. If I hear someone else is courting you, I'll understand."

"I see." Claire opened the buggy door. "*Gut*-bye, Adam." She hurried into the house before Adam had time to set the brake. He turned the horse for home. Without fully understanding why, relief washed over him.

A light shone in Rosa's kitchen window as he pulled into the drive. He took care of his horse, rolled the buggy under the lean-to, then meandered across the yard and knocked on her door.

"Is something wrong?" she asked.

"I didn't want you to be alarmed when a strange truck pulls up to your barn. I have a potential buyer who wants to look at *mei* horses tomorrow."

"I know you've worked hard to train them. I'm glad you've found a buyer."

"*Ya,* well, I won't know that until tomorrow."

"Would you wait a minute? I have something I'd like you to take home." She disappeared behind the door and a moment later returned with a small basket. "Ask your *mamm* if she will give these eggs to the widows tomorrow at their get-together."

"That's very kind, but why don't you join them?"

"Adam, it's late. I need to go to bed now." She said good night and closed the door.

He trekked over the leaf-covered lawn and stomped the dirt and debris from the bottom of his boots before entering the house.

"You weren't gone long." His mother eyed the basket as he set it on the counter.

"Rosa sent some eggs for your get-together tomorrow." He grabbed *The Budget* to scan the newspaper for upcoming horse auctions. He expected his mother to quiz him about Claire but she didn't.

"Rosa is such a thoughtful dear." *Mamm* lifted the cloth covering the eggs. "She needs a husband."

He stared at the newspaper's typed words but hadn't read a line.

"I was thinking Peter Zook would be a *gut* husband for Rosa."

Peter? Had his mother gone *narrisch*? He cleared his throat. "Peter Zook is almost twice her age."

"Exactly."

Mamm wasn't usually this far removed from reality. Peter had married and buried three wives and fathered fourteen children. He certainly didn't need to add Rosa to his lot.

"She's barren," his mother said. "No young man would knowingly marry her. She needs a husband who is beyond child-rearing days. A widower like Peter is perfect."

"*Perfect?*" He folded the paper and stood. One thing he'd learned since watching over his friend's widow, she was stubbornly independent. She wouldn't marry someone who didn't measure up to Uriah—and nobody could.

"Claire made a *wunderbaar* pie, *ya?*"

"I have an early day tomorrow."

Adam left the kitchen. Before going to bed, he stood at his bedroom window and looked toward Rosa's house. He rubbed the leathery area of his neck where he'd been burned.

So much had changed.

Too much.

Chapter Four

Rosa swiped the steamy kitchen window with the dish towel to get a clear view of the truck and horse trailer. She watched as Adam greeted the driver with a handshake and led the man into the barn.

The glass fogged again. She turned away from the window and removed the hissing kettle from the stove, then filled her cup with boiling water and let the lemony tea bag steep while she buttered a slice of bread.

After the barn fire, Adam had spent several months recovering from his burns, and afterward the horses needed retraining. He had put his heart and soul into those horses—a form of therapy for himself, no doubt. At first Rose regretted the decision to let him keep his horses in her barn. The horses had nothing to do with lightning setting the barn on fire, and yet she despised the creatures. But the arrival of the truck and trailer this morning made her realize that she would miss the activity once he sold the stock.

Rosa blew gently over the surface of her tea, then took a sip. She opened the journal where she kept a record of the egg sales, scanned halfway down the list, then stopped. Why did she constantly feel the need to review the list and count her expected earnings? She knew the weekly delivery schedule by heart. Her orders never changed, except when the bakery requested extra eggs over the holidays.

She slapped the journal closed. When had she become so obsessed with tracking money?

Rosa knew the answer. But she couldn't allow the looming taxes to consume her mind. Constantly worrying didn't help the situation.

It wasn't like she had no place to go. *Aenti* Lilly had offered her a place to stay after Uriah died. At that time, Rosa had respectfully declined. Paradise was her home and starting over again in Ohio wasn't something she wanted to consider. But now . . .

She ran her hand over the journal. She needed to sell more eggs in order to keep her house. Or come up with something else to sell.

A horse whinnied, and she rose from the chair and looked out the window. Adam's hard work had paid off. He led the horse up the trailer ramp, then went back inside the barn and came out with another one. By the time the men shook hands, all four of Adam's horses had been loaded into the trailer.

Rosa filled the kettle with more water and set it on the stove. She had enough time to share a cup with Adam before retrieving the eggs.

She smiled at the slight bounce in Adam's step as the truck and trailer pulled away. But instead of coming to share the news, he was heading home.

A heaviness filled her chest. Loneliness was normal—understandable—when it came to missing Uriah. But . . . was she really having that response to Adam?

Rosa rubbed her eyes. She wasn't thinking straight. Probably the lack of sleep or worry over the taxes. Clearly, Adam was moving forward, and by the furtive glances Claire made toward him at supper last night, there probably was more to the horse sale than met the eye. Now he would have money to put a down payment on a place of his own.

Rosa just needed to trust God's provision. He would provide the means to save her farm. Nothing was too difficult for God.

"Nothing," she said, snatching the egg basket from the counter.

She left the house with renewed hope. But when she spotted another dead chicken inside the coop, everything changed.

The lifeless hen made Rosa's stomach clench. She couldn't tell how long the chicken had been dead. Better bury it, just to be safe. She ducked into the barn and retrieved the shovel, then went out back and began to dig. What she really wanted to do was not bury the bird but deposit it on her neighbor's stoop. He should see what his dog did.

She dug faster. She had to get the dead carcass in the ground before she allowed bitterness to take root.

She heard the crunch of gravel and turned to see Hope Bowman climbing out of her buggy. "I'm out here in the garden," Rosa called.

Hope lifted Faith off the bench and strolled over to the edge of the dried cornstalks. "I thought you might stop by after your deliveries."

"I'm running behind. I haven't even collected the eggs." She motioned to the bloody chicken at the bottom of the hole. "Look what I found this morning."

Hope's eyes widened. "You lost another one?"

She drove the shovel hard into the mound of dirt and left it standing. "I still can't believe I slept through the ruckus. The first full *nacht* of sleep I had in weeks, and this happens." Rosa shook her head. "That dog won't kill another one. Even if it means camping outside in the henhouse with a shotgun."

Hope shifted Faith to her opposite hip and bent closer to the chicken. "Are you sure a dog got it?" She stepped back. "I've seen an injured chicken pecked to death by other chickens."

Rosa hadn't considered that possibility. But the other chickens wouldn't have attacked if they hadn't seen blood on her. "I suppose when I finish here I should check all the chickens closer." She grabbed the shovel and scooped a load of dirt. Tossing it into the hole, the dirt landed on the dead carcass with a *thud*.

"I can make some of your deliveries if you want," Hope said. "I told *Mamm* I would *kumm* over and make apple cider, but that can wait until the girls are out of *schul*."

"Could you deliver to Byler's Bakery? Their recipes are dependent on eggs. I don't like to keep them waiting." Rosa finished filling the hole, then patted the top of the grave with the backside of the shovel.

"Sure." Hope bounced Faith to her other hip. "I wanted to ask Becky about babysitting anyway."

Rosa smiled at chubby-cheeked Faith. "I would hold you," she told the infant in *Deutsch*, "but I'm all dirty." She held up her smudged hands and wiggled her fingers, which triggered a drooling smile from Faith. Rosa chuckled. "She's certainly a *gut*-natured *boppli*."

Hope kissed her child's cheek. "I'm blessed."

"*Ya*, you are, Hope Bowman."

Her friend frowned. "I'm sorry."

"Don't apologize. God had a different plan for *mei* life." Rosa couldn't remember how many times she had recited those words. She and Uriah had wanted children. He'd even built a kitchen table large enough to seat ten. But her body rejected every baby she conceived. Four miscarriages left her heartbroken, and she had shared the depth of those pains only with Hope.

Rosa motioned toward the henhouse. "I suppose people are waiting for their eggs. I better get them gathered and washed so I can get on the road."

Hope gasped when Rosa swung the door open to the coop. "It's a wonder the chickens have any feathers on them at all." She scanned the floor.

"Thanks to the dog." Rosa reached into the nesting box and pulled out a brown egg. Hope added the one she collected to the basket and moved to the next nest. It didn't take them long, since there weren't many eggs to gather. Rosa rechecked each box for any missed but found none. She didn't have to count them to know she wouldn't have enough to fill all the orders.

Hope elbowed Rosa's side on their way to the house. "You're awfully quiet. Is something wrong?"

"I don't have enough."

"You can use eggs left over from yesterday to fill the orders, *ya?*"

Rosa shook her head. "I sent them with Eunice Bontrager to take to the widows."

"You'll just have to short someone. At least it isn't the holiday season where everyone is baking more. I'm sure it won't be an issue."

The issue was the lack of income, but Rosa wasn't ready to

confess her tax problems to anyone, including her best friend. She twisted the doorknob and bumped her hip against the back door. She placed the basket on the counter and turned on the tap water as Hope lowered Faith to the floor.

After the eggs were washed, they packed them around a piece of muslin to prevent breakage during transport. Rosa walked Hope to her buggy. "*Danki* for taking these to the bakery." She handed the basket to Hope once she and Faith were seated on the bench.

"Are you sure you don't want me to make any other stops?"

"*Nee.* I'm still not sure who I'm going to short."

Rosa watched Hope drive away, turning over the problem in her mind. She didn't want to inconvenience anyone, but it would certainly be easier for one of her *Englisch* customers to drive into town. The Amish seldom went into town—some only once a month.

She finally decided on the Thompsons, who lived closest to town. At least that was the best reason she could find to short their order. Rosa went into the vacant barn and glanced around. It seemed odd not to run into Adam. He spent most of his day either outside in the fenced area training horses or inside the barn cleaning stalls. But it was probably for the best that he sold his horses so quickly. He would no longer need her barn. Unless she could figure out a way to come up with the money to satisfy the tax lien in time, she might not have a barn to share.

She had already considered selling her plow team. But most buyers waited until spring to purchase livestock to avoid the costly winter feed bill.

And she didn't have until spring.

Her barn should already be stocked with enough hay to last the winter, and it wasn't. The supply in the barn belonged to Adam. He probably sold it along with the horses and it just hadn't been hauled away yet.

Rosa tried not to dwell on dead chickens and revenue loss as she headed down the country road to make her deliveries. She loved Paradise for its towering, leaf-covered canopies along the road and the rich hues of the rolling fields during the different seasons. She drew in a lungful of crisp fall air as Blossom picked up her trotting pace.

Spending a few moments at each stop for a cup of coffee made the morning pass quickly. By the time she knocked on the Thompsons' door to make her last delivery, her heart raced from caffeine jitters.

Camille Thompson sniffled as she answered the door.

"Is everything all right?" Rosa didn't normally pry, but her *Englisch* friend was obviously upset.

Her friend dabbed a tissue against her puffy eyes. "I know I owe you for the last two weeks, but I don't have the money to pay you."

"We can settle up another time." She lifted up the basket. "I only had enough to fill half the order anyway. I'll bring the other half tomorrow."

Camille's eyes watered more. "Rosa, I won't be able to pay you tomorrow either."

Out of all her customers, the Thompsons probably needed the eggs more than anyone. Rosa smiled. "Like I said, we'll settle up another time."

"Thank you," Camille said. "You don't know what a blessing this is."

"I'll see you tomorrow." Rosa returned to her buggy. It was

satisfying to know she was a blessing to someone else. It put her hard times in perspective. At least she didn't have to worry about having food to eat. Had Uriah left her broke and with a houseful of children, it could have been so much worse. As it was, she only had herself.

She clucked to Blossom and pulled out of the driveway. "Lord, forgive me," she whispered, "but I don't want to move in with *Aenti* Lilly."

Rosa scanned the countryside, and her mind scrambled to formulate a plan. If she was going to stay in Paradise, she had to pay the back taxes and buy enough feed for her livestock to get through the winter. She had no intention of telling any of the members in the district about her delinquent taxes. She didn't want anyone to think Uriah hadn't supported her well. Had they not lost their dairy cows, things wouldn't be so grim. "Please, God," she prayed, "show me a way to save *mei* farm."

But when Rosa pulled into the barnyard, the sight that greeted her made her physically sick. One. Two. She scanned the ground and eyed the third dead chicken.

Rosa stopped Blossom at the hitching post and jumped out of the buggy. Feathers littered the lawn. Dog prints. More slaughtered chickens near the corral. Another one next to the *icehaus*.

Rosa searched the cloudy sky. "Why?" she cried out—to God, to herself, to no one in particular. She turned a circle, staring upward. "What *nau*?"

～

Adam paid the cashier at the auction house for the horses he purchased. Unlike the horses he'd just trained and sold, this stock was much younger and would take longer to train. But once they were buggy broken, they would fetch a good profit.

"Can you give me an idea of how long it will be before they're delivered?" he asked the woman behind the counter.

"Mack said to give him a couple of hours."

"That's fine." It would take him more than an hour to get home by buggy.

She picked up her pen. "Do you have a contact number you wish to leave for him?"

Adam shook his head. "I don't have a phone. But I'm less than ten miles up the road. If he has problems following the directions, tell him to stop at any Amish farm and someone will direct him to my place."

"I'm sure he won't have a problem." She set the pen on the paper and pushed it aside. "Next," she hollered as Adam moved away from the pay window.

If he'd only bought one or two horses he would have tied them behind the buggy, but hauling eight would require too many trips. Besides, the three fillies barely weaned were not halter broken. He had no choice but to transport them by trailer.

Adam looked forward to seeing Rosa's expression when she saw the fillies. Since she named all of her chickens, he thought she might like to name the yearlings too. He crossed the vehicle parking and headed toward the grassy area sectioned off for buggies.

"Adam," a man's voice called.

He glanced over his shoulder. Stephen Bowman and his teenage lad, James, headed his way. "Bought up all the horses, *ya*?"

"I left a few old hags."

Stephen nodded at his *sohn*. "See, it's a *gut* thing we didn't bid on any of them." He turned back to Adam. "I told James we would start looking for a buggy horse for him."

A horse was important to a young man, especially once they reached the age to attend the singings. Adam remembered how long it took him to pick out his first horse. He bought a fast horse, but it didn't help him win the *maedel's* attention. Rosa only had eyes for Uriah.

Heat had already started to crawl up his neck. He pushed aside the thought. He'd rather not rekindle that old attraction. As if he could avoid it.

"I might have one for sale in a few months." It wouldn't take long to determine which horse of the eight had the best disposition. Someone as inexperienced as James would need a fully trained driver. Boys his age often raced their buggies.

"How many horses do you own *nau*?"

"Eight, but I hope to have twenty within a year or two."

Stephen nodded. "Is that why Rosa told Hope she's selling her draft team? To make room for your new herd?"

"What?" He hadn't heard anything about her selling the team.

"*Ach*, I thought you were still using Rosa's barn."

"*Ya*, I am."

"*Mei fraa* said Rosa was looking for a buyer. I passed the information along, but you and I both know this isn't the time of year to buy a draft team."

Adam agreed.

"You should tell her if she waits until spring, she'll fetch more money."

"*Ya*, I'll be sure to."

Not that Rosa would listen to him. He'd trained stallions less stubborn.

~

Rosa knocked hard on the neighbor's door. She would have taken care of this earlier, but she had to clean and pluck the chickens. She hung them in the *icehaus* long enough to speak with the neighbor, and afterward she would cook and can them.

She knocked again.

No answer.

Rosa muttered under her breath and knocked again, this time rattling the aluminum screen door with her fist. She planted her hands on her hips and turned, surveying the area. Determination stiffened her spine. She had no intention of leaving without speaking to the owner.

Rosa marched across the yard toward the barn.

By the sound of vicious barking, his dogs didn't like visitors. Large cages were anchored to the back of the barn. She stopped abruptly as several liver-spotted brown-and-white dogs charged the caged run. The fence clattered as the dogs jumped against it.

Rosa backed away, but not before noticing that one of the dog runs was empty. The missing dog must be the one that attacked her chickens. Tate Wade denied his dog's involvement the last time. This time she would show him the empty cage.

The dogs settled down once she was out of sight. She strode around to the front of the barn where she had seen the man working before. She knocked on the door, then eased it open.

A dim overhead light illuminated the small workspace. Tools lined a pegboard on the wall and the bench held an assortment of electrical drills and saws.

The dogs' barking erupted once more. Only this time, instead of vicious protective barking, the yipping sounded excited.

A voice rose over the din. "Can I help you?"

She spun to face Tate Wade.

"You're the neighbor lady." He cocked his head to one side. "What are you doing in here?"

She eyed the double-barrel shotgun in his hand.

"You didn't answer my question—why are you in my barn?"

Panic washed over her as the dogs barked behind her and Tate moved closer. She motioned in the direction of the kennel. "Did you know you have an empty cage? I think one of your dogs is missing."

He crossed the room with a few long strides and opened the door leading to the kennel.

"The last cage on the left," Rosa shouted over the shrill barking. She lifted to her toes and peered around his side.

"They're all there." He closed the door, muffling the sound. "Now, will you tell me what you're doing in here?"

"Maybe you should put the gun down first."

He shifted the shotgun to his other hand. "Let's go outside."

She followed, grateful to leave the barn. The bishop wouldn't be pleased if he heard she spent any amount of time in a closed barn with an *Englischer*.

Tate stopped near the door, squatted, and grabbed two dead pheasants by their feet.

"You shot those?"

He nodded and grinned proudly at the birds dangling from his hand.

That explained the gun, the orange hat, and the whistle around his neck. It also explained why his dogs went after her chickens. Her Rhode Island Reds probably reminded them of game birds. Rosa straightened her shoulders. "Your dogs attacked my chickens, *again*."

"Not my dogs. The two you said were missing from the cage were with me." He turned toward the house and started walking.

She stormed behind him. "That makes eight they've killed."

He continued walking.

"Mr. Wade, my chickens were mangled. What are you going to do about—"

He pivoted to face her. "Two years ago I made your husband a fair offer to buy your property. That offer still stands."

"What are you talking about?" She shook her head. "My farm is not for sale."

He shrugged. "You would be smart to accept my offer now, but I can wait."

"You'll wait a long time."

"Isn't the auction less than a month away?" He grinned. "Twenty days, if I'm not mistaken."

A flash of heat traveled up the back of her neck. "You read my mail?"

"Back taxes are public record." He fixed her with a steady gaze. "All sales are final. You are aware of that, right?"

Chapter Five

Rosa suppressed her tears until she reached her house. Once inside, her knees buckled and she collapsed onto a kitchen chair in sobs.

The heartless man wanted to take her farm. No wonder he wasn't concerned that his dogs were killing her chickens.

"God, do You see what I'm up against? He wants my land." She brushed the tears away with the back of her hand. "Is this Your will?"

It was the same question she asked when the dairy cows caught the respiratory disease. But she'd had Uriah then. Now she had no one.

Anger flared toward her late husband. Had he really considered selling their home without telling her? At one time she would have believed it unthinkable. But he had let the taxes go unpaid without telling her. He had left her unprepared. And alone.

An image of *Aenti* Lilly flashed in her mind. Rosa didn't have to be alone. All she had to do was leave everything she knew behind.

She pushed away from the table and got to her feet. She wasn't going to sit around feeling sorry for herself. If she lost the farm, it wouldn't be because she hadn't done everything in her power to prevent it. There were six chickens out in the *icehaus* that still needed to be cooked and canned.

Rosa slipped on her cape and headed outside. The *icehaus* worked well in the middle of winter or when packed full with frozen foods. Otherwise, the insulated walls were not sealed tight and didn't keep a consistent temperature.

She opened the door and stepped inside, leaving the door propped open for light. Her teeth chattered as a chill passed through her. She snatched the stiff chickens, turned, and bumped into Adam who stood in the doorway.

"*Ach!* You startled me."

"Sorry. I thought you saw me."

"I'm a little preoccupied."

"I see that." He reached for the lifeless hens. "When did this happen?"

"While I was out delivering eggs." She glared at the neighbor's house. "Do you know how many dogs he owns over there?"

"*Nee*, and if you do, I'm *nett* so sure I want to know how you found out."

"Eight."

"It's *nett* illegal." He continued toward the house.

"Do you know what he does with his dogs?" She didn't wait for him to guess. "He hunts *birds*."

Adam climbed the porch steps and paused at the door. "Did you see the dog attack the chickens?"

"*Nee*." She pointed to the muddy paw prints on her porch. "But there's the proof." She nudged the door open with her hip, waited for him to enter, then closed the door and followed him into the kitchen. "You can put them in the sink."

Before going to Tate Wade's house, Rosa had removed the gizzards and plucked the majority of feathers, but the chickens still needed to be washed more thoroughly and cut before she cooked the meat.

Adam set them inside the basin. "Chicken for supper tonight?" He wiggled his brows.

Despite her best intentions, she cracked a smile. "Are you inviting yourself?"

He nodded.

"Hmm."

He smiled. "I'll help you clean them."

"They're plucked. I've already done the hard part."

"I know."

The twinkle in his blue eyes dispatched a jolting current. It was no brotherly look. Goose bumps ran up Rosa's arms, as bumpy as the naked chickens. She forced herself to look away. If she wasn't careful she would fall for his caring and sweet nature.

Rosa turned on the tap and pretended to inspect the chickens. "I suppose I might have missed some feathers."

He edged up next to her at the sink, his shoulder touching hers as he rolled up his cuffs. "I've never prepared a chicken. You'll have to tell me what to do."

Working this close was awkward. Even Uriah hadn't helped her prepare a meal. "You can start by pulling any feathers I missed." She pushed up the sleeves of her dress.

He inspected the first hen, then flipped it over.

"Do you think your *mamm* would want a chicken? I could send it with you."

"*Nee,*" he was quick to reply. "She's already made meat loaf. Besides, she's *nett* that fond of chicken."

She crinkled her brows. "I suppose chicken more than once a week does get old."

"*Nett* to me. I'd rather eat chicken with you than meat loaf any day."

With you. Rosa swallowed hard. He didn't have to work very hard to lift her spirits. "Maybe supper isn't such a *gut* idea."

"There isn't anything wrong." He peered into her eyes. "Friends can spend time together."

Her neck hairs bristled. "I don't want to keep you from spending time with Claire Milner."

"You're *nett.*" He held up the chicken. "This one is ready."

Gut. She needed a distraction. Rosa tapped the cutting board, and he lowered the chicken onto the wooden block. Distracted, she rummaged through the utensil drawer for a knife.

He leaned closer. "So how did I do? Did I miss any feathers?"

She pretended to look it over. "I think you could be a cook's helper."

"*Danki,* but I'll stick with horse training."

"Apparently you're a *gut* trainer. You sold all of your horses." She concentrated on cutting off the drumstick. The lighthearted banter between them faded as her thoughts shifted to the bleak situation with the neighbor. "I'm glad you found a buyer for them all."

After a moment he nudged her arm with his elbow. "Something bothering you?"

Baited words. She was vulnerable enough to spill it all: The years of unpaid taxes, the endless hours of fretting over losing her farm, the prospect of moving to Ohio. Even, if she wasn't careful, the pain of being childless. A red truck pulled into the driveway. Adam lowered the chicken back into the sink and washed his hands. "This won't take long." He wiped his wet hands on the side of his pants as he hurried out of the kitchen.

"Sorry I'm late." The driver climbed out of his truck.

"That's no problem. I was helping a friend with her chickens." Adam went to the opposite side of the trailer as the driver unlatched the ramp. Now that the horses had arrived, he was anxious to get them unloaded so he could show Rosa the fillies.

Adam eased the heavy ramp down as the driver guided the other side. He made a makeshift halter from a piece of rope and led the sorrel gelding into the corral. The fillies were last to leave the trailer and jumpy. One nipped and another one lifted her front hooves and pawed at the air.

"Easy, girls." Adam tightened the hold on the ropes. They were too young and high strung to release into the ring, so he placed them in the larger stall and removed the rope halters. Adam filled the trough with fresh water and tossed them some hay. Pleased with the new stock, he jogged to the house.

"Rosa," Adam called from the back door. "Will you *kumm* out to the barn for a minute?"

She came around the corner, wiping her hands on a dish towel. "It's *nett* another dead chicken, is it?"

"*Nee*, nothing like that. I want to show you something."

Midway to the barn, her eyes locked on the corral and she froze. "You bought more horses?"

"*Ya*. That's what trainers do. Buy, train, sell . . . then buy more. What's wrong?"

She didn't move.

"*Kumm* on. I want to show you the ones inside the barn."

"There's more?" She cringed. "*Ach*, Adam."

He reached for her elbow and gave it a slight tug. This wasn't the reaction he had expected. "You'll love the ones inside."

He directed her to the large stall at the far side of the barn. "What do you think?"

She stared for a moment, then reached between the fence rails. The chestnut-colored filly nuzzled her outstretched hand. "They're beautiful."

"*Nau* I have *mei* girls in the barn, and you have your girls in the coop." He chuckled, but stifled it when it came out sounding nervous. "I thought maybe you would like to name them."

She shook her head, retracting her hand from inside the pen.

"Why *nett*? You name your chickens."

She pushed away from the stall. "I wish you had said something before you bought them."

"This upsets you?"

"I, ah . . ." She brushed past him and headed out the door.

"Rosa?" He followed across the lawn. "Tell me why you're upset."

She walked faster.

He reached for her arm and stopped her before she started up the porch steps. "This isn't like you. Why are you running off?"

"Things changed when the dog attacked *mei* chickens again. You can't keep the horses here."

"What are you talking about?"

"You have to move them." She lowered her head, and he had to bend to look into her eyes.

"That isn't going to be easy. I just bought eight horses."

Her shoulders straightened as she drew in a breath. "You have twenty days to find another place to keep them."

Chapter Six

Adam tried to recall Rosa's exact words. Something about the dog and another chicken attack. But what did that have to do with him keeping his horses? And twenty days. What kind of a notice was that? He couldn't find a place to keep eight horses in that short time.

She turned toward the house and Adam waited, stifling the urge to question her. He had to find out what was going on with her. He wanted to *understand* her. But she said nothing, just disappeared inside without so much as a glance in his direction.

If he remembered correctly, Uriah would drive her to town for ice cream whenever she was upset about something. But Adam doubted she would be willing to go into town with him. Besides, ice cream might make matters worse if it reminded her of Uriah.

Maybe he frightened her by admitting he wanted to have supper alone with her. She had turned somber only moments before the truck arrived.

"Lord, I'm *nett* any *gut* at figuring out women," he muttered. As he plodded toward the barn, he looked back once. But she wasn't standing at the window.

Adam grabbed the pitchfork and stabbed at a mound of hay. He filled the wheelbarrow and carted the feed outside to the horses. He took his time tossing the hay over the fence, talking to the horses, returning the wheelbarrow to the barn. He still had plenty of time before supper. If he arrived too early, Rosa might cancel. He wouldn't risk it.

A handful of clucking hens met him near the barn door and followed him to the coop. The chickens triggered an idea far better than ice cream. If he left now, he might have enough time to get to town before the feed store closed.

He jogged home.

Entering the house, his mother called out from the kitchen, "I'm making meat loaf."

"I was invited to supper," he called back. "I'm heading into town *nau*."

Adam went directly to his room, washed up, and changed his clothes. It was the second time this week he wore his Sunday clothes, and it wasn't even Sunday.

The last canning jar lid popped. The chicken safely sealed, Rosa twisted the ring into place and pushed the hot jars to the back of the counter. After telling Adam he needed to find a new place for his horses, she didn't expect him for supper. And she wasn't hungry either, but the raw chicken wouldn't keep.

Earlier in the day she had gone down to the cellar, brought up carrots and red potatoes, and left them soaking in a pot of salted water. It was more than she could eat, but they wouldn't save for another day. She put the vegetables on to boil, then heated the skillet to fry the chicken.

Someone knocked on the door just as she added the last piece of chicken to the pan.

Adam smiled warmly from the other side of the screen door, as though their earlier conversation had never taken place. "I hope I'm *nett* late."

"*Nee.*" She eyed his white shirt, dark pants, and black hat. He only wore those clothes on Sundays. She looked beyond him to his tied horse. "You drove your buggy from next door?"

"I had an errand to do in town."

"In your Sunday clothes?"

He arched an eyebrow. "I hope we're *nett* going to talk all *nacht* with the screen door between us."

Rosa pushed open the door. "I didn't mean to put you on the spot about your clothes. It was merely an observation."

He stepped inside and leaned closer. "You sound like *mei mudder.*"

True, Rosa was older than he was, but only by two years. It wasn't as if—

She sniffed. "*Mei* carrots!"

Rosa turned toward the stove to see dark smoke curling toward the ceiling. The pot had boiled dry. She grabbed a couple of potholders and carried the hot pan to the sink. "*Nee* carrots for supper."

"That's okay." He sidled up beside her. "Close your eyes."

She turned off the tap water and shut her eyes. Beside her she heard a strange chirping sound and opened her eyes to see a tiny chick cupped in his hands.

"For you," he said.

She shook her head and frowned. *No more animals.*

"What? You don't like *mei* gift?"

The little bird chirped. She wasn't sure which looked more out of sorts, the bird or Adam.

He extended his cupped hands. "I think she's calling you."

She hesitated. Then, unable to resist the baby chick, she tossed the potholders on the counter and reached out for it. "It's cute." She had almost forgotten what it was like to hold a fuzzy peeping chick.

Adam blew out an exaggerated breath. "You had me worried for a minute."

"*Danki*, but I can't keep it." She went to give it back, but he threw his hands up in the air. "Adam!"

He backed up. "You love your chickens."

She stepped toward him.

"Are you really turning it down?" He sighed and took the baby chick from her hands. "I should've brought you ice cream."

"Ice cream?"

He looked down at the floor. "You were upset over losing your chickens . . ."

"What does that have to do with ice cream?"

He shrugged one shoulder. "Uriah used to take you into town for a treat when you were upset over something."

She and Uriah had eaten a lot of ice cream. Every time she suffered a miscarriage. Rosa sighed. "I can't believe he told you about that."

"We were like *bruders*."

Rosa fell silent. She had been so caught up in her own losses that she hadn't given much thought to Adam losing his best friend. "You meant a great deal to him." She cleared her throat. "And you're like a *bruder* to me."

It obviously wasn't the right thing to say. He stared at her, his eyes glazed with sorrow.

She motioned to the chick. "So it was between ice cream and a chick." She sighed. "Ice cream would have been simpler."

He smiled. "But this darling won't melt."

"Where am I going to keep it? It's too young to go out to the coop with the other chickens."

"Hold that thought." He handed her the chick and rushed to the door.

Adam hoisted the oversized wooden crate containing the baby chicks from the back end of the buggy. Now that Rosa had accepted the one, it shouldn't be too difficult to convince her to keep them all.

As he reentered the house with the crate, she stepped cautiously toward him, her head tilted slightly. "Is that more peeps I'm hearing?"

"You wouldn't want to break up the family." He spotted an area out of the way, yet close to the heat of the woodstove, and lowered the crate to the floor.

"Just how large is the family?"

"A dozen."

She gasped.

"You were upset over losing your chickens. I thought you would want to replace them."

"I need laying hens. *Nett* some straight-run batch of chicks from a hatchery. They're probably cockerels, and I certainly don't need more roosters." She rubbed her temple. "I can't afford them."

"I bought feed already." At the time, he thought this was a good idea. Especially since he'd never known anyone to cry so hard over losing a few chickens. But something was wrong. She seemed even more troubled than earlier today, when she told him to find a new place for his horses.

He crossed the distance between them. "I'll build a brooder box."

"It's more than that," she muttered, turning away from him.

"Should I have bought the gallon of ice cream?"

She cracked a smile.

"What flavor do you like? Chocolate? Vanilla? I'll even buy you the fancy stuff with chunks of brownies or cookie dough."

She shook her head. "You're a *gut* friend, Adam."

Friend. Well, he supposed it could be worse. Especially since she had just said he was like a brother.

"I hope this means you'll reconsider allowing me to keep my horses here."

Her smile vanished and she lowered her head.

"Rosa, please." He shifted his feet. "Eight horses are going to be hard to place."

"That's why I gave you almost three weeks."

He groaned.

A barking dog broke the tension.

Her eyes widened. She thrust the baby chick at his chest, rushed past him, and removed the gun from the rack on the wall. Rosa stormed outside as he juggled to keep from dropping the chick.

Adam lowered it to the floor. He would put it in the box with the others later. First, he needed to get the gun away from Rosa.

Before he took his first step, a shot rang out.

Chapter Seven

"Have you lost your mind?" Adam snatched the shotgun from Rosa as the dog's yelp faded into the distance. He set the gun's safety lock.

Rosa covered her face with her hands. "I hit him, didn't I?"

How did she want him to respond? Be pleased for her?

"The dog's *nett* dead, if that's what you're asking." He stormed to his buggy, set the gun inside, then grabbed the lantern he kept in the back and lit it.

"Are you going to look for the dog?"

"*Nee,*" he snapped. "I'm going to check on *mei* horses."

"I'll get another lantern." She whirled toward the house.

"Rosa, just go inside." His horses hadn't calmed down yet, and he didn't want her making matters worse. At times the woman lacked any sort of judgment. "Please," he said. "Wait in the *haus.*"

The startled horses had vaulted to the opposite end of the corral. He lifted the lantern higher and counted, then counted again. None appeared harmed, but they were visibly distressed, and might trample him if he were to crawl through the fence to get a closer view.

Inside the barn, the three fillies greeted him at the stall gate. He checked Bolt and Thunder next. Rosa's draft team was fine, as was her buggy mare. He blew out a breath. The dog's fate might be another issue, but the horses weren't injured.

Adam leaned against the stall. "God, I think the stress of losing Uriah has finally caused her to crack."

He hung his head. Uriah died in the barn fire to save him, but he couldn't save his friend's wife from herself. How could losing a few chickens trigger that type of erratic reaction?

The door creaked on its hinges and lantern light flickered from the opposite side of the barn. He groaned under his breath as Rosa approached.

She stopped a few feet from him. "Is everything all right?"

"The horses are fine." Her sudden timid stance tore at his heart. He stepped closer. "We should leave them alone."

"I'm going to look for the dog," she said, looking off into the field.

"*Nee*, you're *nett*." His tone was firm.

She snapped up her head. "Adam, I have to. The dog yelped, that means it's injured."

"Did you see the dog? Do you even know if it was your neighbor's?"

"You sound like Tate Wade. He refused to admit his dog killed *mei* chickens. *Nau* look what happened."

"And I suppose if you killed his dog, you're even. Are you pleased?"

"*Nee!*" Her glassy eyes flickered with lantern light.

A stretch of silence passed between them. He cleared his throat.

"I don't want you searching for an injured animal. They tend to attack."

"*Ya, mei* chickens," she muttered under her breath.

"What's done is done." He placed his hand on her shoulder and turned her toward the house. "Go back inside."

She lowered her head and shuffled away.

"Rosa?"

She turned. "*Ya?*"

"Do you have any more guns in the *haus*?"

She shook her head.

She wasn't getting this one back either. Not until he was certain she wouldn't shoot at something else. As she slipped into the house, he removed the twenty-pound bag of chick feed from his buggy and left it on her porch next to the door.

He had so looked forward to eating supper with her. Now he just wanted to go home.

Rosa sipped her coffee as she waited for sunrise. Adam was right. She had lost her mind. She'd spent most of her sleepless night praying for the dog, its yelping cry replaying in her mind. How could she have let anger take control of her actions? She was ashamed of her lack of self-control. She hadn't intended to shoot the dog, only to fire into the air. The gun went off accidently while she was loading it.

Still, if the dog died . . .

Rosa glanced out the kitchen window. The sky was turning a lighter shade of blue. She pulled her cape off the hook next to the door, pushed her feet into a pair of shin-high mud boots, and headed outside. No matter what Adam said, she was going to search for that dog.

The cool morning air frosted her breath as she walked. She slipped under the pasture fence and plodded over the furrowed ground. Birds chirped as she entered the woods. She hiked the winding, red- and yellow-leaf-covered path and stopped at the creek. The dog wasn't anywhere in sight.

Perhaps it didn't run off to the woods to die. Maybe it was all right. Even so, she had to keep searching. She chose a different path home, weaving around the towering oaks and maples with no success.

Finally, she tromped out of the woods, but instead of coming out on her property, she found herself on her neighbor's land. She had already cut halfway across the field when she decided to double back. Since Tate Wade's dog pens were on the backside of his barn, it wouldn't be too difficult to count the number of dogs in the kennels.

As she neared the cages, the dogs charged and she jumped back, clutching her chest. This wasn't a good idea. The noisy commotion was bound to draw attention. She took a quick count. One missing.

Behind her, a man cleared his throat.

She turned toward him, smoothing out the wrinkles on the front of her dress with her hands. "Good morning, Mr. Wade."

"Mrs. Hostetler." His tone was as cold as his unblinking, dark eyes. "What do you plan to do, destroy my other dogs?"

"I, ah . . ."

He crossed his arms over his chest. "I had no idea how cruel you were. I thought Amish people didn't believe in violence."

She flinched. No one had ever described her that way. Then again, she'd never taken a shot at someone's dog. She lowered her head.

"My prized German shorthaired pointer's leg was shot."

"I'm sorry. It was an accident."

"For your sake, he'd better recover. His champion bloodline will cost a great deal to replace." Rosa watched, alarmed, as his face flushed a dark red.

For your sake? Was that a threat?

"I do hope your dog makes a full recovery," she said. "But I'd like him to *live* on your side of the property line, not mine."

"I don't want to see you near my kennels again."

Rosa nodded. "Again, I'm sorry." She circled to leave. The quicker she could get home, the sooner her heart would stop pounding so hard.

"I'll let you know when I receive the final bill from the vet."

She turned and traipsed across the pasture that separated their properties and came up on the backside of her barn. He expected *her* to pay? She had suffered losses too.

"The dog might be a champion, but he's also a killer," she muttered under her breath. "The man doesn't care about the chickens I lost."

Rosa stomped closer to the fence talking to herself. Even as she fumed, she realized that this wasn't about evening the score. The gun might have misfired, but that didn't erase the fact that she shot the dog.

Adam looked up from cleaning a horse's hoof. "What do you do, go to bed mad and wake up even madder?" He lowered the mare's front leg and straightened his back, hoof pick in hand. His stare followed her as she closed the gap between them.

Last night he was too upset to eat supper, or to even let her know he'd left the chicken feed on the porch. She didn't want him upset with her today. *"Guder mariye,"* she said, keeping her voice calm.

He stepped closer. "Were you out looking for that dog?"

She nodded.

"Rosa . . ." He shook his head.

She winced at his tone. "I felt awful. The gun went off accidently." Her throat tightened as her mind reeled with what could have happened.

"That's a *gut* reason for you *nett* to have a gun in the *haus*. You don't know how to use it."

He was right. Rosa had never shot a gun before last night. She didn't want to admit that she nearly dropped the gun when it kicked.

"I've never seen you like this." He softened his tone. "I'm worried."

She forced a smile and pulled her emotions back. "I'm going to put a pot of *kaffi* on after I feed the chickens. Would you like a cup?" She fully expected him to decline.

"Sure."

"Oh . . . okay." Rosa motioned to the barn as she started walking in that direction. "I have to feed the chickens first."

Inside the barn, she leaned into the barrel and scooped up the last remnants of corn. In a pinch, she could use some of the chick feed, but it contained additives that she didn't like to feed to her egg-producing chickens.

The feed barrel was a metaphor of her life—empty. She was at the bottom of the barrel, both figuratively and literally. Financially and emotionally, she was barely scraping by.

She stepped outside and shook the can. Several hens flocked around her as she rattled the grain. One of her noisiest hens, Gabby, was missing. So were Chuckles and Chops. She tossed the remaining grain and hurried into the coop. Gabby was on the ground dead.

Rosa gritted her teeth and turned her eyes to the heavens. "Why, God?"

She felt a tug on her arm and turned to see Adam at her side. *"Kumm* on."

"I have to . . . gather the eggs . . . and . . ." All her reserve failed her, and the tears came.

"Shh." As though she belonged in his arms, he steadied her against him and guided her head to his shoulder. "I'll bring the eggs inside."

She closed her eyes and breathed in the scent of soap. For a moment she just rested there, comforted by the feeling of his arms around her. Then she opened her eyes and caught a glimpse of his mother staring in their direction as she hung laundry on the line.

Rosa pushed away from him and ran to the house. The only man to have enfolded her in his arms was Uriah. She never believed another man would hold her.

A few moments later Adam knocked on the back door and came into the kitchen. "Had you already gathered some eggs?"

"Nee, why?" She got up and prepared the teapot. Anything to calm the jitters.

"I only found six." He extended his hands, each holding three brown eggs.

"What?"

"I looked through all the roosting boxes."

"How can that be?"

He shrugged. "Maybe the dog traumatized them. I wouldn't worry about it. You'll have eggs tomorrow."

"I *am* worried. I have deliveries scheduled. People are relying on those eggs." As it was, the six he collected were the ones she had promised to the Thompsons to make up what they'd been shorted.

"Folks will understand."

She shook her head.

The lines on his forehead crinkled. "Do you want me to look again?"

"I'll do it." Without putting on her cape, she went outside.

Adam followed her into the coop. She searched each nesting box, but he was right. All forty-some chickens had stopped laying.

~

Adam washed down the last bite of peanut butter sandwich with a drink of milk. His mother had paced the kitchen since serving him lunch. He wasn't sure if he should ask her why or pretend she wasn't fretting about something.

"What did Claire and her *mamm* prepare for supper last *nacht*?"

"I didn't have supper with the Milners."

His mother didn't look too surprised. Perhaps she'd heard the gunshot and the commotion in Rosa's yard. She wrung her hands together, busied herself at the counter for a moment, then turned to face him. "You're spending a great deal of time at Widow Hostetler's *haus*."

The widow reference wasn't lost on him. His mother liked Rosa, or he thought she did. The only negative comment he'd ever heard was about Rosa's inability to have children. Perhaps his mother viewed barrenness as a curse.

"I wish you wouldn't spend so much time with her."

Adam pushed his chair away from the table. "I promised Uriah I would look after Rosa."

"Isn't it asking a lot for Claire to wait for Rosa's time of mourning to pass? I'm sure Uriah didn't expect you to spend so much time—"

"Before you finish, you might want to look again at this." Adam jerked the hem of his collarless shirt down and pointed to the burn scars on his neck. "Uriah died trying to save me."

"And I'm grateful. It's just that . . ."

He glanced out the window at the empty lot where the barn once was. "Rosa's life wouldn't have been turned upside down if I had died in that fire instead of Uriah."

Mamm bowed her head.

Adam swiped his hat from the table. "I'm going into town."

He needed to buy a roll of chicken wire. Something he should have done after the dog attacked Rosa's chickens the first time. Erecting a fence was the only way to keep the flock safe, and even that wasn't a guarantee.

Tomorrow was Sunday. Rosa needed to get away from the farm, to spend time in fellowship. Lately, she'd become so consumed with her chickens that she'd almost lost sight of the people who cared about her. If he didn't put up some fencing, she'd spend Sunday services at home watching over those hens.

He wanted to blame sleep deprivation for her odd behavior, but it had to be something more. She had pulled away when he held her. He could only conclude that she was repulsed by his scars. Thank goodness he hadn't tried to kiss her.

Still, the memories of holding her lingered. It felt right to have her in his arms. Her head nestled on his shoulder, her warm breath driving fire to his core.

He shook his head.

She didn't share the same feelings. She would never fall in love with him, not the man who was to blame for her husband's death.

Chapter Eight

After another sleepless night, staying attentive during the three-hour church service proved challenging. Rosa shifted on the wooden bench. The same thoughts of Adam that had assailed her mind last night continued to vie for her attention today. But every time she recalled the warmth of his embrace or the thumping of his heartbeat against her ear, she thought about Eunice, standing at the clothesline gaping at them.

She could only guess what Eunice thought of her now, after seeing that public display of affection. Rosa had wilted against him as if she belonged in his arms.

But Adam was just a kind man, that was all. A man who would offer a comforting gesture to anyone in distress.

Rosa felt a poke in her ribs and glanced sideways at Hope. The service had ended and the members were starting to stand. Rosa stood and stretched. Hope thrust Faith into her arms.

"Will you hold her while I get *mei* potato casserole out of the buggy?"

"Of course."

Rosa cradled the sleeping infant and fought against a rising tide of jealousy. It was hard not to be envious of her best friend. Four beautiful daughters and a fine son, not to mention a loving husband. Everything Rosa wanted, Hope had.

Becky Byler appeared with her arms outstretched. "Do you want me to take her?"

"Don't you want to join your friends?"

Becky shrugged. "It doesn't matter." But her downcast expression and slumped shoulders didn't match her words. It did matter.

Most of the unmarried girls congregated together during the fellowship hours. Even as they helped with the meal preparations, they stayed tight-knit, whispering among themselves. Becky Byler didn't fit in with that bunch.

Rosa released Faith into Becky's arms. If the girl needed something to do instead of interacting with the other young folks, Rosa wouldn't monopolize time with the infant. Besides, she hadn't planned on staying for the meal. She didn't want to leave the chickens unattended for too long.

Rosa spotted Hope coming from the house and walked across the lawn to meet her.

"I'm going to head home," Rosa said. "Becky Byler is watching Faith."

"Home already? Are you *nett* feeling well?" Hope eyed Rosa suspiciously.

"I feel fine." She leaned closer. "I don't trust the neighbor to keep his dogs in the kennel, and I don't want to lose any more chickens."

"Oh, Rosa, listen to yourself. You're willing to sacrifice

Sunday fellowship to watch your chickens? Don't let a dog control your life."

"It isn't just *mei* laying hens. I have to feed *mei* chicks."

"When did you get new chicks?"

"A gift from Adam."

Hope's brows lifted.

"Don't read anything into it," Rosa warned. "He felt bad that I had lost so many chickens."

Hope smiled. "Adam's sweet, *ya?*"

Rosa had already said too much. This wasn't the time or place to talk about Adam. "We can chat one day next week after I make *mei* deliveries."

"*Ya*, it sounds like we have some catching up to do."

"Don't be mapping out a spot in *mei* garden for a celery crop," Rosa said. "It isn't like that."

The reference to celery, traditionally served at their weddings, made Hope laugh.

Rosa turned toward the row of parked buggies. "I'll see you soon."

"You need to consider building a fence for your chickens."

"Adam already built one." She kept walking, ignoring Hope, who was demanding to hear more.

Halfway to her buggy, Rosa heard someone call her name. She turned. "*Hiya*, Peter."

He ambled closer. "I heard you wanted to sell your plow team."

"*Ya*, are you interested?" Normally buying and selling were not discussed on Sunday, but she took it as a sign from God to keep hope that she could raise the money she needed.

"Maybe. I'd like to look at them. Say tomorrow?"

"Sure. I get back from *mei* egg deliveries around ten."

"I'll see you then." He turned back toward the crowd.

Danki, God. The money from the draft horses plus her savings would more than cover her taxes. She caught a glimpse of Adam in the distance, carrying a bean crock in one arm and guiding Widow Esther by the elbow with his other. Since her stroke, Esther wasn't too steady. Adam showed great patience walking beside her, matching his stride to her short, shuffling steps. The other unmarried men were hanging around near the unmarried women, Claire Milner among the group.

Rosa continued toward the parked buggies. She had reached Blossom when she heard footsteps behind her.

"You're *nett* leaving already, are you?" Adam asked.

"Ya." She untied the reins from the post.

"I saw you talking with Peter Zook . . ." His voice trailed and he looked down at the ground and toed a stone.

"He's interested in buying *mei* plow team."

"I heard you might be selling them." He looked up at her. "I don't think it's wise. You'll get a better price if you wait until spring."

Spring was too late. "I have to sell them *nau*. I can't afford to feed them this winter if I don't have eggs to sell."

The womenfolk were busy taking food into the barn while the men loitered in a circle by a piece of farm equipment. They were not within earshot, but she still didn't want to continue discussing the sale of her horses. It wouldn't take much to figure out she was broke and selling the team was a necessity.

"How did your new girls do in the brooder *haus* I built?"

Rosa smiled. "Fine, but I still think there are a lot of roosters in that flock."

"Maybe so." A grin split his face. "I like chicken dinner."

Looking past him, she caught sight of Claire and Mark Raber talking next to the barn. Rosa must not have disguised her shocked expression, because Adam turned to see what she was looking at.

He stared silently.

"You better get back to the group." It hadn't been that long ago that whispers had spread of Adam sitting with Claire on her parents' porch swing.

He faced her. "I'd rather talk with you."

"I have to check on *mei* chickens."

"Your chickens are safe. Besides, if you leave *nau*, what will you eat?"

"Probably chicken."

"Rosa." He frowned.

"I also want to see if they laid any eggs," she said. "You said that the fence would give them a sense of security and they'd start producing again."

"You hover over those boxes like you expect them to lay a golden egg." He unearthed another stone with the tip of his boot. "Do you remember the *nacht* a bunch of us stood under that old oak?" He motioned to the large tree on the far corner of the property.

As children, they had played under most every tree in the district at one time or another.

"It was raining." He shoved his hands into his pockets. "I asked to drive you home from the singing. You don't remember?"

"You were joking."

"*Nee*, I was serious." Adam leaned toward her ear. "If we walked over to that tree and I asked you today, what would you say?"

She looked at him. Her heart began to race as if she were nineteen again. "We're too old to attend the youth singings," she said, and climbed into the buggy.

⁓

Adam watched as Rosa's buggy rolled away. He couldn't have made his intentions any more direct, and she rejected him, just as she had so many years ago. He understood the past. Later that same night she accepted Uriah's invitation. But now . . .

Adam sighed. She hadn't been interested in him then, and she wasn't attracted to him now. He rejoined the others for the meal, but his appetite was gone. There was only one thing on his mind: how could he fulfill his promise to Uriah to look after Rosa, while keeping his heart at a distance?

Chapter Nine

The next morning Rosa received another delinquent tax notice in the mail. She opened the kitchen drawer and added the latest reminder to the stack with the others. "I'm running out of time, God. I need a miracle." She had said those same words earlier when she found the nesting boxes empty again.

Maybe she should go ahead and write her aunt a letter, just in case. It was a last resort, but she was almost there, and she didn't think she should show up on *Aenti* Lilly's doorstep unannounced.

Rosa reached for a pen and notebook from the drawer, but instead picked up her ledger book and began flipping through the list of her egg customers "God," she said, "this isn't just about me. What about the widows? I've never charged them for eggs, so it's an unexpected expense for them. This is the middle of October. Soon it'll be Thanksgiving and Christmas. Everyone bakes more during the holidays." She paused. "But I guess I don't have to tell You about the widows' needs. You have provided for them, and You will continue even without *mei* eggs."

Rosa scanned the income log. With nothing to record, the tally hadn't changed. She'd never be able to pay the taxes before the auction day. She closed the book and slipped it back into the drawer. Unless she sold Bolt and Thunder . . .

Did she dare hope that was part of God's plan? It would make sense. If she sold the horses, not only would she be able to pay her taxes, but she wouldn't have winter feed to buy.

God would provide. He often worked in mysterious ways.

A buggy pulled into the yard. Rosa craned her neck at the kitchen window and saw Peter Zook climbing out of his buggy. She opened the door before the man knocked. *"Hiya."*

"Wie geht's?"

"Fine, *danki*." Now with the formalities accomplished, she wanted to whisk him out to the barn and show him the horses. "Let me get *mei* cape, and I'll take you out to see Bolt and Thunder." She yanked her wool cape from the peg and slipped it on as she left the house. "They're a *gut* team. I want to sell them together."

"How old are they?" She had to think. Uriah bought them the year after they married, and they were three at the time. "Nine."

He opened the barn door, waited for her to enter, and followed her to the stalls. "I didn't realize you had so many horses."

"These aren't mine. Adam Bontrager is using *mei* barn." She stopped in front of Bolt's stall. "This one is Bolt and the next stall over is Thunder."

While he inspected the draft horses, Rosa checked on the fillies in the nearby stall. She ran her hand over one filly's silky coat. The smaller of the three nuzzled her cape while the one with the white star on its forehead nipped at her elbow. Under different circumstances, she would love to spend more time with them.

Maybe those circumstances would change today. Selling the team would improve everything. She wouldn't lose her farm. Adam wouldn't be forced to relocate his horses.

Peter came outside of Bolt's stall and entered Thunder's. "They packed on some extra weight, *ya?*"

"They gained a little." A lot. They were fat and borderline lazy. Sometimes when a horse wasn't worked it lost its stamina, and often its value as well. "The only planting I've done is in the garden. So they haven't been worked in two years. But they're a strong team."

"*Ya*, so I see."

She breathed easier.

Peter closed the stall gate. "I'm interested if I can pay on time."

"How much time do you need?"

"I would have all the money by spring. Maybe early summer."

The air left her lungs, her hope along with it. "I wanted to sell them this winter."

He looked into the stall as if recalculating their worth. "You could take them to the auction, but you'll get pennies on the dollar for them. It'd be a shame."

Exactly what Adam had told her too. *Lord, this wasn't how I thought You would answer* mei *prayers.*

"I could give you a down payment at the beginning of next month."

That wouldn't help either. The tax sale was in eighteen days.

"I'll be honest with you." She fought to control the quiver in her voice. "I don't have the money to buy hay. I can't wait until spring to sell them."

He nodded. "If it helps, I'll take them *nau* so you're *nett* out the winter's feed bill. And I'll pay your asking price on payments."

One way or the other she had to sell the team. She couldn't move them to her aunt's place in Ohio. She wasn't even sure when the next livestock auction was scheduled.

She swallowed down the lump in her throat. "*Ya*," she said, "I'll accept your offer."

But all the while she was wondering, *Where is God?*

Adam stood next to the barn and directed Stephen Bowman as he backed up the hay wagon. The load wouldn't fill the loft, but it should carry both his and Rosa's horses through the winter. At least now she could wait until spring to sell the team.

Adam held out his hand to signal Stephen to stop. "That's far enough."

Stephen set the wagon brake and jumped down from the seat. His son, James, followed.

Adam slipped his hands into a pair of worn leather gloves. With Stephen and his son helping to unload the wagon, the hayloft would be loaded in no time.

And none too soon, if the storm clouds on the horizon were any indication. This late in October, any rain could turn into sleet. Rosa's buggy was missing from the yard. He worried she might get caught in bad weather.

Stephen cranked the engine on the gas-powered conveyor belt. "We should get started, or we might *nett* get this hay undercover before it rains."

Adam went into the barn and climbed the wooden ladder into the loft. He stood at the opening and waited for the bale to reach him. With both Stephen and James tossing bales on the belt, Adam wasn't able to keep up with the volume reaching him. Every other bale fell off the belt while he carried another one by the twine over to the stack. It didn't matter so much that they weren't piled nicely, what mattered was getting them under cover.

From his elevated view, Adam spotted Rosa's buggy a quarter mile down the road. The wagon was half unloaded when she pulled into the yard. She looped Blossom's reins around the post and nodded a greeting to Stephen and James. Then her gaze carried up to the loft, and her smile quickly turned to a frown. She shook her head as she went into the house.

An hour later they unloaded the final bale just as the drizzle turned to sleet. Adam leaned out of the loft opening. "*Danki* for helping."

"What about stacking? Should we *kumm* up?"

Adam shook his head. "I'll be fine. You two should be on your way. It's getting *kalt*." He shot them a quick wave, then wrapped his fingers around the twine and hoisted the bale on top of the pile.

Stephen's wagon had barely rattled out to the end of the drive when Rosa's screen door slammed. Adam glanced out as she marched toward the barn. A few moments later she stood at the bottom of the ladder, arms crossed, calling his name.

He shimmied down the ladder. His foot landed with a *thud*, and when he turned, he met her glare. "Something wrong?"

"What are you doing putting hay *in* the barn? You should be taking it out."

He wiped his shirtsleeve across his sweaty forehead. "You said you were worried about getting through the winter." He picked loose hay off his shirt.

"I told you. You have to find another place for your horses. All the hay too."

"Rosa, be reasonable."

"I don't have that option," she said. "And neither do you."

He followed her outside. "There's enough hay to last the winter for all of our horses. You don't have to sell the team either."

"They're already sold. Peter is picking them up later this week."

"I don't understand the problem." Unless it had something to do with him wanting to court her. "I've used your barn for a couple of years *nau*."

"And it was supposed to be temporary."

He groaned and followed her into the house. "We need to talk about this."

"It's too late." She stressed the words. "I didn't have any eggs again today." Her eyes brimmed with tears. She whirled away and darted into the kitchen.

"I told you, it takes time."

She turned on him with fire in her eyes. "I don't have time. I have sixteen days to pay *mei* delinquent taxes or I'm going to lose this farm." She bowed her head. "When the cows got sick, Uriah let the taxes lapse. When they came due, I wrote a letter to the county clerk explaining that *mei* husband was deceased, but it didn't matter. They said the taxes were too far behind."

He pulled a handkerchief from his back pocket and handed it to her. "How long have you known?"

"Since the beginning of the year." She swiped at the tears. "If *mei* chickens hadn't stopped laying . . ."

"I wish you had told me sooner. I spent the last money I had on hay. I won't have an income until the horses are trained."

"I won't ask anyone for money. You included." Rosa crossed her arms and turned her back on him. "I don't want anyone to think Uriah wasn't a *gut* provider."

"He would never have wanted you to go through this alone," Adam said. He felt his stomach twist into a knot. He'd made a promise to Uriah to take care of Rosa, and he'd fallen short of fulfilling his vow. "There's a widow's fund. Maybe you should speak with one of the elders—"

She spun to face him, her eyes narrowed. "I would never ask for money from that fund. It's for the widows."

"*Ya.* You fall into that group."

She shook her head. "There are women in much greater need." She locked eyes with him. "And don't you say anything about this—to anyone."

He buried a groan under his breath. Pride would devour her if she continued on this path. "Rosa—"

"I mean it. I won't ever speak to you again."

"Things will work out. God has a plan."

"*Ya.* Apparently His plan is for me to go live in Ohio with *mei aenti.*"

He shook his head. "I can't let you go there. How would I watch over you?" He inched closer and touched the wet streak on her cheek. "Have faith. God will see you through."

Her shoulders slumped and she sniffed.

"He will, Rosa. Trust me. Trust God."

Adam believed what he said. But he knew he had to figure out some way to help, or her eyes would haunt him forever.

⌒

Rosa poured *kaffi* into two cups as Adam leaned against her kitchen counter. She wanted to break the silence between them, but her thoughts were a jumbled mess.

He rubbed his jaw. "So how much money do you need yet?"

"A lot." She set the pot on the stove.

"Even after selling Bolt and Thunder?"

She cringed. "Peter didn't have the money." Rosa handed him a cup of coffee. "He's going to make payments." Right or wrong, she'd already agreed to the terms. These past two years without Uriah had proven unbearable, and battling the delinquent taxes left her weary and questioning God's will more than ever.

"How does that help you? I wish you had talked to me first."

"I couldn't afford to feed them all winter, so taking payments was the only choice I had."

"Why don't we sit down and go over what you owe? Maybe we can figure something out." He pulled out a chair and tapped the seat.

Rosa hesitated.

"You can't do this alone. Please let me help."

She opened the kitchen drawer and removed the stack of notices from the County Tax Bureau, along with the book she used to record her income. She handed the information to him, then sat in the chair next to his. "The top envelope is the most recent."

He unfolded the letter, and as he scanned the page, his expression turned hopeful. He set the paper down. "It says you only have to pay twenty-five percent by the auction date."

"I'm aware of that."

He pointed to the clerk's letter. "That's the amount you're trying to raise?"

"*Ya,*" she said. She opened the log book and pointed to the first column. "This is how much I have saved. In this row I've listed what I had counted on from egg sales."

He blew out a short breath.

"It's hopeless, isn't it?"

"Nothing is beyond God's help." He reached for her hand and gave it a gentle squeeze. "I'm glad you shared this with me."

She was too. Even knowing he lacked the financial means to help, it still comforted her to know she wasn't alone.

He sipped his *kaffi* and set down the cup. "I guess we have some work to do."

"*Ya.* I need to pack, and you need to find a new home for your horses."

He shook his head. "I meant horse training. I'll pick the one that shows the most promise. Lord willing, there's a chance I can find a quick buyer once he's trained."

"Really?"

"Don't you think that would be God's will?" He shrugged. "I do."

She found a ray of hope in his faith and smiled. "I'm blessed to have a friend like you." She patted his hand. "I mean that."

He placed his other hand over hers, opened his mouth as if

he wanted to say something, then closed it again. Adam released her hand and pushed away from the table. "I'm going to pick out a horse."

"You really want me to help train?"

"Of course I do." He winked. "I like your company. Besides, you'll find working with horses will get your mind off your problems. Make sure to wear old clothes."

When Adam left the house, Rosa dashed upstairs to change. She hadn't felt excitement like this since Uriah had convinced her they could make a go of dairy farming.

She changed into the old charcoal gray dress she saved to wear for spring cleaning. It was spotted white where bleach had splattered, with the hem tattered beyond repair. The dress should have gone into the rag pile long ago. Rosa hurried down the stairs to the door where she kept her work boots. She had one boot on when someone knocked on the door.

Rosa opened the door. "Mr. Wade! What—what can I do for you?" She hopped on one foot, trying to get the other boot on.

He thrust a piece of paper toward her. "Here's the vet bill."

She glanced at the charges, and her heart plummeted.

"Had the dog not lived, the amount would've been higher. As it looks now, the vet says he'll eventually be able to compete in hunting competitions. So I guess you're lucky."

Lucky? She'd paid less for Blossom than the price of this vet bill. She extended the paper toward him.

"Keep it. That's your copy." He made to leave but turned back. "If I have to file a lawsuit, you'll have court costs tacked on to the vet bill."

Rosa closed the door and stared at the long list of charges. Fifty dollars for bandages. Three hundred for each night at the animal hospital. Over two hundred for medications and IVs alone. She flipped to the second page as the itemized costs continued.

Paying this would leave her destitute.

Chapter Ten

Rosa lagged behind Adam as he headed toward the corral. He had said working with the horse would take her mind off her problems, but he failed to warn her how achy she'd be at the end of the day. She was stiff and sore from sitting on the fence, and even a thick application of arnica ointment didn't alleviate her soreness.

Every night she dropped into bed exhausted. But as worn out as she was physically, she still wrestled with the empty nesting boxes and the neighbor's vet bill.

She hadn't slept in three days. Not since Mr. Wade had given her a copy of the bill. Last night she got down on her knees and prayed for wisdom . . . and forgiveness. Every time she thought about taking up that shotgun, she wondered how she could have exercised such poor judgment. She could have killed the dog—or one of the horses—or even worse, a person.

It was true that the dog was on her property and had attacked her chickens, but that was rationalization. She felt prompted by

God to hold her tongue, make amends with the neighbor, and pay the vet charges.

But even with that strong conviction and sleepless nights, she couldn't bring herself to deplete her savings. She prayed that God would show her another way. So far, she hadn't received an answer. Not even a hint.

Rosa climbed up the fence rail as Adam adjusted the harness on the sorrel gelding. He hitched Flapjack to the open buggy and took a seat on the bench. Adam clicked his tongue and ordered the gelding forward. Flapjack sidestepped but quickly calmed down under Adam's tone of voice and steady actions.

Adam steered the horse around the corral, the first lap walking, then trotting. Rosa marveled at the level of skill Adam demonstrated. After making several laps of stopping and going, walking and trotting, and changing directions, Adam pulled up next to the fence railing. "Would you like to take him around a lap or two?"

"Sure." She climbed off the fence too quickly. The horse jerked his head up. "Sorry." She reached her hand to his neck and the horse flinched again. "Maybe this isn't a *gut* idea. I don't think he likes me."

"He's a little nervous yet." Adam slid over on the bench, making space on the driver's side.

"Are you sure I can hold him?"

"I'll be right beside you." He extended the reins.

She eased onto the bench.

"Give him a tap and tell him to go," Adam said.

The horse's ears perked at the sound of Adam's voice. Rosa only had to click her tongue for Flapjack to move forward. Except for the young gelding stretching his neck to gain more reins, his gait was smooth. They completed the lap and she pulled back on the reins. "I think you've done an amazing job training him so fast."

Adam smiled. "You can take him around again."

She wasn't sure if the ripple in her stomach was from the thrill of driving a newly trained horse or simply sitting shoulder to shoulder next to Adam. She clicked her tongue and lightly tapped the horse's rump. Taking the first bend, the horse pulled on its lead and at the same time increased his pace.

"Slow him down," Adam said calmly.

Flapjack ignored her command and didn't respond to her yanking on the reins. Rounding the corner, the buggy tipped. Her body slammed against Adam.

He reached over her and took control of the reins. "Whoa." His arm muscles tightened as he held the reins taut. Flapjack obeyed.

"I guess he got away from me," Rosa said once she caught her breath.

"He's a little cantankerous. I was premature letting another driver take him."

Flapjack pawed at the ground. He was lathered in sweat and foaming around the bit. He jerked his head up, but Adam kept him in check.

"It isn't good to end the lesson after a horse gets away," Adam said. "If you want to get out, I'll take him for a few more laps, then we can give him a break."

She climbed down from the bench and crawled between the fence railings to get out of the training area. "I'll go make lunch."

Eating lunch together had become part of their daily routine.

The long hours they spent together was stirring up feelings Rosa didn't want to admit. Adam was a pillar of strength, a reservoir of support. But respect and admiration for someone wasn't the same as love. She couldn't allow her heart to be fooled.

Adam Bontrager was a good man. He needed a wife and family.

She kicked her boots off beside the door. Her house cleaning had suffered over the last few days of working with him. The women would be appalled at her floors. Even with Adam stomping his boots on the outdoor mat, it would take a hard bristle brush and scrubbing on hands and knees to clean all the dirt tracked in.

Rosa had a fresh pot of coffee and sandwiches prepared by the time he tapped on the door.

"It's open." She set the sandwich plates on the table as he entered the kitchen. He washed his hands while she set the table. Then he sat in the chair opposite hers. After spending this time with him, it was going to be difficult to go back to eating every meal alone.

She caught a glimpse of Flapjack tied to the fence post. "You didn't remove his tackle?"

"*Nee*, he needs to get used to standing for long periods with it on."

That made sense. She'd often wondered how horses tolerated the long Sunday services and the extended mealtime afterward. "How do you think his training is going?"

Adam shrugged. "He's *nett* ready to go on the road yet." He must have seen the disappointment in her expression because he quickly added, "We'll know more by the end of the week."

She smiled but doubted it masked all her worry. There weren't many days left. Less than two weeks didn't seem like enough time to train a horse, let alone find a buyer.

"Don't worry," he said.

She traced the rim of the mug with her finger. "You know me too well."

"You spend too much time worrying about things you need to give to God. All of this is in God's plan. His provisions will meet your need."

"I know." She was thankful for his faith. Even Uriah had never stood so boldly. When the cows became ill with the bovine disease and it looked as though they would lose their dairy herd, Uriah had told her not to worry, but his voice shook and the wrinkles across his forehead indicated otherwise. Adam's faith was stronger than anyone she knew, and it reassured her.

"What else are you fretting over?" Adam took a bite of the sandwich.

The answer leaped to her mind immediately: she was worried about falling in love with him. But to that, she couldn't admit.

He pressed on. "Ever since the neighbor stopped over the other day, you've been acting strange."

Rosa sighed. "I might as well tell you. He showed me his vet bill. It's more than I paid for Blossom and her harness."

"It would have been cheaper to build a pen his dog wouldn't escape from."

"It was foolish to take the gun off the rack. I should have chased the dog off with a broom."

Rosa knew her impulsive actions weren't pleasing to God. The scripture she had read that morning played in her mind: *Forgive those who trespass against you.* God's Word was clear. She prayed the neighbor would forgive her for shooting his dog.

"What's done is done. You can't do anything about it now."

"He expects me to pay the expenses. He called me cruel."

Her neighbor wasn't interested in a mere apology. He wanted payment. Payment that would deplete her savings, cement the loss of her farm, and force her to move to Ohio.

"His dog was on your property." Adam pushed his empty plate aside and moved his *kaffi* cup forward. "Should I wait for you to offer me a cookie or just help myself?"

She retrieved the jar from the counter and handed it to him. "Since the chickens haven't laid any more eggs, I haven't been able to make another batch."

"I need to go to town later. I'll pick up a dozen eggs for you."

"*Nee.* I can't pay you."

He dug his hand down to the bottom of the jar and pulled out a broken cookie. "You just did."

She smiled. If her chickens started laying again, she planned to make him a double batch to take home.

He stood. "Flapjack is waiting. Are you going to *kumm* back out?"

"You don't need *mei* help."

"But I enjoy your company."

Warmth spread over her face.

"Pink is a *gut* shade for your cheeks," he said. "It brightens your eyes."

She had warned herself not to pry, but she couldn't keep from doing it. Adam had to have seen Mark Raber and Claire talking after the Sunday services last week. "Aren't you a little concerned about *nett* spending enough time with Claire?"

Adam strode to the kitchen entry and stopped. "Don't lose sleep over me and Claire. She and Mark Raber are courting *nau*."

~

Adam untied Flapjack from the post as Rosa took her place on the rail. He wanted to take the gelding around the corral a few times before letting Rosa drive again. So far, the training had gone better than expected. He had pushed Flapjack harder than normal, but he had to. He couldn't let Rosa lose her house without doing everything he could to help.

It bothered him that she made him promise not to tell anyone in the community. She had spent her life helping others; if anyone deserved help from the widows' fund, it was Rosa. But he couldn't bring himself to breach her trust either.

Adam clicked his tongue, encouraging Flapjack into a faster trot. If all went well, he would take the horse out on the road tomorrow and try some country roads to avoid heavy traffic. Maybe even show him to a few people he knew were looking to buy a buggy horse.

An engine revved next door. Flapjack shied. It took a great deal of strength for Adam to regain control.

In the distance he saw Wade working on his truck. How could he expect Rosa to pay the vet bill when his dog killed her chickens? Perhaps if he talked with the neighbor, he could convince him to let the matter drop.

~

"Here you are," Eunice said to Rosa. "I knocked on your door, but there was no answer."

Rosa jumped off the fence. "I was helping Adam."

"*Mei* son has an assistant *nau*, has he?"

"I just watch usually."

"I wanted to return your dish." She held up an empty dish in her hand, the one Rosa had used for the chicken casserole.

"*Danki.*" Rosa motioned to the house. "I could use a cup of *kaffi*. How about you?"

"Maybe a half a cup. I can't stay long. I'm meeting some of the other widows in town at the fabric store. You know we like to get together."

Rosa smiled.

"Did you want to join us? We could ride together."

"*Nee*—I couldn't." The answer sounded unnecessarily abrupt, so Rosa tried to temper her response. "I have some things already planned for this afternoon." She had promised Hope she would babysit if Becky Byler wasn't able.

"Our group is very supportive," Eunice said. She stepped into the house, her eyes roaming the sitting room. "I don't have to tell you how lonely—"

The peeping chicks caught her attention. She spotted the crate across the room and lifted her brows.

Rosa kicked off her boots. "*Boppli* chicks," she said. "A gift from Adam. He built that brooder box too. They'll soon be old enough to go outside."

Surely this wasn't the first time she'd seen chicks in the house. It wasn't as though they were running around loose. "Here, let me take that." Rosa reached for the dish. When she saw the state of the kitchen, she cringed. She should have taken a few minutes to clean up after lunch.

Rosa set the casserole dish on the counter, then hurried to clear the table. Bread crumbs on the counter, dirt on the floor, deplorable to someone like Eunice. Her house was always in order.

"I wish you would reconsider going into town with me. It isn't about picking out material as much as enjoying fellowship. And you must be lonely living here alone."

"I'm sure it's a *wunderbaar* gathering." Rosa placed the coffee-pot on the stove and willed it to boil. Truth be told, she despised participating in the widows' gatherings. They were a loving group of women and had welcomed her after Uriah's death, but Rosa couldn't manage to feel comfortable among them. As it was, it had taken her two years just to get beyond cooking for two and not jumping out of her skin every time the century-old farmhouse creaked. Despite the widows' certainty that she would adapt to living alone, she hadn't.

Besides, all of the other widows had children or grandchildren to help pass the long hours of silence. She had neither.

"I just think if you had group activities, you wouldn't depend so much on Adam," his mother said.

Rosa moved the pot to a hotter spot and avoided looking at Eunice.

"I know he feels it's his duty to look after you." She sighed. "Please don't take this the wrong way. Adam is a thoughtful *sohn*, and I'm very pleased he has such a giving heart. But I worry he is missing the opportunity to find a *fraa*. And I so want *kinskinner*."

Rosa had dreamed of having a houseful of children and grand-children too. She pushed down the pain, plastered on a smile, and faced Eunice. "I understand completely."

"*Ach* dear, I wasn't thinking." Eunice covered her mouth. "I'm so sorry."

"You didn't say anything wrong," Rosa said. "Did I tell you *mei* chickens still haven't laid any eggs? Please tell everyone I hope to be able to bring them some soon." She shifted her attention back to the stove. More kindling would heat the pot faster. She opened the side compartment and peered in at the dying embers. "I'm afraid the fire is almost out."

Eunice glanced at the wall clock. "If you don't mind," she said, "could we have *kaffi* another time? I don't want to be late to the frolic."

"I don't mind at all." Rosa hoped the relief in her tone wasn't too obvious.

Once Eunice left, Rosa washed the dishes, scrubbed the counters, and mopped the floor. She added oil to every lamp in the house, rearranged the canned goods in the pantry, and still she couldn't erase the conversation with Adam's mother.

She was filling the chicks' pan with fresh water when someone knocked on her door.

"Did you walk off the job?" Adam stomped the dirt from his boots on the mat before entering the house. "I waited for you."

She wiped her hands on her apron. "I needed to clean the house."

"I'm done for the day. Would you like to go to town with me?"

"I can't." She disappeared into the kitchen long enough to grab the watering pan.

Adam went over to the box and lifted the wire lid. "What did *mei mamm* want?"

Rosa eased the pan inside. "She invited me to the widows' gathering."

"So you're going?" He smiled.

"Nee."

His smile faded. "Are you upset about something?"

"Do you think the neighbor revved his engine purposely to spook Flapjack?" That wasn't the only thing upsetting her, but it was the only thing she was willing to share with him.

"Don't let him upset you. Anger's a sin."

"I thought you were going into town." She walked to the door, knowing he would follow. "I think we might be spending too much time together."

He closed the distance between them. "I don't."

"I really appreciate everything you're doing for me, but—"

"Don't say it."

"Adam, I don't want *mei* problems to interfere with your life."

He opened the door. "Get some sleep tonight, and don't fret over the neighbor."

Don't fret over the neighbor.

There was only one way she was going to stop fretting over the neighbor: she had to make amends with Tate.

Chapter Eleven

Rosa counted out the money down to the last penny for the vet charges. After wrestling all night with what she felt God was directing her to do, she had to obey. She closed the lid on the canning jar filled with coins. *God, I don't know where the money will* kumm *from for the taxes, but I can't live with the animosity either.* She slipped on her cape and headed across the yard. *If there's another way, stop me, please.*

Tate answered the door after the second knock.

Before he said anything, she pressed the coin jar against his chest.

"It's all there," she said. "I'm sorry your dog was injured."

"Thank you. Do you want the jar back?"

"No. That's yours to keep."

He stared at her. She couldn't breathe. She needed air. Without a word, she pivoted on her heel and fled.

A gust of wind and a sudden pelting of hail sent a chill through her bones. She cut through the garden. The moment she stepped inside the house, a blast of heat from the woodstove hit her. She kicked off her shoes and padded into the kitchen to make a cup of tea.

As the kettle heated, she looked out the window. Hail pinged against the brown lawn. Freezing rain mixed with snow would come next. Through the window she caught a glimpse of Adam as he traipsed from his property over to hers. He must have seen her, because he waved on his way to the barn.

Shouldn't she feel better? She had done the right thing, so why wasn't there some sort of relief?

Well, whether she felt better or not, it was over. No matter what happened now, she wouldn't be able to pay the taxes. One way or the other, she was going to lose the farm.

She opened the drawer and pulled out the letter she had started to *Aenti* Lilly. Everything she had saved was gone. It was time to make other plans.

She jotted a couple of sentences about the change in weather, then put the pen down. Her mind reeled in all directions. Traveling by bus would limit how much stuff she could bring. She would have to sell most of her belongings and ship the rest to Ohio.

Rosa left the kitchen and roamed through the house, trying to inventory what would have to be left behind. Parting with the rocking chair her father had made would be difficult. The bed Uriah had crafted so lovingly by hand wouldn't ship either.

She wandered back downstairs. The dishes held no sentimental value; she would find someone in need of them. The table for ten only mocked her with lost dreams. She ran her hand along the fine wood grain. She had wanted a large, noisy, happy family. What God had given her instead was grief and solitude.

Rosa started pulling jars off the shelves. Living alone, she hadn't eaten much in the past two years, yet she'd put in an oversized garden and canned as if she had a huge family to feed. Even if by some miracle she didn't lose the house, she wouldn't eat this much food in twenty years. Someone else could use it.

She had a good portion of the pantry unloaded before Adam tapped on the door and entered.

"It's too dangerous to work the horse today," he said. "I'm sorry. I tried, but Flapjack kept slipping."

That didn't surprise her. Judging by the amount of mud on his boots, the rain had softened the ground. "You look *kalt*."

"I could use a cup of *kaffi*." He took one step in, then looked down at his boots.

"Don't worry; mopping gives me something to do." She shrugged. "I mopped at three this morning when I couldn't sleep. The floors weren't even dirty."

He followed her into the kitchen. "Rosa, you can't keep losing sleep."

"I couldn't get the dog out of *mei* mind," she said. "I really feel terrible about how quickly I lost *mei* temper." Her lips quivered. "I don't know what happened to me. I'm *nett* a violent person."

"I know you're *nett*."

"The neighbor doesn't. Do you know what he said to me? He said he had always heard that the Amish were nonviolent. Until he met me." She shook her head. "What kind of a life have I portrayed? *Nett* one that resembles Jesus."

"You don't need the neighbor's approval."

"It's God's approval I want." Her vision blurred. None of her actions lately exemplified Christ. Worry, fear, and anxiety ruled over her.

"Jesus said, 'In Me you have peace.' He tells us plainly to expect tribulation."

She nodded. "I know. Jesus overcame the world."

"And you will overcome this." He reached out and took her hand. His fingers were frigid. "Things will work out if we put our trust in God."

Adam's soft voice had a way of touching her soul with reassurance. She didn't want to spoil his hope by telling him the vet charges emptied her savings. The kettle hissed. Rosa removed two mugs from the cabinet.

He glanced at the table. "Were you unloading your cupboards in the middle of the *nacht* too?"

"I made that mess a few minutes ago." She filled the mugs with *kaffi*. "Do you think the weather will clear so we can work with Flapjack later this afternoon?"

"I suppose it's possible." He moved in front of the window and stared outside. He rubbed the back of his neck and sighed.

She handed him a cup. "The horse isn't going to be trained in time, is he?"

"I wish you would let me talk with the bishop. The widows' fund is intended to—"

"*Nee.*" She shook her head.

"I know you've given to that fund."

"Sure, we've all added to the offering. But that doesn't mean I'm entitled to draw from it."

He groaned under his breath. "You *are* a widow."

Her eyes welled with tears. She set her cup on the table and fled the room.

"Rosa!" He followed her to the foot of the stairway. "You're *nett* thinking straight. You haven't slept in days."

She ran up the steps and into her bedroom and slammed the door. Dropping onto the mattress, she buried her face in her pillow.

Adam tapped on the door. "Can we talk?"

"Later." What was there to talk about? She wasn't going to ask for money without having a way to repay the fund. This mess was created while her husband was alive. He should have told her he didn't pay the back taxes. He had to have known the county would auction the farm.

She punched the pillow. *Why did Uriah die and leave me in this jam?*

But no answer came. Only the sound of Adam's footsteps retreating down the stairs.

Chapter Twelve

Adam spent a restless night petitioning God on Rosa's behalf. He climbed out of bed in the morning not sure what he would say to Rosa's neighbor to change the man's outlandish payment demands but believing God would provide the right words.

Adam crossed the neighbor's property line just as Wade pulled up in his pickup truck. He waited while the man shut off the engine and opened the door.

"Can I talk with you a minute?" Adam said.

The man got out of the truck and turned to face Adam. "Who are you?"

"I'm Adam Bontrager. I live on the other side of Rosa Hostetler. I wanted to talk with you about your dog."

He smiled. "Nice of you to ask about him. He'll probably be in the cast a few more weeks, but—"

"I'm more concerned about Rosa's chickens. Your dog killed several and traumatized the others."

Tate narrowed his eyes. "Now that she's put up a fence around her coop, it's no longer an issue."

"I hope that's true." Adam shifted his feet. "Rosa is a widow. She sells eggs to make a living, and because of everything that's gone on recently, her chickens have stopped producing."

The man stared without blinking.

"I heard you've asked her to pay the vet bill." He continued without giving Tate time to acknowledge. "I don't believe it's her responsibility. If you had kept your dog on your property, he wouldn't have killed her chickens, and he wouldn't have been injured. She's not a cruel person."

"She admitted to shooting my dog."

"The gun went off accidently. But your dog was on her property attacking her chickens." To his credit, Tate Wade didn't try to deny or rationalize this. Adam figured he'd better get the rest of it in while he had the chance. "As a widow, she needs to keep her expenses to a bare minimum. She doesn't have money to pay vet bills, *especially* since she hasn't had any eggs to sell."

Tate reached for the doorknob. "I'll be back in just a minute." He disappeared inside his house and a moment later stepped back outside. "She already settled the vet costs." He handed Adam an empty, gallon-size pickle jar. "She told me to keep the jar, but I don't need it."

He stepped back into the house and shut the door in Adam's face.

Adam's mind reeled. *I don't understand, God. I thought You sent me to talk with him.* He plodded back across the field clutching the empty jar. *I thought You would have prepared his heart to see reasonably. Was that only wishful thinking?*

He reached Rosa's steps, drew a deep breath, and knocked.

The door opened. *"Guder mariye,"* she said.

"Is it really?" He brushed past her and went into the kitchen. Setting the empty jar on the counter, he turned to her. "We need to talk."

"Where did you get that?"

Adam ignored her question. He opened the drawer where she kept her records, removed the logbook, and flipped it open. A quick scan to the bottom entry on the page explained everything. She was broke.

Rosa snatched the book from his hand. "This isn't your business." She jammed the book back into the drawer and slammed it closed. "I didn't designate you as my keeper."

"Nee, but Uriah did."

She glared at him.

"Rosa, why didn't you talk to me—to anyone—before paying him a dime?"

"I didn't know any other way to make amends." She began to sniffle, and he pulled a handkerchief from his pocket and gave it to her. She blew her nose and wadded the handkerchief up in her hand. "I didn't want to disappoint God by being bitter and angry, and I was. I was so upset with Tate Wade that I couldn't sleep."

Adam sighed. "I should have talked with him earlier. I could've made some sort of arrangement with him."

"Adam," she said softly. "I'm all right with *mei* decision."

"Well, I'm not."

"I sent a note to *mei aenti* in Ohio about living with her."

He couldn't bear the thought of her moving so far away. "Rosa, let me talk with the bishop. This can all be taken—"

"I've decided to butcher the hens. If they're not going to lay eggs, I might as well." She headed to the door, darted outside, and marched toward the shed.

Her stubbornness had stretched his patience thin. Adam trailed her to the woodshed and stopped her as she grabbed the ax. "Why are you doing this?"

"I told you they're *nett* laying eggs. I won't be able to take them with me to Ohio . . . and people are hungry. Earlier I took some canned goods over to one of *mei Englisch* egg customers whose husband is out of work, and she really appreciated the food." She paused. "Helping others is the right thing to do, and these chickens will go a long way."

Adam swallowed back tears. In the midst of all her struggles, she was thinking of ways to help other people. *Lord*, he thought, *I don't want her to move to Ohio. Isn't there a way?*

"Let me do it." He reached for the ax. "You can get the water boiling."

Rosa added a pinch of salt to the pot of water simmering on the stove. She was adding wood to the stove when the back door opened and Adam called, "Rosa, *kumm* quick."

She wiped her hands on her apron and rushed to the door.

"You have to see this." He took hold of her elbow and guided her outside.

The gusty wind made her shiver. She wanted to double back for her winter bonnet and cloak, but his eagerness piqued her interest. "What's this all about?"

Adam unhooked the fence around the henhouse. "They're laying again."

She followed him into the coop. Adam pointed first to one nesting box, then another, and another. She'd never seen so many eggs. "It's a miracle!" She spun around and flung herself into Adam's arms.

Stirred up by the commotion, the chickens flapped and clucked around them. His eyes bored into hers and he leaned closer.

She pulled away just before his lips touched hers. "I should get a basket." She ran to the house, her heart hammering.

When she returned, he gently lowered the ones he had collected into the basket. Rosa focused on gathering eggs from another nesting box. The basket quickly filled, almost overflowing.

"I've never had this many eggs," she said as they entered the house.

"A miracle like you said, *ya?*"

She smiled. "*Ya,* so it is."

Rosa set the basket on the counter next to the sink. "Once I get these washed, I'm going to make *mei* deliveries." She chuckled. "Won't they be surprised to see me so late in the afternoon?"

"Do you want me to drive you?"

Unbidden, an image rose up in her mind—Adam leaning toward her in the coop with those piercing eyes. But his mother made it clear she disapproved of Rosa. She didn't want to upset Eunice more.

"*Nee.*" An expression of utter disappointment filled his face, and she tried to explain without using his mother's name. "*Danki* for the offer, but I don't know what people would say."

He motioned to the door. "It stopped raining. I think I'll work with Flapjack."

She laid a hand on his arm to stop him from turning away. "Adam," she said, "I don't normally . . ." She lowered her head. "I've never thrown myself into a man's arms like that before."

"Maybe that's another miracle," he said.

Chapter Thirteen

Adam coaxed the gelding around the ring one more time, but his heart wasn't into training today. He'd kept a safe distance from Rosa since she pitched herself into his arms and then gave him a gibberish apology for her impulsive behavior. He'd been just as excited to see eggs in the nesting boxes. It meant God had answered his prayer— one part. He was still praying for someone to buy Flapjack.

If he hadn't tried to kiss her yesterday, maybe he wouldn't feel so awkward today. It was plain that she didn't share the same feelings for him. He needed to accept that they would only be friends.

Rosa left the henhouse toting two baskets and a wide smile. The count must be even higher today.

Danki, *God, for providing another abundance of eggs. Please show me how I can help her. She's going to need more customers.*

Rosa hoisted the oversized egg basket into the buggy seat and climbed in beside it. "Lord, You provided the eggs," she murmured, "*nau* please provide the buyers."

The blue sky was a welcoming sight. So was seeing Adam in the corral working with Flapjack. She shot him a quick wave, but he was preoccupied with the horse and didn't see her.

Byler's Bakery was first on the list. Becky was busy sorting pastries at the back counter when Rosa entered. She swiped her hands on the front of her apron and stepped to the register.

"What can I help you with, Rosa?"

"*Mei* chickens surprised me with an overabundance again today. I was hoping the bakery could use more."

Becky peered into the basket. "Wow, that is a lot." She smiled. "I've been wanting to try some new recipes. I suppose we could use another dozen or two." Becky disappeared into the kitchen area and returned with a container.

"I really appreciate you helping me out." Rosa counted out two dozen. Her basket was still full. "So what new recipes are you planning to try?"

"I have one for an apple turnover, and I need to use up the pumpkins from the garden, so I thought I would make some muffins."

"Sounds delicious. Let me know how they turn out." Rosa didn't have as much success selling to her other customers. She landed at Hope's house with more than half her basket unsold.

"I'll buy a dozen," Hope offered after hearing Rosa's dilemma.

"You raise your own eggs. You don't need to buy mine." Rosa plopped down on her friend's kitchen chair. "But I suppose I am desperate to sell them."

Hope poured two mugs of *kaffi* and set them on the table. "That's exactly what Adam said last *nacht* when he stopped over to talk with Stephen about buying his gelding."

"He did?" Rosa toned down her excitement when Hope's brow arched. "He's a *gut* trainer."

"And . . ."

"And Flapjack will make a fine buggy horse."

"You have feelings for Adam, don't you?"

Rosa's cheeks warmed and she shifted on her chair.

"You can't hide it from me." Hope reached across the table and patted Rosa's hand. "I'm glad you're ready to move forward."

If she didn't find a way to pay her taxes in the next few days, Rosa would be moving, all right. But she didn't exactly consider Ohio as moving forward.

Hope smiled. "He gave you the chicks and put up a fence around your coop."

"Adam has . . . become a *gut* friend since Uriah died. It was hard at first, but through prayer, God helped me put aside *mei* anger about the fire. I don't blame Adam for Uriah's death. But I don't see us as more than friends either."

"Uriah would want you to be happy. And from what I've heard, you and Adam have spent a lot of time training that horse together."

"Did Adam say something about us working together?" *About my taxes?*

Hope shrugged. "If you started attending the sewing frolics, they would talk about someone else. Probably Becky Byler. You know how every woman in the settlement has something to say about her size."

Rosa wanted to ask if the sewing circle gossip was Eunice, but she resisted. Instead, she asked about Becky. "Do you think that might be why she's withdrawn?"

"I've been praying for her to feel accepted."

Rosa nodded. "I find it's easier to pray than to risk giving the wrong advice. I think she's tried every diet, and working around all those sweets must be difficult."

Hope wouldn't be distracted. "It's difficult for you to accept you're falling in love again, isn't it?"

"It wouldn't work. I can't have children. I already lived through seeing the disappointment in Uriah's eyes every time I miscarried. I couldn't bear it again."

Faith's cry rang out from the other room and pulled Hope's attention away. Just as well. The inability to have children was the least of Rosa's worries. She needed to sell eggs and find a way to pay her taxes, and that was as far into the future as she was willing to go.

"I better get moving." Rosa reached into her basket and removed a dozen eggs. "If you hear of anyone who needs eggs, please send them over."

Adam met Rosa outside the henhouse and helped her carry the eggs into the house.

"Have you ever seen so many eggs from so few chickens? It takes two of us to carry them all." Rosa beamed. "What am I going to do with them all? I practically had to beg everyone to buy extra yesterday."

"God answers prayers, all right," Adam said. "And He never gives us more than we can eat." He grinned. "I like egg salad sandwiches."

"I'm serious. What am I going to do with all of these?"

He set the basket on the table. "Let's get this straight. You pray for a miracle, get it, and then question what you're going to do with it? Do you think God made a mistake? Or maybe He forgot to tell the chickens they could stop laying eggs?"

She bowed her head sheepishly.

"Remember how God brought quail to the Israelites? So much quail it came out of their nostrils. This was after they complained of only having manna to eat."

"I complain too much, don't I?"

"Nee." He winked, then held up his index finger and said, "I'll be right back." He jogged out to the barn and grabbed the Eggs For Sale board he had painted earlier.

Rosa's eyes lit up. "What a great idea. But we don't live on a busy road. Do you think I'll get many customers?"

"I think the only reason the chickens laid so many eggs is because God has buyers already lined up. You'll see." He tapped the board. "I'll get this put up."

Adam carried the sign out to the mailbox, and even before he finished nailing it to the post, a vehicle entered Rosa's driveway. As that car pulled out, another one pulled in.

Rosa should be pleased. For a road without much traffic, God seemed to be sending people to buy her eggs.

Adam had another idea for increasing the sales, but it involved his mother. He hiked home while Rosa was busy with customers.

"If you're hungry there is stew to warm up," *Mamm* said as he entered the kitchen.

"Okay, maybe later. Rosa's chickens laid a bunch more eggs today."

"That's *gut*. I know for a while they haven't been laying anything."

"I was hoping you could spread the word that she needs to sell them." He paused, debating how much to tell her without breaking his vow to Rosa. "Maybe the women in your group will buy them this week."

Mamm studied him silently for a moment. "Is she hurting for money?"

He looked down at his boots. Maybe saying something wasn't a good idea. "Like everyone, she has expenses. She's always been so *gut* about giving eggs to the widows . . ." He shrugged. "She's also a widow and not with much income."

"I know how it is, *sohn.*"

"But don't most of the widows have adult *kinner* who help pay expenses? Rosa has no one."

Mamm sighed. "*Ya,* it's a shame." Her brows rose. "I'll suggest a bake sale. That will give everyone a reason to buy plenty of eggs."

Adam hoped he wouldn't regret getting his mother involved.

Chapter Fourteen

Rosa's customer list grew daily—and so did the number of eggs her chickens laid. Since Adam put up the road sign, she had sold out every day before noon. Days away from the tax deadline, she'd begun to believe Adam was right. God would provide the tax money.

Rosa carried a quart of water out to the training ring for Adam. She perched on the fence rail as Adam removed his coat and draped it over the horse's head.

"He needs to trust me completely," Adam said. He boarded the buggy and clicked his tongue, but Flapjack hesitated. With some verbal coaxing from Adam, the horse lurched forward. They made one complete circle before the horse's gait smoothed out. Several starts, stops, and turning repetitions later, Adam halted the buggy. He kept the head covering in place, tied Flapjack to the post, then strode over to the fence.

"I thought you could use some water." She handed him the quart jar.

"Danki." He leaned against the fence and took a drink.

"Why did you cover Flapjack's head?"

"Blind trust," he said. "It trains him to listen to his master's call." He took another drink, then handed her the empty jar. "Like God wants us to trust Him."

"So I've discovered."

"Have you counted your money again?"

She shook her head. "*Nett* since your suggestion." Adam had pointed out that she fretted more when she constantly tallied her sales. He challenged her to wait to count it again until the morning of the auction. It took restraint, but she followed his advice. She didn't even keep a mental tally.

Behind them, the Bowmans' horse whinnied as their buggy entered the driveway. Rosa jumped off the fence and waved as she and Adam crossed the drive.

"*Hiya,*" Rosa said.

Adam greeted Stephen as he climbed off the bench.

"Stephen and James wanted to check out Adam's horses." The girls clambered out from the back and the women meandered to the house. Adam, Stephen, and James headed toward the corral.

Once inside, Rosa gave the girls some paper to draw on while she and Hope chatted over tea. Rosa hadn't seen her friend since Hope's mother took ill. "Is your *mamm* better?"

"She isn't coughing as much."

"That's *gut* to hear."

"And I hear your chickens are still laying a lot of eggs." Hope sipped her tea.

"More every day. I've been able to sell them all too. *Danki* for passing the news."

Hope shook her head. "I've been so busy with *mei mamm*, I haven't spoken to anyone but Becky Byler when she came over to babysit."

"That's odd. Lately everyone in the district has needed extra eggs."

"Probably for the bake sale."

"When is the sale?" Rosa had been preoccupied, but she would certainly find time to bake for the sale. Most of the sales benefited a family who had health care burdens or who had lost their home in a fire. She hadn't heard about any families that had fallen on hard times.

"The sale was today. I dropped off some pumpkin pies on the way to *mei mamm's*." Hope reached across the table for Rosa's hand. "I'm sorry I've been tied up so much with *Mamm* and we haven't had much time to talk. Is there anything I can do for you?"

The men entered the kitchen. Stephen smiled at Hope. "James *nau* owns his first buggy horse, *fraa*."

Rosa's heart skipped. "Flapjack?"

Adam nodded. "He still needs several more weeks of training to get him road ready, but James wants to help me work with him."

"We should head home, *fraa*," Stephen said.

Hope nodded and walked her cup to the sink. "I'll talk with you soon," she said to Rosa before leaving.

Adam waited until the Bowmans left before showing Rosa the wad of cash. "It isn't the entire amount you need, but it should help." He added the money to the jar. "I told you I didn't want to move *mei* horses."

She didn't want him to find a new place for his horses either. "I don't know what to say."

"Just praise God."

"Praise God, indeed." Rosa peered at the jar. "Should we count it *nau*?"

Adam shook his head. "You only have a few more days to wait. God will provide." He motioned to the door. "I need to tend the stock, but maybe afterward we can have *kaffi* and a cookie?"

She nodded. "I'll make a fresh batch."

Rosa mixed up Adam's favorite peanut butter cookies. The first batch was cooling on the counter and another pan was in the oven when someone tapped on the door. Eunice and two women from the widows' group stood on the stoop.

"We wanted to give you this," said Mrs. Lehman, the shortest of the three. She extended an envelope toward her.

Rosa peeled open the flap and removed the cash contents. "I don't understand."

Eunice stepped forward. "You know how the widows' group enjoys working together on a project. These are the funds we raised from our bake sale."

"From your eggs," Enos Mast's widow said.

Rosa caught a glimpse of Adam as he came out from the barn. The moment their eyes connected, he ducked back inside. Rosa looked at Eunice. "Did Adam say something to you?"

"He mentioned you had too many eggs and sort of suggested that we buy them."

"That's why none of you would accept them for free? You felt obligated to pay for them?" Adam's good intentions settled in Rosa's stomach like a rock at the bottom of a pond. "Did he suggest you have a bake sale too?"

"Nee," the women said in unison. "That was our idea."

Rosa stared at the money.

Dorothy Lehman patted her hand. "You've been so *gut* to all of us, giving us eggs when you could have sold them. We wanted to help you."

"We don't have husbands to look out for us, but we have each other." Adam's mother squeezed Rosa's arm. "You're a member of our group."

Rosa smiled, and suddenly her skewed view of being a widow shifted. It wasn't a life sentence of loneliness. Loneliness was not sharing herself with others. Perhaps God was leading her to embrace being one of them.

"Maybe you could *kumm* to our next get-together," Eunice said.

"Ya," Rosa said without reservation. "I'd like that."

Chapter Fifteen

On the morning of the tax deadline, Rosa emptied the jar onto the table and sorted the money. Adam counted bills and she counted the change. Once they finished, she tallied the amount.

Twice.

Adam slid his chair back. "Money must have dropped on the floor."

It hadn't, but she didn't stop him from searching.

"Let's count it again," he said.

Numbness settled into her core. She had fully expected that the needed amount would miraculously be there. Just as he had. "We already recounted."

Adam rechecked the count, then slumped farther down in his chair. He rubbed his eyes. "I can't believe it."

Neither could she.

Like a hammer driving a nail, Adam had repeated over and over: *Have faith. Just have faith.*

But faith had failed her.

She got up and went to the sink—not because she was thirsty, but because she needed space around her. She needed to find a way to silence the voices in her head.

"Rosa." Adam crossed the room and gathered her into his arms.

She twisted away from him. "Take the money you gave me from selling the horse."

"We can worry about that later."

"Later?" She stared at him. "Don't you understand? There is no *later*. Time is up." She sighed. "I should have been packing all along."

"There's a chance no one will bid on the property. We can always hope—"

"Hope?" she said. "I'm fresh out of hope." She couldn't even bring herself to apologize for her lack of faith.

"All I'm saying is, it wouldn't be unlike God to—"

"Adam, I'd like to be alone."

He stared at her a moment "It's *nett* over, Rosa. You're still working your way up the mountain."

"What's that supposed to mean?"

"Remember when God commanded Abraham to sacrifice his son Isaac? God provided a ram as a substitute for the boy. But it was on the top of the mountain. Not at the bottom."

Adam left, and Rosa sank down at the table to give over to her despair. She cried until she had no tears left. She didn't know how long she sat there, or whether she dozed, only that when she sat up and looked around again, the day seemed half gone.

She was alone. The house was quiet. But Adam's final words still echoed in her ears. Abraham. Isaac. The mountain. The ram.

She reached for her Bible and turned to the story in Genesis.

Isaac spoke up and said to his father Abraham, "Father?"

"Yes, my son?" Abraham replied.

"The fire and wood are here, but where is the lamb for the burnt offering?"

Abraham answered, "God himself will provide the lamb."

~

Three days later, Adam was dumping a wheelbarrow full of horse manure on the compost pile when he spotted the mail truck pull up to Rosa's house. Why was the driver hand-delivering the mail?

He watched from a distance. Rosa ripped open the letter and turned away from the door as the mail truck drove off.

Adam wasn't sure she would welcome him inside. Since the day of the auction, she had kept her distance. But he decided to risk it. He left the wheelbarrow upended and headed for the house.

Adam tapped on the door. No answer. He knocked harder this time. When she still didn't answer, he let himself inside. His stomach knotted. Obviously she'd been busy. Boxes lined the walls of the sitting room.

He found her sitting at the kitchen table with her face buried in her hands and a letter open before her. "Are you okay?"

She didn't look up or even answer.

He caught a glimpse of the letterhead on the official-looking form: *County Tax Claim Bureau:* NOTICE TO VACATE. He didn't need to read any more.

"Rosa?" he said.

No response.

"I, um . . ." He cleared his throat, but words wouldn't come.

She lifted her head and stared at him with bloodshot eyes. "You need to unload the hay in the barn and move your horses." She stood, reached for the jar of money on her counter, and thrust it at him. "Take out what's yours. Apparently it's God's will for me to move to Ohio and live with *mei aenti*."

"This isn't how——" He wiped his clammy hands against his pant legs. "You don't have to."

She waved the eviction notice in his face. "What choice do I have?"

He swallowed hard. "You can stay and . . . marry me."

Her eyes closed and she shook her head slowly. Then she pushed her chair away from the table and stood.

Adam followed her out of the kitchen. She stopped at the door, opened it, and motioned for him to exit. He paused in the threshold. "I don't want you to move to Ohio."

"Your loyalty to Uriah is commendable," she said. "To think you would feel such indebtedness."

He rubbed the burned side of his neck. Indebtedness? Is that how she saw it? A debt that needed to be settled, the price Uriah had paid to save Adam's life?

She shut the door behind him and left him standing alone on the stoop. He felt empty, hollowed out. His legs trembled under him, and he sat down on the top step.

"God," he said, "I don't understand any of this. I assumed You were providing the money to pay her taxes when the chickens over produced. Like a fool, I even assured Rosa that was Your plan. Please forgive me." He got up and stalked toward the barn, kicking at a stone in his path. "I messed up *mei* proposal too. She thinks I'm doing it out of obligation. God, You know that isn't the truth. Can You somehow talk to her for me?"

A raw November wind chapped Rosa's face as Blossom trotted along the road. But she didn't care; maybe the drive and the cold and the damp would help clear her head.

"Lord, please forgive me," she prayed out loud as she drove along. "I trusted and relied on Adam's faith instead of standing on *mei* own faith in You. He wasn't wrong to believe—but I was wrong to believe in his word rather than seeking Yours. I accept Your will for my life and I will move to Ohio. I only ask that You help me make amends with Adam before I leave."

The road in front of her blurred as tears welled in her eyes. "I never realized just how attached I had become to him." She wiped her face with the back of her hand. "I've—well, I might as well admit it—I've fallen in love with him. But, Lord, how could I marry him when I know I can't have children? I would only disappoint Adam."

Rosa took the long way home and returned to find a note stuck in her doorjamb. When she unfolded the paper, money fluttered to her feet. She bent down to pick it up. The note said that the money was to buy eggs for another upcoming bake sale the widows had planned.

She glanced next door. Eunice's buggy was parked in its usual spot. This was as good a time as any to take the eggs next door and return the money. Rosa packed more eggs than requested into a container and headed to Adam's house.

Eunice opened the door. "I see Adam gave you *mei* note." She waved her in. "Have a cup of tea with me. I'd like to talk with you about a few things."

Rosa hesitated.

"Adam's not here, if that's what's concerning you."

"All right. Maybe a half a cup." She followed Eunice into the kitchen. "I just thought of it *nau*, but I have extra flour and sugar I'd like to donate to the bake sale."

"That would be great." Eunice dunked a tea bag in one cup, then transferred the bag over to the next one. She set the cups on the table. "I would like to apologize," she said. "I was selfish when I talked so adamantly about wanting *kinskind*." She paused for a moment. "I thought you and Adam were growing close and, well, I know you've had miscarriages in the past."

"Four," Rosa clarified. It wasn't a secret, nor did it matter now.

Eunice sighed. "I thought if I discouraged you from becoming involved, *mei sohn* would—"

"You don't have to worry any longer." Rosa set her cup down and stood. "I'm moving to Ohio."

"Rosa, I was wrong to interfere."

"I have to finish packing." Rosa got up and rushed blindly to the door—and bumped directly into Adam.

He kept her from falling but said nothing.

"Danki." She rushed across the yard and into the house, gasping for air. Surely this would all be over soon. Surely the feelings she had for Adam would subside once she had moved.

Minutes later Adam stood on her stoop. Hands deep in his pockets, he shuffled his feet. *"Mei mamm* sent me. She said something about flour and sugar."

Rosa opened the door wider and stepped aside. "Come in." She took a few long strides to the kitchen with him trailing behind her and opened the pantry. Almost all the canning jars were gone, but some of the staples still lined the shelves. "Flour," she mumbled, grabbing the ten-pound bag.

"Rosa."

His husky voice caught her off guard and she turned.

"After Uriah pulled that burning rafter off me in the fire, he made me promise him that I would take care of you. But that isn't why I asked you to marry me." He reached for her hand. "I love you, Rosa."

"Adam . . ." Her voice shook. *I love you too*, she wanted to say, but the words wouldn't come.

"I thought you shared the same feelings for me." He rubbed his neck. "*Mei* scar reminds you that I'm the reason you lost Uriah. He should've survived, *nett* me."

At last she found her voice. "I don't blame you for Uriah's death. Please believe that." Rosa lowered her head. "I have fallen in love with you too."

"Then marry me."

Her heart screamed yes, but she shook her head no. "I've had four miscarriages. That's why Uriah took me into town for ice cream all those times, to try to cheer me up. But you need to know. I can't carry a *boppli*." She swallowed hard. "I saw the pain it caused Uriah. I won't put you through that."

He inched closer. "If you want children, we can adopt."

"You say that, but—"

"I mean what I say." He cupped her face in his hands. "Last year you did all that research about foster families for Hope. Why can't we be a foster family?"

She opened her mouth to respond, but his kiss hushed her words.

"I love you," he said, his warm breath feathering against her cheek.

"I love you too."

Adam trailed kisses across her cheek to her ear. "Will you marry me?"

She pulled back. "Your mother wouldn't approve. She wants—"

"She wants what's best for me. And that's marrying you." He swept his hand over her cheek. "Rosa, say that you'll marry me."

"Yes." Tears clouded her vision. "Yes, I will marry you."

He twirled her around the kitchen, then kissed her again.

They were interrupted by a knock on the door. Rosa pulled away. "I better see who it is." She adjusted her dress as she walked to the door.

Adam followed.

Tate Wade stood on the other side of the screen door.

"Can I help you?" she said.

"I wanted to talk to you about your house," Tate said. "I'm the one who bought it."

Rosa motioned to the boxes stacked against the far wall. "As you can see, I'm packing. I'll be out in—"

"Wait." He held up his hand. "Please hear what I have to say. I'm willing to sell it back to you. For the same price as I paid."

Rosa glanced at Adam.

"Mr. Bontrager," Tate said, "I couldn't get it out of my mind, what you told me about Rosa being a widow and the eggs being her only support. Growing up, I watched my mother struggle after my father died. There were days we had very little to eat." His focus returned to Rosa. "I'm sorry for the pain I've caused you. I hope you can forgive me."

Rosa stared at him for a minute or two. "Apology accepted."

"Good. The guilt was eating me up." He exhaled a pent-up breath. "So, do you want to buy the place or not?"

"Yes! I want it." She glanced at Adam, then back to Tate. "I mean, we want it."

"Fine." He nodded. "I buy houses at auction all the time. I'm a real estate developer, so we can work out the paperwork later. I've reinforced the kennel so my dogs won't get out again. And I'll reimburse you for your chickens. I hope from now on we don't have any neighborly issues."

He turned to leave, then stopped and faced her. "One more thing. The property is currently zoned commercial. Apparently at one time it was a dairy business. If you petition to have it rezoned, you'll cut your taxes to a fraction of the cost. Buy some cattle and have it zoned under agriculture, and you'll save even more." He nodded. "Well, I'll be off. I hope you both have a good day."

When Tate was gone, Rosa closed the door and turned to Adam. "Can you believe what just happened?"

"It's a miracle." Adam pulled her into his arms. A glint of light danced in his eyes. "Tate said guilt changed his mind, but what really happened is that God softened his heart."

She swiped at her eyes. "And God provided a way to keep the *haus*, even after *mei* faith failed."

"I thought I had it all figured out," Adam said. "But God didn't pay much attention to my plans."

Rosa laughed. "From *nau* on we will be patient and trust completely in His provision."

"Always," Adam said.

She closed her eyes as his lips brushed against her forehead. In that moment she knew that no matter how much she had lost, her life was full and complete. Everything she needed had been provided.

Joy instead of mourning. An end to grief. The beginning of a new life.

Light. Love. Home. A place to belong.

"Always," she repeated. "We will trust God's provision. Always."

Always Beautiful

BETH WISEMAN

Chapter One

Becky stood on the bank of the creek, her bare feet clutching the rocky ground beneath her, knowing that with one more step she'd plunge into the rushing rapids and be carried away from her troubles. Forever.

As tears streamed down her cheeks, she wondered how different her life might have been if she hadn't always been so fat. She knew what people said about her. She had heard it again just this afternoon when Annie Lapp and two other girls were standing at the counter of Byler's Bakery.

"She's huge," Annie whispered, but loud enough for Becky to hear. "And she just keeps getting bigger and bigger. She's never going to get a husband." Annie laughed. "Maybe she needs to stop working at the family bakery and do something else."

Everyone talked about her. It had started the first day of school. *Fatty, fatty, two by four, Becky can't get through the old barn door.* Her mother had always said that Becky was just healthy, and during her younger years, she'd tried to ignore the finger-pointing and snickering. But now, at eighteen, she was as big as a house, and the whispering still hadn't stopped.

People were nice enough to her face, but she didn't have any real friends. Only Elam. He was her best friend, and his self-image wasn't any better than Becky's. Elam wore thick, gold-rimmed glasses. His eyeballs rolled around all over the place, often making it hard to tell where he was looking. Becky was so used to it, she didn't think that much about it, but Elam was self-conscious. The eye doctor had said he couldn't have surgery on his eyes until they'd quit changing.

Becky thought Elam was incredibly handsome, even though she'd never had a romantic interest in him. He was tall and thin with dark brown eyes and wavy black hair that curled on the ends when it got too long. She loved Elam—the same way she loved her brother. Besides, even Elam couldn't possibly want to spend his life with someone who took up three times as much space as the average person.

Trembling, she watched as each wave crashed against the boulders below. Occasionally a small limb or twig was carried by the current and over the steep drop-off, submersing for a few moments before popping up downstream. But the real threat was around the bend. Any time it rained more than a couple of inches, the creek filled and the rapids thrashed along a bank filled with jagged rocks. No one ever went near the rapids, and Becky usually avoided the creek altogether since she couldn't swim.

A part of her wanted to jump, to stop the pain that overwhelmed her these days. She was tired of standing out in a crowd, tired of people whispering about how big she was, tired of the painful reality that she was never going to have a husband. The bishop might preach against pride and vanity, but even Plain people were human like the rest of the world, and physical attraction was important.

But taking the easy way out would destroy her parents—and Ruben and Lena. Her younger siblings loved her unconditionally, as did her parents, but Ruben and Lena had always been thin, and neither of her parents struggled with their weight either. She really couldn't blame it on the family business, since *Mamm* and Lena both worked at the bakery with Becky.

Why me? Why do I have to be so big?

More tears fell as she shivered on the bank, feeling alone and hopeless. Taking her own life would be a great sin. But to jump and survive would be the greatest humiliation of all. She couldn't possibly face the community, never mind facing herself in the mirror, knowing that she had failed even at this. And despite her suffering, she was sure she couldn't do it.

She looked up at the sky and lifted her arms. "Please, Lord. I beg You. Make me thin. I don't want to live like this anymore. Please, dear God . . . I want to be skinny and beautiful."

As she spoke the words aloud, she could almost feel God frowning. It shouldn't be important how she looked. Heaven knows everybody had told her enough times. But it was easy for folks who weren't overweight to say it didn't matter.

Becky lowered her arms and in that split second of inattention, lost her footing. She teetered out over the edge, glimpsed the blur of the rushing water below her, and braced herself for the fall. Just when she knew she was doomed, she slipped backward and collapsed on the bank. She sat there for a long time, gasping for breath, terrified at how close she'd come to doing something stupid.

"God, help me," she whispered. "Please."

She sat there another few minutes until her tears dried up. Then sun rays eased through the clouds and lit the water below, glistening in a way that Becky hadn't noticed before. A peaceful feeling settled over her.

God had heard her plea. She wasn't sure how she knew, but He was going to answer her prayer.

She'd never been so certain of anything in her life.

~

Elam ran full tilt toward Becky and slid up beside her. He cut it close, just short of accidentally pushing her into the water. But he could hardly be blamed for being distracted. Her beautiful face was aglow with a smile—the same smile he thought about even when she wasn't around.

He fought to catch his breath and struggled to focus as he stared at her.

"What are you doing out here?" he asked "What if you had fallen in and no one was out here to help you?" He pulled off his hat and ran a hand across his forehead. "Look at the water, the way it's rushing. And the falls are just around the corner. I'm not sure I could have saved you if you'd fallen in."

"I'm fine, Elam." Becky clasped her hands in front of her and raised her shoulders, dropping them slowly. "I'm actually better than fine." The warmth in her smile echoed in her voice. "I'm great!"

"*Ya*, well, get away from the creek."

Elam gently guided her a few feet from the water's edge. He shuddered to think what would have happened if she'd fallen in.

He'd already lost someone dear to him a few years ago. A car had slammed into his father's buggy and killed him instantly. Becky Byler was the most special girl in the world, and he couldn't bear losing her too. He'd loved her since they were kids. Someday he planned to marry her if she'd have him. But she'd been so depressed lately about her weight that Elam hadn't considered encouraging anything more than friendship.

Becky was gorgeous, but he wanted her to see that for herself. He didn't know anyone who was better with children than she was. No one could cook as well. She grew the biggest, tastiest vegetables in their district. And he'd been told that she could sew circles around even the elderly women.

For Elam, those were all just bonuses. Becky was a gentle soul who loved everyone, and more than once Elam had been pushed to come to her defense when someone poked fun at her weight. Fighting wasn't their way, but twice Elam had gotten physical on the school grounds when they were young. Fortunately things didn't turn violent these days, but the whispering behind Becky's back continued, and Elam fought to control his temper when he could tell Becky's feelings were hurt. He'd marry her today if he could.

They started walking back to where both buggies were tied to the same tree.

Becky turned to him, still smiling. "How'd you know I was here?"

"I didn't. I was on my way to Rosa Hostetler's *haus* to get some eggs. *Mamm* says it's easier to get 'em from her than to mess with chickens ourselves."

Becky was quiet for a few moments, then she slowed down, stopped, and turned to him. "I know it's hard—just being you and your *mamm*. I've told you a hundred times that *mei* family can help out more." She paused, sighing. "I know you're busy tending the fields by yourself, and with no other *kinner*, your *mamm* is bound to be plumb tired all the time."

Elam forced a smile, knowing Becky was right. He often wondered how his mother would fare when Elam got married and moved out some day. "We do all right, and going to get eggs ain't no big deal."

"Well, Rosa drops off eggs at the bakery every day. I can always get extra and cart them to your *haus*." Becky untied her horse from the tree.

"Maybe I'll take you up on that offer." It would be a good excuse to see her.

He offered her his hand and helped her into her buggy. "I was worried about you being out here. I mean, it wondered me why you came out to the creek all by yourself like this." He paused, forced his eyes forward, and studied her face—her rosy cheeks, dark hair, and amazing deep brown eyes. She was still glowing and smiling, but Elam was worried about how depressed she'd been.

"I'm *gut* now. I had a talk with God, and I know He heard my prayers." She pulled her dress inside the buggy, and Elam shut the door. "I know you've been concerned about me, and I love you for that. But everything is going to be just fine."

She picked up the reins, flicked them gently, and started away. Elam was still reeling.

Did Becky Byler just say she loved him?

Chapter Two

Becky loaded the last tray of whoopee pies into the glass cabinet that ran the length of the bakery. Most of their visitors were tourists, but a few folks in their district came to Byler's Bakery just for convenience's sake. More and more Amish women were working outside the home, and some of the ladies stopped by on their way home from work to pick up breads, desserts, noodles, or a jar of chow-chow.

Becky's little sister, Lena, came out of the kitchen carrying a tray of apple fritters. For a ten-year-old, she was small and slight, and the heavy tray was almost too much for her. Becky gave her a hand sliding the tray in next to the whoopee pies. "Why aren't you eating a cinnamon roll?" Lena said. "You eat a cinnamon roll every morning."

Becky wiped her hands on her black apron. "Because I don't want one."

Lena shrugged. "Okay, but there might not be any left later." She ran the sleeve of her green dress across her sweaty forehead.

"Whew, it's hot back there." She pointed toward the kitchen, where the ovens worked nonstop.

Summers in Lancaster County were brutal, but at least the Bylers had air-conditioning at the bakery during the day. Five years ago when Becky's mother wanted to open the shop, Becky's father had the idea to partner with an *Englisch* man named Danny Kaspar, a retired police officer looking for an investment. The *Ordnung* forbade air-conditioning, of course, but if one of the partners in a business was *Englisch*, it was allowed.

Becky was glad for the loophole—especially on a day like today when the temperature was predicted to be in the nineties.

She was cleaning the glass countertop when her mother came from the back. Lena was sitting on the bar stool near the cash register eating a cinnamon roll.

"There's a mud sale at the firehouse today, so I expect lots of people will be out and about this morning." *Mamm* rounded the corner of the counter and went to peer through the glass door. "I hope it doesn't rain." She flipped the door sign to Open and returned to the counter. "But I guess that's why they call it a mud sale. Silly *Englisch* folks, mostly. I wouldn't slosh around in that mess."

"Maybe it won't rain," Lena said around a mouthful of cinnamon roll.

Mamm opened the cash register and filled it with money. "Lena, finish eating, then come help me in the back. There are pots and pans to be washed and four loaves of bread still in the oven that we need to keep an eye on."

Becky eyed the racks filled with baked goods. The yeasty aroma of fresh bread baking drifted from the back of the shop. Her mouth watered. Any other time she would probably have been gorging on cinnamon rolls, just as her little sister expected. But she had prayed for God's help, and if she expected God to work, she needed to cooperate.

She was busy daydreaming about what it would be like to be thin when the bell on the door rang and Matt King walked in. Becky swallowed hard. The very idea of Matt caused Becky's heart to flutter, and she blushed every time he was around. He wasn't just handsome—he was also the kindest person she'd ever met. He always treated her as if she were the prettiest girl on the planet, even though Becky was sure it was just his nature to be nice. She'd had a crush on him for as long as she could remember.

"*Wie bischt*, Becky?" Matt strolled up to the counter, his tall, muscular body moving with easy grace. His face was bronzed from the summer sun and thick blond bangs hung down over his forehead. When he smiled, tiny lines feathered from the corners of dark blue eyes, making him look a bit older than his nineteen years.

"I'm *gut*, Matt." Becky forced a smile. She could feel her face flaming. Again. She tried to avoid his gorgeous eyes, but he held her gaze, and she just couldn't look away. "What can I get for you?"

Matt finally pulled his eyes from hers and began studying the baked goods in the glass display. "Hmm . . ." He drummed his fingers on the counter. "*Mamm* said to pick up some pumpkin whoopee pies. She has an *Englisch* friend coming for lunch who loves them, but she didn't have time to make any this morning."

Becky leaned down, thankful for the baggy dress she wore, but wishing it did more to hide her flabby body. She pulled out the tray with pumpkin whoopee pies. "How many?"

"Four."

Becky took out the pies, placed them in a bag, and rang them up on the cash register. "Anything else before I total?"

"Ya." Matt paused, and Becky looked up at him, waiting for him to go on. "Are you going to the singing this Sunday?"

"Huh?" She thought she heard him wrong. "I meant, is there anything else you want to buy?"

Matt shook his head. *"Nee.* Nothing else." He handed her a twenty-dollar bill, Becky gave him back his change, and he picked up the white bag with the pies. "So, are you?"

"Am I what?" Becky sat down on the stool behind the counter.

"Going to the singing?"

She shook her head. *"Nee."* Becky had only gone to a few singings over the years. Most recently, she'd gone a couple of weeks ago because it was at the Bowmans' house and she'd promised Hope Bowman she would attend. As a rule, she didn't normally attend social gatherings unless she had to.

"Oh," Matt said. But he didn't leave. He just stood there staring at her with the bag in his hand.

Becky was sure her face was on fire, and her heart was doing somersaults in her chest.

Finally, Matt dragged his eyes away and shrugged. "I was just wondering if you were going." He looked back at her. "You're such a *gut* singer. I like hearing your voice."

Becky looked down. *"Danki,"* she finally said.

Matt sighed. "Anyway, if you were going, I was going to offer to give you a ride."

Becky felt her mouth drop open, but no words would form.

"Okay then," he said after a minute. "*Danki* for the pies. See ya." Matt gave a quick wave, turned, and headed for the door.

Becky stared through the glass door and watched him disappear around the corner. Everyone knew that when you rode to or from a singing with someone, it was an indication that the couple was interested in each other. A sign they were going to start dating.

She twisted the strings of her prayer *kapp*. If Matt King had been trying to ask her out, then it must have been a joke or a dare. He could have any girl he wanted. They probably would have showed up at the singing together, and he would have left her there for another girl. Or his friends would have handed him a wad of cash and congratulated him for daring to take out the fat girl.

She tried to dismiss the conversation as she doodled stars on the receipt pad. Her mother would scold her about it later. It was an awful habit she'd had since she was young. She'd doodle stars on just about anything.

Maybe because I'm such a dreamer.

Matt flicked the reins. Black clouds loomed above, and he was hoping to get home before the rain started.

He had stunned her speechless by asking her if she was going to the singing. And to tell the truth, he had surprised himself as well. He'd been trying to work up his nerve all week.

She hardly ever went to the singings, but a couple of weeks ago at the Bowmans' house Matt sat as close to her as he could so he could hear her above the others. She had a voice like an angel. And the way she smelled! Heavenly. Maybe it was her soap or lotion, or maybe she was secretly using perfume. He didn't know, and he didn't care. Whatever it was, he liked it.

And Becky was just so sweet. Good to everyone. A few people poked fun about her weight, but she had a really pretty face. He'd spent time with plenty of girls in their community since his *rum-schpringe* started a few years ago. Gorgeous girls with great figures. But despite the fact that they'd been brought up to avoid pride and vanity, all they seemed to care about was their appearance.

Becky, on the other hand, wasn't the least bit vain, and even though she was a big girl, there was something alluring about her. But over the years when Matt had tried to get to know her better, she had always avoided him. She was the only girl in the district who shied away from him.

As he pulled into the driveway, the rain was just starting, barely a sprinkle, but by the time he got the horse watered and in the barn, it had turned into a downpour. He ran to the house, shielding the bag of pies beneath his shirt.

"Here are your whoopee pies," he said to his mother as he stood dripping on the kitchen floor, handing her the bag.

"Danki, sohn." She waved an arm toward the stairs. "Go get dried off, then see if you can find your *daed*. He'd planned for you to help him paint the back fence before this rain started, but I'm not sure what he's doing now."

The rain had cooled things off a little, but now he just felt clammy. Matt headed upstairs, dried off, and put on fresh clothes. He bumped into his older sister on the way back down the stairs, and she ran past him like the house was on fire.

"What are you in such a hurry for?"

Marie didn't even turn around. "None of your business!"

Matt shrugged and started back down the stairs again. The only boy among six sisters, he was used to being the odd man out. None of them ever shared much with him. Which was okay, since all they ever talked about was who they were dating, when they hoped to get married, and a whole bunch of other girly stuff that didn't interest him in the least.

He walked into the kitchen and picked an apple from the fruit bowl. Saturday afternoon, and saved by the rain. He hadn't been looking forward to spending the day painting the fence. He didn't mind hard work, and he loved being outside, but painting was his least favorite thing to do.

"Where is everyone?" he asked his mother. "I saw Marie running up the stairs, but other than that it sure is quiet around here."

Mamm wiped her hands on a kitchen towel, then leaned against the counter and faced him. "As I said, I don't know where your father disappeared to, but the rest of the girls went to the mud sale." She shook her head. "Miserable weather to be at a mud sale."

"What's wrong with Marie? She looked mad."

Mamm sighed as she shook her head. "She and John had words, I think. She's not saying much about it, though."

Matt finished off the apple and tossed the core in the trash can. "I'm sure it's something to do with the wedding."

"*Ya*, probably so. Marie has been planning her dream wedding since she was a little girl, and I don't think John shares her enthusiasm about the details."

"Every wedding I've been to looks the same." Matt poured himself a glass of iced tea, chugged it down, then used a paper towel to dab at the sweat on his forehead. "I don't see what there is to have words about."

Mamm sat down at the kitchen table. "Every bride wants things to go perfectly on their special day."

"Well, she's got three months to get it all together." Matt poured himself a little more iced tea.

"October will be here before you know it." *Mamm* pulled a piece of paper and pen from her apron pocket. "*Danki* for getting the whoopee pies." She scratched it off her list. "Guess I better get started on lunch for Claire. She only comes through town about once a year."

Mamm stood up and pulled two lunch pails from the refrigerator. "Except for Marie, the other girls are eating at the mud sale, and *Daed* said you two would eat on the park bench on the other side of the garden." She handed Matt the two lunch pails. "Not sure what his plan is now, but here are your sandwiches. Chicken salad, a peach, and those awful chips your father likes."

"Have fun with your friend." Matt grinned as he left the room and walked onto the porch. He liked the extra spicy chips his father often requested. He watched the rain come down and wondered briefly where his father might be, but his head was filled with thoughts of Becky Byler.

Chapter Three

Two weeks after that day on the creek bank, when she'd prayed to God for help, Becky went with Elam to the pizza place off of Lincoln Highway. There wasn't anything she liked more than pizza, so this was a true test of her will power. Becky slid into the booth across from Elam—the same booth they'd been sitting at for years.

"I got the same one we always get. Large with everything but onions and mushrooms."

Becky had skipped breakfast this morning, and she'd only had some fruit for lunch. Pizza sounded good, and she didn't want to hurt Elam's feelings by not eating any. Normally she'd eat four or five slices, about half the pizza. This time she chose the smallest wedge.

Twenty minutes later Elam had polished off half the pizza, and Becky was still working on her first piece.

"I know that's not all you're going to eat," he said with his mouth half full. He pushed his glasses up on his nose.

Becky nodded. "*Ya.* This is all I want."

Elam swallowed his food, then frowned. "Are you sick?"

"*Nee*. Just not hungry."

It wasn't the truth. Not the whole truth, anyway, if the growling of her stomach was any indication. But her desires had changed. She was determined not to make a pig of herself as she had in the past.

Elam stared at her for as long as he was able, before his eyes drifted in opposite directions. Then he shrugged and started in on her half.

Becky had never held back eating in front of Elam. He had certainly seen her eat a lot over the years. And that was just what he *saw*. Not even her own family knew about her late-night visits to the refrigerator.

When the waitress brought the bill, Elam quickly snatched it up.

Becky tried to yank it from his hand. "It's my turn to pay,"

"*Nee*. You didn't even eat anything."

Becky looked down at the pizza crust she'd left. She wasn't even tempted to finish it. "It's still my turn."

"I'm not having my date pay for supper."

Date? Becky and Elam usually went once a week to eat somewhere, and they had always split the bill or taken turns.

They walked outside into the afternoon sun, and Becky immediately started to sweat. Summer wasn't giving them any break as August drew near. The heat and humidity were awful.

She waited until they were on the road before she broached a subject she'd been thinking about. "Matt King asked me if I was going to the singing this weekend." She watched for Elam's reaction. If there was more going on in his head than friendship, she was going to need to nip that. "He offered to take me."

Elam pulled back on the reins and slowed the horse to a steady trot. A muscle flicked in his jaw. "What?"

"I know." Becky laughed. "I'm sure it was a dare, a joke . . ." She shrugged. "Something."

"Why do you say that?" Elam kept glancing back and forth between Becky and the road ahead. He always said he could see well enough to drive the buggy, but sometimes he made her nervous.

Becky grunted. "Why else would someone like Matt King ask me out?" She shrugged again, as if it didn't matter. "He can have anyone he wants."

～

Elam's stomach churned as he thought about how to respond. He didn't want to say anything that might encourage Becky to go out with Matt, but he didn't want to hurt her feelings either. It wasn't surprising that Matt saw what Elam saw in Becky. Becky had no idea what a wonderful and beautiful person she was, inside and out.

Elam had always known that she didn't have any self-confidence. And although part of him wanted to build up her self-esteem, most of the time he did little to make her feel better about herself. It was selfish, he knew. But he enjoyed their friendship, and he wanted more. What he didn't want was somebody like Matt swooping in to take her away from him.

"I'm sure it wasn't a joke or a dare," he finally said. "But I thought he was going out with Mary Stoltzfus."

"I did too." Becky shrugged. "I don't know why I even mentioned it. It was just weird."

They were quiet for a while, but Elam couldn't let it go. "Did you want to go to the singing with Matt?"

"He didn't exactly ask me if I wanted to go. He just said that if I was going, then he was going to ask to take me." She turned to face him.

Elam took a deep breath. "But . . . I mean, did you *want* to go?" He slowed the buggy as he pulled into Becky's driveway. She opened the door on her side, stood up, and turned to face him.

"*Danki* for supper." She smiled. "You should have let me pay, though." She gave a quick wave, then walked into the house, leaving him without an answer.

Matt and his father quit working in the fields early. It was starting to sprinkle. They were dog tired and hungry. But as they neared the house, Matt counted the buggies pulled up outside. Six.

"What's going on?"

Lucas King stopped abruptly and slammed a hand to his forehead. "*Ach,* I forgot. Your *mamm* and all your sisters are having a gathering this afternoon to talk about Marie's wedding." *Daed* shook his head. "This wasn't the best day to take off early."

His father let out a heavy sigh and started walking again. Matt followed, knowing he would have to be polite, but hoping he could hurry upstairs and get an early bath before supper. They could hear the chatter long before they hit the front porch.

Matt and his father stopped right inside the front door. *Mamm* sat on the couch next to Marie, and the mother of the groom, Esther Zook, was on the other side of Marie. The rest of his sisters were scattered around, some sitting on the floor. Matt followed his father's lead by saying hello and nodding in every direction. Rosa Hostetler was there, along with Hope Bowman and her little one, Faith.

Then his eyes landed on Becky Byler, and no one else in the room existed. What was it about her? Why was she so compelling to him? She was the only girl in the district who never seemed interested in him.

He was still standing there gaping at her when his father tapped him on the shoulder. "Let's leave the ladies be."

Matt tipped his hat. "Nice to see you all."

The chatter started right back up once Matt hit the stairs, but he turned once to get another quick look at Becky. She was staring right at him. He grinned at her and dashed up the stairs.

In record time, he was clean and dressed in fresh clothes. He rushed back downstairs, hoping Becky was still there. The crowd seemed to have thinned out. Hope Bowman and the baby were gone, and some of his sisters had left the room. To start supper, he hoped. Matt's stomach was rumbling.

His adrenaline spiked when he saw Becky sitting in the same chair as before. He wished there was a way for him to talk to her alone. She seemed to avoid him at every turn.

Rosa stood up. "Becky, I can take you home since your *mamm* had to leave early."

Becky stood up, and Matt took a few steps toward her. "I can take Becky home, Rosa. It's not really on your way."

"*Nee*, I don't mind," Rosa said.

Matt tried to lock eyes with Becky, but she wouldn't look at him. "I have to go out anyway. I—I need to go to the store, and it's right on the way to Becky's *haus*. I can take her home."

Rosa's eyes twinkled. "Well, all right, Matt. Then you can take Becky home."

Matt looked at Becky. Her eyes darted around frantically, making her look like a snared animal desperate for escape. Matt hoped he was doing the right thing. Maybe she just didn't want anything to do with him.

Either way he was going to need to stop at the store so he wasn't caught in a lie. *Surely there is something I need.*

~

Becky climbed into Matt's buggy and fluffed her dress so it didn't cling to her big belly. She tried sucking in her stomach, but that didn't help.

"This really isn't necessary. Rosa could have taken me home." She tensed every muscle trying to make herself smaller. But it didn't work. She took up so much of the seat that she was almost touching Matt's leg.

"I don't mind." He paused, clicking his tongue to move the horse into action. "Poor ol' Buttercup hasn't been out in a couple of days anyway."

"She's a beautiful animal." Becky could feel the heat in her cheeks. She didn't dare look at him.

"Can I ask you something?"

Becky swallowed hard. "Okay."

"You always smell *gut*." He chuckled, turning to face her. "I know that's a weird thing to say, but you do. Is it some special soap or lotion?"

Becky ducked her head and smiled. "It's goat's milk soap, but we add a fragrance oil that's a mixture of rosemary and lavender."

"Well, it sure smells *gut*."

"*Danki. Mamm* and Lena and I use it, but *Daed* says it smells too feminine, so *Mamm* makes a different kind for him and Ruben. She puts a tiny bit of honey in theirs."

Becky knew her mother's recipe for soap was special. This wasn't the first time someone had told her she smelled good, but it was the first time the comment had come from a man. "*Mamm's* recipe came from her *mammi*. The milk comes from my goats."

"We don't have any goats. *Mamm* makes soap using goat's milk too, but she buys the goat milk either in cans or from other farmers." He narrowed his brow. "But *mei mamm* and sisters must not make it the same way."

"Secret recipe." Becky smiled. "I love goats. We have Boer goats. We're up to twenty-six now, and I have names for all of them."

Matt laughed. "Really?"

"*Ya*. Each one is special. *Daed* was going to take some to auction, but I cried until he finally gave in and said he wouldn't."

She was babbling, but she couldn't seem to help it. She dabbed at the sweat on her forehead, thankful for the topless buggy they were in. At least there was a breeze.

"I've given a few of my goats away to people I knew would take *gut* care of them," she said. "And we've lost a few to coyotes or sickness." She shook her head. "It's awful when that happens."

"We've got horses, pigs, sheep, and chickens." Matt slowed the buggy down to a trot. "But no goats. *Mamm* had a bad experience with a billy goat when she was young. She got rammed pretty bad and said the males get mean sometimes. She's never wanted any part of goats"

"Aw, they make such *gut* pets. We drink the goat milk too. It's better for you than cow's milk. And we make cheese." She paused. "But we do have to separate the males until breeding time. Some of them do get a bit ill-tempered."

"So . . . you don't eat any of them?"

Becky brought a hand to her chest. "Bite your tongue. No way!"

They both laughed, and Becky realized that the nervous fluttering had stopped, and she was really enjoying talking with him.

Matt pulled into her driveway, his eyes fixed on the herd. "Last time you had worship service at your *haus*, I don't remember seeing that many goats."

"It was winter the last time we had service here. They were probably in the barn keeping warm." She waited for him to come to a complete stop before she stepped out of the buggy. "*Danki* for bringing me home."

"Sure."

She turned to walk inside, her step a bit lighter. She wondered what it would be like to date someone like Matt King. He was so handsome. And so nice.

Just the kind of fellow who would break her heart.

Chapter Four

Becky pulled the scale out from under her bed, anxious to see how much weight she'd lost over the past month. Her dresses were loose, and she was guessing at least ten pounds. She had a lot more energy too.

As she reached under the bed, she dislodged a red suitcase filled with *Englisch* magazines. Once she had loved poring over the pictures of the models, fantasizing about what it would be like to be thin. But the comparison made her even more depressed, so she hadn't looked at them lately.

She shoved the suitcase aside, stepped onto the scale, and gasped. Twenty-three pounds.

Before she had a chance to celebrate or even comprehend the number, someone knocked on the door. She scrambled to put on her shoes and socks and slipped the scale back under the bed.

"Come in."

Ruben walked in. It was hard for Becky to believe that her fourteen-year-old brother would be entering his *rumschpringe* in two years. He was a handsome kid and was surely going to break some hearts.

"*Mamm* said one of your goats has her head stuck in the fence. We can hear her hollering." Ruben rubbed his nose. "And breakfast is ready."

"Okay. I know I overslept this morning. Tell *Mamm* I'll be down in a few minutes." Not the best way to start the day—with a goat in distress. There were several sections of the fence where the smaller goats could stick their heads in the hog wire, then because of the way their horns jutted backward, they couldn't get out. Becky and her father had added tight meshed chicken wire in the spots where the goats often got stuck, but the whole fence really needed to be done.

She pinned her hair, put on her *kapp*, and hurried downstairs.

"Sorry I'm late, *Mamm*." She didn't stop as she walked through the kitchen. "I'll get the goat and be right back."

She rushed across the yard to the pasture where she kept her goats. Peaches was the one who was stuck. Becky couldn't see her yet, but she recognized her voice. The babies bleated when they were first born, then the sound turned into more of a long whine before they actually sounded like full-grown goats. Peaches was born three months ago, and she was just the right size to get her head stuck.

Becky found Peaches on the far side of the pasture. "It's all right, girl," she said. She maneuvered the spiked horns until the kid was free, and Peaches quickly ran back to her mother.

Becky knew she was going to have to come up with a way to keep her goats from getting stuck. Surrounding the entire pasture with chicken wire would do it, but when would any of them have time for a project that big?

After she gave most of her pets a rub on the snout, she hurried back for breakfast.

"*Daed*, what should we do about them getting their heads stuck in the fence?" She sat down across from where Ruben and Lena were sitting at the kitchen table. "It only happens until they get big enough that their heads won't fit, but they manage to poke through the wire in the same places to get to those bushes they love."

Daed reached for a piece of toast on a plate in the middle of the table. "They'll die in this heat if one of them gets stuck and no one is around to free them."

And it would be my fault. Becky stared at the scrapple, eggs, bacon, and toast. She took one small spoonful of eggs and one piece of bacon.

"Those Boer goats with their spiked horns have always gotten stuck in the fences," her father went on. "I've pulled the buggy over on the side of the road and freed plenty of them over the years." *Daed* scooped up a spoonful of scrapple. "When I was growing up, we duct taped a stick to their horns, and that kept them from being able to fit their heads through the fence when they were young. Never seemed to bother any of them."

"Just run the stick from one horn to the other and tape it to the horns?" Becky broke off a tiny piece of bacon and ate it.

"*Ya*. I'd try that. Those goats of yours keep finding a way to get to those bushes. I'd say cut the bushes down, but there are plenty more along the south fence." *Daed* pushed his chair back from the table. "Ruben, you ready?"

Ruben nodded, swallowed a mouthful of food, and chugged down his glass of milk. He followed their father out the back door. Lena left the kitchen to go upstairs and get dressed.

Becky finished her eggs but left the rest of the bacon. She was about to stand up and help clean the kitchen when her mother walked up to her, hands on her hips, and stared at her.

"Why aren't you eating, Becky? Don't try to deny it; I've been watching. Are you ill?"

Mamm was a full-figured woman, and she ate plenty. But she was not fat or even chubby. As a child Becky had been certain she was adopted, but in reality she looked too much like her younger sister for that to be possible.

"I've been dieting." Becky stood up, brushed past her mother, and put her plate in the sink. *Mamm* followed her, plugged the sink, and started running hot water.

"*Ya*, well, I can tell you are losing weight. Especially in your face." *Mamm* stacked the plates in the soapy water. "But don't overdo it. You don't want to be like those *Englisch* girls who get so thin that they die." She shook her head. "I read about that in a magazine once. Anorexia is what it's called."

Becky laughed aloud. "*Mamm*, are you kidding me? I'm huge. I'd never be that thin." *But I sure would like to be.*

Mamm shook her head. "Becky, you see yourself as much bigger than you really are. You always have." She paused as she handed Becky a clean dish to dry. "You are a beautiful girl."

In the face. How many times had she overheard that over the course of her life? *Becky Byler has a lovely face, but . . .*

"Anyway, I'm trying hard to lose weight."

Becky paused. She wanted to tell her mother the whole story—how she had prayed, how God had granted her a miracle, how she was going to be thin and beautiful. But she knew her mother would not approve.

Vanity and pride. She had been taught to live by the *Ordnung* her entire life, and everyone knew that the *Ordnung* forbade taking too much notice of your looks or accomplishments. *Still, we are made in God's image,* Becky thought. *Wouldn't God want us to be the best we could possibly be?*

"Just do it in a healthy way. Don't stop eating altogether." *Mamm* handed Becky the last dish, then pulled the plug to let the dishwater drain.

"I hear people whispering, *Mamm*. About how fat I am." Becky blinked back tears as she recalled all the times her feelings had been hurt.

Her mother turned to face Becky and gently latched onto her arms. "You listen to me. It is a shame that a few folks don't see you for the beautiful person you are. Your beauty shines from the inside." Her mother paused. "But you are also very beautiful on the outside, Becky." *Mamm* dropped her hands to her side and shrugged. "*Ya*, I know. It shouldn't matter. But I think the Lord knows that we like to feel *gut* about ourselves. He just doesn't want our looks controlling our lives. We strive to all be equal in His eyes. So keep that in mind while you're trying to lose weight."

Mamm kissed her on the cheek. "Besides, I think you're perfect the way you are."

Elam finished his chores early, and once he was cleaned up, he went and found his mother in the mud room running their clothes through the washing machine. "I'm going to town. Do you need me to pick anything up?"

"*Nee*, I don't think so." She laid one of Elam's wet shirts in the laundry basket. "I'm going to get these hung out to dry and then work in the garden." *Mamm* pulled another shirt through, let out a heavy sigh, and then dabbed her forehead with a handkerchief she kept in her apron pocket.

"Do we need more eggs from Rosa?" Elam recalled Becky's offer to deliver eggs to him and his mother. He didn't have any pressing business in town. He just wanted to see Becky. He needed to brave up and tell her how he really felt about her. Especially if Matt King might be interested.

"*Nee*. Not yet."

"Okay. I'll be back before supper."

It was too late into the year to ask Becky to marry him. Not enough time to have the announcement properly published or to plan a wedding. Even though Amish weddings were uniform, every bride still had her own special way of making it unique, and he wanted Becky to have that opportunity too. But maybe if they officially started dating, then they could marry next year in October or November.

Fifteen minutes later he pulled up to the bakery. Young Lena was behind the counter with her mother, but Elam didn't see Becky. Rosa was counting out eggs to Sarah Byler, and there were two people in line. He recognized Esther Zook from the back by the way she was slumped over, but it wasn't until Mary Stoltzfus turned around that he recognized her.

Elam waited patiently, hoping Becky would come out from the back and wishing he could strike up a conversation with Mary to find out if she was dating Matt. Rosa smiled at Elam as she brushed by him on her way out, and Lena was busy totaling up Esther's order. He tapped Mary on the shoulder.

"Hi, Elam." Mary batted her long eyelashes over bright blue eyes.

The tall girl had been gorgeous since she was young. With her rosy red cheeks and full red lips, she looked as if she wore makeup similar to the *Englisch* girls. But Mary was a natural beauty. She'd be a perfect match for Matt.

"*Wie bischt?*" Elam forced a smile as he wondered how he could ask the question on his mind. If he recalled correctly, Mary's mother had been ill for the past couple of weeks. "How's your *mamm*?"

"Much better. *Danki* for asking." Mary turned back around and placed her order with Lena, then spun to face Elam again. "The doctor said it was bronchitis, and she really is a lot better, but not back to her old self yet. I'm doing as much as I can, but today I'm cheating and ordering two loaves of bread." She smiled. Elam had to admit she was mesmerizing, with her perfect white teeth and full lips. Surely she and Matt were an item and no one knew about it yet. That was the way it was done when things became serious. The couple was hush-hush about it until after the news was published.

"I'm glad to hear she's doing better."

Mary smiled, then handed Lena her money and was waiting for change. Elam was going to miss this chance if he didn't ask her.

"Hey, I was wondering . . . ," he whispered from behind her. She twisted the upper half of her body to face him.

"*Ya?*"

"Are you and Matt King a couple?" Best to just find out, he decided. "I mean, I heard rumor of that, and I was wondering if we'd have another wedding to look forward to soon." He rubbed his stomach. "Nothing like a wedding meal to make a man happy."

Mary laughed. "We all know that you men live for the meals on wedding days. But *nee*, there are no wedding plans for me." She tapped a finger to her chin. "Marie King and John Zook's wedding is in October, then a few weeks after that, Rosa Hostetler and Adam Bontrager will exchange vows." She shrugged, smiling. "Those are the only weddings I know of."

Elam nodded, but he couldn't help but notice that Mary hadn't answered the question of whether she and Matt were dating.

"*Danki*, Lena," Mary said to the young girl as she took her loaves of bread and turned toward the exit. She gave a quick wave to Elam as she left.

"What can I get for you, Elam?" Lena leaned her elbows on the glass countertop and smiled. She looked so much like Becky with her dark hair and big brown eyes.

"Uh . . ." He should have thought of something while he was in line. "I guess . . ."

Lena let out an exaggerated sigh. "Just wait here. I'll go get Becky."

Elam flinched with embarrassment, but at least he'd get to see Becky. She came from the back with splotches of flour all over her black apron. An apron that showed off a shrinking middle.

"Wow. You're really losing weight." It was a good starting comment since he knew how much Becky's weight bothered her.

Her face lit up as she bounced up on her toes behind the counter.

Lena had disappeared as soon as her older sister came out. "*Danki* for noticing. It's a miracle. The pounds are just dropping off." She reached over the counter and touched Elam's arm, which sent a little thrill up his spine. "I prayed about it, Elam. I asked God to make me lose weight. And He did." She let go of his arm, stepped back, and looked down at her smaller self. "I can't believe it."

"I thought you were perfect just the way you were." Elam forced a smile. Was she losing weight so that she could be with Matt?

Maybe he was blowing this entire thing out of proportion. Maybe Becky misunderstood Matt's intentions when he mentioned the singing. Matt King was a much better match for someone like Mary.

"So, what brings you here?"

"I just wanted to see you. And I wanted to ask you—"

The bell on the door chimed. Becky's face lit up, and Elam turned to see Matt.

Chapter Five

Matt was disappointed but not surprised to see Elam Miller chatting with Becky. Those two were together all the time.

He stopped beside Elam at the counter. *"Wie bischt,* you two?"

They all exchanged pleasantries. Matt was hoping Elam would leave, but he folded his arms over his chest and leaned against the counter as if he might stay all day. Elam had weird eyes that roamed all over the place, but otherwise he was ample competition for the ladies in their district. Matt was hoping he hadn't latched onto the one girl Matt hadn't had an opportunity to spend time with.

"Remember awhile back when I took you home, Becky . . . you told me all about your goats?" She nodded, and out of the corner of his eye Matt caught the scowl on Elam's face. "You said that sometimes you give them to *gut* homes. I talked to *mei daed,* and we both think having a few goats would be *gut.* And *Mamm* said she'd go along with it as long as I take care of them. Would you consider selling one buck and three of the does?"

"I think I could spare a few knowing that they'd be well taken care of," she said. "Only thing is, with these Boer goats, they tend to get their horns stuck in the fence when they're young because of the way the horns point backward. They push their heads through, then the horns get locked and they can't get their heads out. We struggle with it when the kids are young." She paused. "Does it matter to you if they are babies or older goats?"

"As long as they produce milk, I don't think it matters."

Matt felt the urge to reach across the counter and brush off a smudge of flour on Becky's cheek. And he should have, since only seconds later Elam did.

"Flour," Elam said as he pushed his thick glasses up on his nose.

Matt was sure Elam liked Becky as more than a friend. Maybe she was already spoken for. If that was the case, he didn't want to get in the way.

But Becky sure wasn't acting as if she and Elam were courting. "Do you want to come to the *haus* after I'm off work and take a look, see which ones you might want?" She laid her palms on the glass counter and smiled. "But remember, they're all special. You have to keep their names."

Matt grinned at her. "I will. And that sounds great. I'll see you this afternoon."

He left the bakery, still wondering about Elam and Becky. He wasn't paying much attention when he bumped into Mary Stoltzfus in front of the bakery.

"*Ach*, Mary, I'm sorry. I was lost in thought and not watching where I was going." Matt leaned closer. "Are you okay?"

"*Ya*. I'm fine. I just realized that Becky's little sister, Lena, gave me a twenty-dollar bill as my change, and it should have been a one-dollar bill. I need to go back in and tell them."

Becky's heart fluttered, and she didn't think the end of the day would get here soon enough. She couldn't believe it. Matt might actually be interested in her.

Elam cleared his throat and nodded toward the glass storefront. "I guess the rumors are true." He pointed to Matt and Mary standing outside talking.

"Just because they're talking doesn't mean they are dating," Becky snapped back a little too quickly. "I mean . . . we don't know that."

Elam frowned. "You don't have an interest in Matt, do you?"

"Of course not." Becky rolled her eyes. "Why do you say that?"

He looped his thumbs under his suspenders. "Just wondering."

As Becky watched Matt and Mary laughing and talking, she couldn't help but wonder if Elam was right. Mary was a good match for Matt.

She turned back to her best friend, the one she could always count on. "Now, what did you want to ask me earlier?"

Elam took a deep breath. "This isn't really the place to talk. Can we get together one night for supper?"

Becky stared at him. "What's wrong?"

"Nothing." He raised his eyebrows. "Nothing is wrong. I just have something I want to talk to you about."

"Okay. How about Thursday?"

Elam nodded. "Sounds *gut*. I'll pick you up about four."

After Elam left, Mary came back in the bakery to straighten out a cash mistake Lena had made.

"I told *Mamm* more than once that Lena isn't very good with the money," Becky said. "But *Mamm* insists the only way she'll ever learn is to let her keep running the cash register."

"It's okay." Mary chuckled. "At least most people around here are pretty honest."

Becky spent the rest of the day watching the clock. When she got home, she rushed upstairs. She had just lathered up with lavender soap in the bathtub when there was a knock at the door.

"Becky?"

"Yes, Mamm."

"Why are you up here bathing before you tend to those goats? Your father got worried about them, so he got off the plow early and worked on the fence. You need to go see what he's done. And they need to be fed."

"Okay," Becky yelled. "I'm coming."

"And don't forget to thank your *daed* for all that fence work. You know how hard it is on his back."

"I will." Becky dried off and pulled her damp hair into a bun. She dressed, put on her *kapp*, and ran down the stairs. Matt was just pulling up in his buggy with a small enclosed trailer in tow.

Becky swallowed hard as the realization hit her: she was about to lose four of her pets. She had given some away before, but first she had visited her kids' future homes and given the new owners detailed instructions about how to feed and take care of them. With Matt, she'd just said 'sure' and that was the end of it.

"*Mei daed* worked on the fence today, and I need to go check it. Do you mind walking with me across the north side?" She paused. "Or if you're in a hurry, we'll find which goats you want first."

"*Nee.* Let's check out the fence." He fell in step with Becky, and they started across the lush green field. "I'm going to leave it to your expertise anyway. You probably know which ones are best for us."

"I've been thinking about it since you came into the bakery. Ram definitely wouldn't be a *gut* choice for the male." She chuckled. "He has that name for a reason. But we have a younger buck that has been a fine breeder. His name is Chester."

"How'd you come up with that name?"

"It just popped into my head. No particular reason. He just looked like a Chester when he was born." She glanced up at him and was struck again by how handsome he was. "Pilgrim was born the week of Thanksgiving. Cupid was born right before Valentine's Day, and my most recent triplets are Sugar, Cinnamon, and Spice." She shrugged. "No rhyme or reason sometimes."

Three of her friendliest kids came running toward them. "That's Cupcake and her two does, Ginger and Coco." She pointed toward them.

Matt laughed. "Lots of food names."

Embarrassment swept over Becky in a wave. Had her entire life revolved around food? She decided in that instant that she would never name another kid anything food related. She was quiet as they kept walking, then stopped when Cupcake and her does reached them.

Matt reached down and petted Cupcake, then the babies. "I like their names. It's cute." He glanced around. "Where are the bucks?"

"They're fenced off on the other side." Becky pointed to her left, where her bucks were grazing. They started walking again, but Becky picked up speed when she heard one of the goats wailing. "Oh no. Somebody must have her head stuck again!" She started running, and so did Matt, but as she drew closer, she recognized the agonizing sound. "Someone's in labor!"

"Now?" Matt stayed by her side as they ran.

Becky struggled to catch her breath as she reached Popsicle. *Ach. More food.* The doe was standing and crying out.

"She's far along. She's going to kid any minute."

"Right now?"

"*Ya.*" Becky squatted down to have a better look. "They usually deliver at night or when no one is around. I think they prefer it that way, or at least that's what I've read. I've helped deliver at least a dozen." She shrugged. "But sometimes the mommies just show up at feeding time with a new baby in tow." She pointed. "Here it comes. Look close and you can barely see the tiny hooves."

Matt squatted down next to Becky. "Wow."

"Honestly, I didn't even know that Popsicle was pregnant. She's had four kids, and it's hard to tell when they're expecting—except with the first one, because that's when they get their udders for the first time."

Matt leaned even closer. "I see two hooves."

"It won't be long before we see the nose. Twins are the norm, but plenty of the does have had single births, and I have three sets of triplets."

Matt's eyes narrowed. "She sounds like she's dying. Are you sure she's okay?"

"Childbirth is painful. Or so I've heard." She paused when Popsicle fell onto her side. "This is it."

"Is that normal?" Matt asked again. "I mean, for her to just fall over like that?" He grinned. "I told you I didn't know much about goats."

"I've had a few actually deliver standing up, but most of them lie down like this right before they kid." Becky touched Matt on the arm. "There's the nose!"

Matt's jaw hung low as he stared, but when he covered her hand with his, Becky jerked her hand back. *What was I thinking?*

"Uh-oh." Becky rubbed the goat on her back as she wailed.

"What's wrong?"

"She's having trouble pushing. See the tongue hanging out of the kid's mouth?"

"Is the baby dead?"

"*Nee.* But I'm going to help her." Becky gently latched onto the tiny hooves and nose the way she'd done several times before. "Just so you know, you should never do this until you see the nose. Don't ever pull on just the hooves." She easily pulled the doe out, cleared the sack from her tiny face, and then laid her near Popsicle's head. "There you go, Momma. It's a girl."

She looked back at Matt. His eyes widened, and he grinned. "Do you have one named Jellybean?"

"*Nee.*" Becky bit her bottom lip. "Do you, um . . . want to name her Jellybean?"

"I think that's a great name. What do you think?"

I think you are the most wonderful man on the planet. "I think that sounds great."

Matt chuckled and pointed. "I can't believe Jellybean is already standing up."

"It doesn't take long. She'll latch on and start nursing soon, but—" Becky pointed at Popsicle, whose belly had begun to contract again. The doe cried out, and Becky looked at Matt. "Here we go again."

They both sat down next to Popsicle. Almost an hour later she had delivered two more kids.

"I think we both missed supper," she said when the last of the babies stood up and started nursing.

"It was worth it, though. Wanta go check out your fence now?"

"*Ya.* Then we'll find you three does. I'll pick out ones that have birthed before and are *gut mudders.* I've had a few that weren't very responsible. They'd just go off and leave their babies. It doesn't happen too often, but I'd feel better giving you older does who shouldn't have problems delivering, and ones that are also *gut* milk producers."

"So you think one buck and three does is okay?" Matt got in step with her as they resumed their trek to the fence.

"*Ya,* I think that would be *gut.* I keep the new *mudders* and babies away from the herd until the babies are ready to be weaned, which is usually two or three months."

Becky pulled on the fence where her father had been working. "See how *Daed* added chicken wire here? The goats can't get their heads stuck when there is chicken wire."

Matt nodded.

"They love eating off the bush on the other side of the fence in this particular spot, so this is usually where they get stuck. So *Daed* covered this area with chicken wire on top of the hog wire." She let out a heavy sigh. "But they get stuck in other areas too. We need to have chicken wire running the length of the fence to really keep them all safe." She shook her head. "But that's a huge job, and hard on *Daed's* back. And Ruben works with James, Hope's boy, on Saturdays. They mow lawns for several *Englisch* families in town to make extra money." She laughed. "Although now that James is sweet on a girl, he apparently isn't as interested in that extra money. It might end up being just Ruben's job. Either way, I'm going to talk to *Daed* about hiring someone to put chicken wire all around. That's the only way the problem will be solved."

Matt raised an eyebrow. "I'm looking for an extra job. Maybe I could do it? I could work Saturdays and in the evenings after supper. This time of year it stays light longer."

Just the thought of Matt being at her house almost every day made Becky quiver. "Really? It's hard work, and it's really hot."

Matt pushed back his straw hat and winked. "I'm your man. Talk to your *daed* and let me know. I could start right away."

"I will." She smiled. "Now, let's go find your goats."

Chapter Six

Becky fought to contain her excitement when her father agreed to hire Matt, starting on Saturday. But tonight she was having supper with Elam, and she wondered what was on his mind.

She was sitting on the porch steps when he pulled up, and she hurried to the buggy. These days she was feeling lighter and lighter. She'd already taken in her dresses several inches.

"I thought we'd go somewhere new tonight. We always go get pizza or burgers. I thought we'd try the new place farther down Lincoln Highway, the one with the big red sign. It's a steak place."

"Elam, I've heard that place is fancy. And expensive. We don't have to go there."

Elam laughed. "You're worried because you think it's your turn to buy. I already told you that I won't have my dates buying meals."

Becky twisted her mouth from side to side. "When did we go from being best friends to . . . dating?" She squeezed her eyes closed for a moment, unsure how Elam was going to take the comment.

"That's what I want to talk to you about. But let's wait until we get to the restaurant."

"Okay." Becky fell silent. She had ten minutes to figure out a good reason for not dating him. *Because I really like Matt. Because I love you like a* bruder. *Because you're my best friend, and I don't see you that way.*

Nothing sounded good. *Why would Elam want to date me anyway? Things are good the way they are. And I'm fat.*

"Elam, this is way too fancy," Becky whispered as the waitress ushered them to an empty table in the far corner of the restaurant. "What would the bishop say? And this is going to cost a fortune." She eyed the cloth-covered tables, each one with a lit candle in the middle and a vase of fresh chrysanthemums. Soft piano music was playing in the background.

"No worries," Elam whispered back before they took their seats.

This was the type of restaurant where someone would propose. *Surely not.*

As soon as the waitress handed them each a menu, Becky scanned the prices and let out a small gasp. "Elam!" she said. "Let's leave."

"*Nee*, it's fine, Becky." Elam glanced up at her over his menu. "And would you please *eat*? I know you're dieting, but I want you to enjoy a *gut* meal."

"I'm really not very hungry. I'll just get a salad." *For $8.99.* She shook her head.

When the waitress returned, Elam ordered a twenty-three-dollar entrée, something Becky had never heard of, but she was pretty sure he pronounced it wrong. The waitress grinned and nodded. Becky ordered the salad.

"What do you want to talk to me about?" Her stomach churned and she clenched her hands at her sides. "Is something wrong?"

Elam took a sip of water. "*Nee*, nothing is wrong. I wanted to bring you somewhere nice. And . . ." He hesitated. "I know we've been good friends for a long time, but . . ."

Becky held her breath. All she'd ever wanted was to be loved by a man. But now that the moment was upon her, she could think of nothing but Matt. Even if Matt never took a romantic interest in her, would it really be fair to settle for Elam as second choice?

"I love you, Becky."

There it was. She kept holding her breath.

"I've loved you since we were little, and I know you love me too. But I want to . . ." He paused. "I want to marry you someday."

Becky sent up a silent prayer of thanks that Elam wasn't actually proposing today. But she knew that no matter how she relayed her feelings, Elam was going to be hurt.

"Why would you want to marry me, Elam?" Becky looked down at herself. She was noticeably thinner but still had a good forty pounds to lose before she'd feel good about herself.

"What?" He forced both eyes to focus on her face. "Because I love you. That's why."

"But you could have your choice of anyone in the district. Why pick the fat girl?"

Elam adjusted his glasses. *Does Elam think he can't get anyone else because of his eyes?*

"I mean, I'm not proposing or anything. I just know how I feel, and maybe next year—"

"Stop." Becky held up one hand. "Elam, you are right. I do love you." A smile spread across his face. "But—"

He hung his head. "Not the same way I love you."

"Right," she said softly.

"I'm getting my eyes fixed someday soon."

"Elam, this has nothing to do with your eyes." Becky spoke as tenderly as she could. "You're handsome, smart, funny, and would be a great catch."

Elam grunted. "I don't know about that." He stared long and hard at her. "Do you have romantic feelings for someone else?"

She didn't want to lie, but if she told Elam the truth, she was afraid their friendship would end. And the chances were good that Matt would never ask her out, even if she did get thin.

She must have taken too long to think about it.

"I guess that answers my question. And I'm guessing Matt King holds your heart."

Becky hung her head. Not only was Elam springing for this expensive meal, but she was also ruining his day. "Why would someone like Matt want me, looking like this?"

It came out all wrong, but she couldn't take it back now. Elam blinked rapidly, and Becky actually thought he might cry.

"*Mei* sweet Becky. You are the most beautiful person I know, inside and out. I should not have let you go this long with such low self-confidence. I should have told you more often how pretty you are, how kind you are, what a *gut mudder* you will be." He focused hard and stared into her eyes. "But I was always afraid of losing you."

If Becky had a nickel for every time someone had told her that she had a pretty face, or that she was pretty on the inside . . .

They were both quiet. There really wasn't anything left to say. And as they sat in the silence, a sadness was burrowing down inside her.

As if she'd just lost her best friend.

Matt fed all the farm animals, including his four new goats, then loaded his tool kit into the buggy. Becky's father had told him that he would have all the chicken wire onsite when Matt arrived Saturday. He was anxious to get started, for more reasons than one. A couple of women from town ran Byler's Bakery on Saturday, so the chances were good he might see Becky.

As he headed to the Byler farm, he recalled a conversation he'd had with his mother several years ago. They had been sitting on the couch by themselves—a rarity in a household of nine. She held both his hands in hers and told him, "Matthew, you have a gift, a true blessing from the Lord. You see people for who they really are. You see their souls and identify what it is about them that makes them beautiful. Most of us cannot walk through this life with such pureness of heart."

Matt couldn't remember why they'd had that conversation, but he'd always remembered his mother's words. He wasn't sure if he had any special gifts or not, but he knew one thing: the beauty of Becky Byler shone through clearly to him.

He had always liked her and wanted to get to know her better, but only recently had she opened up to him a little. Watching her deliver the goats had been the highlight of his week. Maybe his month. Or the whole year. She was so capable and tender and kind.

He was glad to see her sitting in a rocking chair on the front porch when he pulled into her driveway on Saturday morning. Her father was standing next to her.

"I have all the supplies in the barn," Abram Byler said as he shook Matt's hand. "I feel like I should be out there helping you, but Sarah has me loaded up on projects around here that are a little easier on the old back."

"I'm happy to have the work." Matt glanced around Abram and said hello to Becky.

She crossed the porch and walked down the steps to where Matt and Abram were standing. There was no mistaking how much weight she'd lost. And although her size had never mattered all that much to him before, she was breathtaking now with her big brown eyes, curvaceous figure, and gorgeous smile. He swallowed hard.

"Matt, *Mamm* said to tell you that we'll be serving dinner at noon. So please come to the *haus* and eat with us."

"*Danki*, I will." He had a lunch pail in the front seat of his buggy, but he was sure that a home-cooked meal would be better than the sandwich his mother had sent with him. Especially with Becky sitting across the table from him.

She smiled. "How are my babies?"

"They all seem fine." He paused. "I'm not sure I'm milking them correctly. I didn't get as much milk as I thought I would."

"Just like milking cows," Abram said. "I guess. That's what Becky says anyway. Those goats have always been hers. Did you know they all have names?"

Matt grinned. "*Ya*. She told me that. I can tell she's fond of them all."

Becky took a few steps closer. "Did you bring a thermos of cold water? It's going to get hot out there."

Matt sighed. "*Mamm* left one on the counter for me, and I just realized I forgot it."

"I'll bring some out to you in a little while."

"*Danki.*" He blew out a breath. "Well, I'm going to get to work, then."

"Holler if you need anything." Abram took a sip of iced tea. "I'll be in the barn repairing a chair leg. Then after that, I will start checking off honey-dos on Sarah's list." He gave a quick wave as he walked across the yard and toward the barn.

Matt smiled at Becky. "See you in a little while."

Becky forced herself to wait an hour before she took Matt a jug of cold water. As she made the trek to the fence line, her does followed. Several times she stopped to pet one of them. As she approached, Matt looked up and smiled.

"Here you go." She handed him the jug.

"*Danki.*" He took a large gulp, then nodded at the goats. "One, two . . ." He counted sixteen.

"Plus the adult bucks over there." She pointed to her left.

"That's cool how they follow you like that."

"There's no trick to it. When they see me, they think food." She laughed. "The fence looks *gut.*" He'd done quite a bit in the last hour. She wanted her goats to be safe, but she wasn't anxious for him to finish the job too fast either.

"Who's that?" Matt pointed to a young buck who was jumping on his mother's back and trying to keep his balance, then he would fall and roll over.

"Popcorn," Becky muttered. She avoided Matt's eyes.

Matt laughed at Popcorn's continued attempts to ride on his mother's back. "They're so playful."

"*Ya*, goats are fun. And useful." She dug her shoes into the thick grass. Staring at the ground, she wiggled her toes inside the leather flats. Even her feet felt thinner. What a miracle she'd been granted.

"Can you hold this?" Matt held up a corner of chicken wire. "I'm having trouble doing this one corner stretch by myself."

"Sure." Becky held the wire in place while Matt secured it to the fence. She wanted to stay and help him all day, never take her eyes off of him. Reluctantly, she said, "I better go. See you at noon."

Her goats followed her all the way across the pasture, making their hungry noises. "I already fed you all," she said as she closed the gate behind her.

When Becky walked into the house, Lena was sitting on the couch with a coloring book.

"What are you coloring?"

Lena didn't look up as she pressed down with a red crayon. "A *haus*." She paused and held up the picture for Becky to see. "I want a *haus* like this when I get married."

"That's a big place. And red?"

"It's brick."

Becky sat down beside her sister and propped her feet up on the coffee table. "There's not a lot of houses like that around here. You must be planning on building a brand-new house when you get married. Don't you want to live in a big farmhouse like this one?"

"I'm not going to be Amish. I'm going to go live in the *Englisch* world."

Becky pulled in her feet and sat up straight. "What?"

"You heard me. I'm not going to be baptized when I'm older. I'm going to marry an *Englisch* man and live in the city."

Becky forced herself to remain calm. Lena was only ten years old. By the time she was old enough to make those types of decisions, she wouldn't feel the same way. But her parents would be very upset to hear Lena talk this way.

"Do *Mamm* and *Daed* know that you don't plan to stay in our community?"

Lena stopped coloring and pressed her lips together. "*Nee*, and don't tell them."

"You'll change your mind."

"*Nee*. I won't. Now, promise."

Becky wasn't sure that was a promise she could keep. Lena seemed so sure, so committed.

But she decided to let it go.

For now.

Chapter Seven

Matt prayed silently with Becky's family, then loaded his plate with meat pie. It was one of his favorite dishes, although his mother rarely made it. She said it was too much work to make enough pies for nine people. Matt loved brown gravy drizzled atop the pie filled with roast and potatoes. He reached for the ladle at the same time Becky did.

"You go ahead," she said as she pulled her hand back.

He generously poured gravy atop the pie, then took his first bite. "This is great, Sarah." Matt smiled at Becky's mother before he scooped more onto his fork.

"Becky gets the credit," Sarah said. "This was *mei mudder's* recipe, and Becky adds her own touches, so I let her make it now." Sarah smiled. "Besides, I enjoy a break from the kitchen now and then."

Matt glanced at Becky's plate. She had taken one small spoonful of the pie and some green beans. Not very much at all, and no butter bread.

She was really taking this diet seriously. He wanted to tell her not to worry about her weight so much, but he wasn't sure how. And he surely wouldn't do it in front of her family.

Abram spooned some chow-chow onto his plate. "How's the fence coming?"

"*Gut.* If the weather holds out, I think I can be done in a couple of weeks."

"I would say there's no rush, but I know Becky worries about those goats." Abram bit into a thick slice of bread.

"Becky said you took four of the goats," Sarah said. "How do they like their new home?"

Matt had tried to pay Becky for the goats, but she wouldn't take any money. "They seem to be okay. *Mamm* was glad to have fresh goat milk this morning."

They continued chatting as they ate. Becky pushed her food around on her plate, but Matt noticed that she didn't actually eat very much.

Dessert was key lime pie. "Did you make this too?" Matt asked Becky as she served him a slice.

"*Ya,* I did." She doled out slices for everyone except herself.

Matt took a bite. Becky wasn't just beautiful, kind, and nurturing. She was also a great cook. "Well, it's very *gut.*"

"*Danki.*"

Matt hadn't been around Becky's little sister, Lena, very much. The girl said almost nothing during the meal, but she stared at Matt a lot.

When he was finished, Matt eased his chair back. "*Danki* for the meal. I better get back to work."

As he crossed the field back to where he'd left off, a handful of the goats followed, but most of them were busy grazing and didn't give him much notice. He could see why a person would have goats. Not only did they provide nourishment and soap, but they were playful little critters.

For the rest of the afternoon he stretched chicken wire and continued repairs on the fence. But every few minutes he'd look toward the house, hoping that Becky would come visit him again.

～

Elam sat alone on the couch. His mother had taken the buggy to town, and he was taking the opportunity for some time alone. He hadn't talked to or seen Becky since their fancy supper on Thursday night. How was their relationship going to change now that she knew how he really felt about her?

Confessing his feelings had been a stupid thing to do. Somewhere deep down, he knew she didn't feel the same way about him, but he had remained hopeful.

He plunged a spoon into the tub of homemade vanilla ice cream. He missed Becky already. He'd almost gone to the bakery yesterday but decided against it. So instead, he had opted for ice cream.

Lots of girls ate when they were unhappy, and he could see why. It was comforting.

As he shoveled another heaping spoonful into his mouth, the front door opened and his mother walked in carrying two shopping bags. She stopped in the middle of the living room, shook her head at him, then made her way to the kitchen.

Elam followed her. "I wasn't going to eat it all."

His mother pulled out a sack of sugar from one of the bags, tore it open, and poured it into a large plastic container. "Becky isn't the right girl for you, Elam. You'll find your perfect match."

Elam took off his glasses and rubbed at his eyes. "I guess."

The truth was he couldn't imagine being with anyone else. He had always felt safe with Becky, and now that he thought about it, he wondered if it was because she was too big to attract the attention of anyone else. It was an ugly thought, but it had surfaced just the same. Now that she was losing so much weight, Elam had noticed a lot of guys checking her out. She would land a husband soon, even if it wasn't Matt King.

While he was lost in thought, his mother put a plate of leftover spaghetti and meatballs on the table. "Sit. You need to eat." She pointed a finger at him. "Something besides ice cream."

Becky or no Becky, Elam had to admit he was hungry. He dug in, rationalizing that starvation wouldn't help him focus on something else.

His heart would heal. Logically, he knew this. But it was going to be a long and painful process.

~

It was two o'clock when Becky took Matt a large glass of iced tea. She couldn't believe what a fast worker he was. This job wasn't going to take two weeks.

"*Danki.*" He took the glass and swiped at the sweat beading on his forehead.

"This is the hottest part of the day, so I thought you might enjoy some tea." She glanced toward the water jug on the ground nearby. "Do you need me to refill that?"

He shook his head. "*Nee*, I still have some. But you can stay out here and talk to me while I drink this tea." He smiled, and Becky felt herself blush.

There were about a dozen goats surrounding them, but they were busily munching on the plentiful grass they had this time of year. "Okay." She leaned against the fence.

Matt took several long gulps of tea, then stared at Becky long enough for it to become awkward. She looked away.

"You've lost a lot of weight." He frowned a little, which seemed odd, but then added, "And you hardly ate anything at lunch."

This is so embarrassing. If he only knew how she had begged God for a miracle. "I've, uh . . . been on a diet."

"I thought you looked fine before. I mean, you look real pretty now too," he added quickly. "But I don't think you need to lose any more."

You don't? In Becky's mind, another thirty or forty pounds would make her the perfect size. And she'd gotten used to not eating much. She'd dealt with some hunger pains in the beginning, but God was in control. He had given her self-discipline and granted her the miracle she'd begged for. Otherwise she would still be big as a house and depressed. She was feeling better about herself, more confident. Becky reached over and scratched Jellybean's head between the two tiny knots that would be horns in a few weeks. "I still have quite a bit of weight I want to lose," she finally said.

"Isn't it hard? I mean, not eating what you want? I don't think I'd be very *gut* at it." He chuckled. "I like to eat too much."

Becky really didn't want to have this conversation with him— or anyone else, for that matter. "It's not so hard."

"Uh-oh." Matt looked up at the sky. "That doesn't look *gut*."

"I didn't think it was supposed to rain today." Becky watched the dark clouds rolling in. "I better let you get back to work." She smiled and gave a quick wave. "Stay dry."

She hurried back toward the house, trying to analyze the conversation they'd just had. If she didn't know better, she might have thought he was flirting with her, but since she'd never been flirted with before, it seemed unlikely. By the time she got to the front porch, it was starting to sprinkle.

It rained for a solid week.

Becky missed seeing Matt, and since this was the first day with no rain, she kept expecting him to show up to work on the fence any minute. For the past hour she had been running out to the clothesline to take the clothes down, just to be available if he appeared. But if he didn't show up soon, she was going to have to start hanging them back up again.

She was going as slowly as she could when she finally heard the *clip-clop* of a horse's hooves. A buggy rounded the corner and turned into the driveway. She pushed back a few loose strands of hair that had escaped from her *kapp* and tucked them back in as best she could.

She waved when the buggy got closer, but her heart sank when she realized it wasn't Matt. She folded the shirt she held and laid it neatly in the basket, then walked with dragging feet toward Elam's buggy.

"*Wie bischt?*" Elam smiled, but it wasn't the same kind of smile she used to get from him.

"I'm okay. What about you?"

He shrugged. "Okay, I guess. I've just missed you." He held up a palm. "Don't take that the wrong way. It's just that . . . well, I did."

"I missed you too." It was true, and even though Becky didn't share Elam's romantic interests, she wanted more than ever for them to stay friends.

"I can't stop thinking about you, and I know that I should say that we're going to still be friends, and that nothing has changed . . ." He looked past her out into the field. "But things have changed, and I don't know where we go from here."

"Things don't have to change." She touched him on the arm, but he backed away. "Elam—" She choked back tears. "We're still going to be friends and hang out, right?"

Elam's eyes clouded. "I don't know, Becky. I just knew that I had to see you. I wanted to make sure that you were okay. I didn't have time to stop by the bakery. Chores have built up at home due to all this rain, and the roof started leaking in the kitchen—"

"Oh no. I'm sorry to hear that." Becky wasn't sure what to do or say, but she didn't want to lose Elam as a friend. She wished he had never told her how he felt.

She looked around him when she heard another buggy turning in.

"Your new boyfriend?"

"*Nee*. He's putting chicken wire on the fence so that the goats won't get their heads stuck. *Daed* is paying him."

Elam kept his head down as he kicked at the grass with one foot. Becky wanted to hug him but feared that would only make things worse. He finally looked up at her.

"You look beautiful." Elam moved closer, kissed her on the cheek, then wrapped his arms around her and whispered, "I hope he takes *gut* care of you."

"I told you. Matt is not my boyfriend."

Even though there is nothing more in the world I want.

"I'll see you around." Elam turned back toward his buggy, and on the way he met Matt. They shook hands. Becky waited for Matt to come her way, but he just gave a quick wave and headed toward his project.

She picked up the basket of clothes and watched him for a few moments, but he didn't turn around.

Finally, she walked toward the porch, her steps heavier than they had been in weeks. She wasn't sure what she was more upset about—Matt not greeting her after having been away for a week or her conversation with Elam.

Both issues weighed heavily on her heart.

Chapter Eight

Church was held at the Bowmans' house on Sunday, and both Matt and Elam were there. Becky had seen neither of them since the last worship service two weeks ago. Matt had finished the fence, and neither Elam nor Matt had stopped by the bakery.

She arrived at worship service feeling blue, but it didn't take long for her spirits to rise. After worship she overheard people talking about her weight loss, and several folks spoke directly to her, telling her how great she looked. Over the past two weeks, she'd lost even more weight, and she was quickly approaching her goal. Her mother had voiced concern over how much weight Becky had lost—and so quickly—but Becky knew that it was the answer to her prayer.

She was standing in the kitchen helping prepare the noon meal when Hope Bowman walked in with Faith balanced on her hip. "You look so *gut*, Becky. It's just amazing how much weight you've lost."

"*Danki.* I feel much better too. I have so much more energy."

She walked outside where small groups were gathered and

looked around for Matt. He was nowhere to be found, but she caught sight of Elam right away. He was talking to Mary Stoltzfus and Hope's boy, James. Everyone had noticed how Hope's son, whom she'd given up for adoption when he was a baby, was wearing Amish clothes now, driving a buggy, and learning the *Ordnung*. Becky knew how much Hope wanted him to become a baptized member of their community someday. Such a blessing it was for them to have found each other.

Finally, she located Matt, took a deep breath, and walked to where he was standing alone near the barn.

"Hi. How are the goats doing?" She shifted from one foot to the other. What she really wanted to say was, *Please notice how much weight I've lost.*

"*Gut,*" Matt said. "We're getting more milk, and even *Mamm* goes out and pets them."

Becky nodded. "Well, I didn't get to talk to you much the past couple of weeks, so I just wanted to check on them."

"How's the fence? Is the chicken wire working, keeping them from getting their heads stuck?"

"*Ya. Danki.* I'm glad I don't have to wake up every morning worried that someone is stuck."

"Do you have any plans this afternoon?" Matt avoided her eyes and looked past her. "I mean, if you and Elam are doing something together . . ." He shrugged. "It's no big deal. I think Cinderella might be pregnant, and I was wondering if you'd be able to tell. I know you said that sometimes you can."

Becky burst out laughing and bent slightly at the waist. "I'm sorry. It's just funny to hear you calling her Cinderella. It's such a girly name." She raised one hand in a gesture of benign authority. "I hereby grant you permission to change her name, if you'd like."

Matt laughed. "Well, Chester I can live with. But what about the other two does—Princess and Butterfly."

"Well, they aren't food names." Becky smiled. "But as I recall, you seem to like the ones named after food."

"Actually, they all answer to their names—just like dogs. So I guess I won't change them."

"I can ride over with you if you want later. I might be able to tell if she's going to kid anytime soon."

"Uh, is it okay with Elam?" Matt looked past her again, and Becky twisted around and saw Elam with the same group.

"Why wouldn't it be?"

Matt shrugged. "I don't know. I guess I thought you two were a couple. I saw him kiss you that day in your front yard."

So that's what was wrong with him. He saw the kiss and made an assumption about her and Elam. "Only on the cheek," Becky said. "We're just friends."

The corner of Matt's mouth rose a little. "Does he know that? Because I've always thought he liked you, more than just friends."

Becky felt as if she were walking on clouds. Two months ago she never would have been having this conversation with someone like Matt. But now she was thin—or thinner, anyway—and she had not one but two men interested in her.

It felt good. It felt amazing, in fact.

Then it occurred to her that maybe Matt would try harder to win Becky's affections if he thought Elam was interested too. Maybe a little jealousy could work in her favor.

"Elam would *like* for us to be more than friends." She raised her chin a little, fighting the smile that threatened to spread across her face.

"And you don't?"

There was a sense of urgency in Matt's voice. Becky felt something inside of her swell with pride.

"As I said, there's nothing between us at the moment. So if you want me to go check out your goats . . . I just need to finish helping with cleanup."

"Okay." Matt grinned. "Meet you back here in thirty minutes?"

Becky nodded and walked back toward the house. She wasn't quite sure what had just happened, only that she felt taller, thinner, and infinitely more confident than she had a few minutes ago.

Matt pulled the buggy up in front of an empty house, glad that the rest of his family was still at the Bowmans'. He and Becky had managed to sneak away from church without being seen, but the family would be home soon. His six sisters would be all in his business if they saw him with Becky.

They walked past his mother's garden and toward the barn. "I have them fenced in back here," he said, pointing. "And this fence is okay. They can't get their heads stuck, and *Daed* and I got everything we need for milking."

"Hi, babies!" Becky called. "Come see me!"

"They know your voice." Matt smiled as he watched the goats come running. She gave each one an equal amount of attention. "Chester is over there by himself. When should I put them all together?"

Becky didn't look up from where she was squatting, rubbing Cinderella between her horns. "Gestation is five months. This is September, so I'd wait a month so that they'll deliver in the spring. But Cinderella could be pregnant since I had them all together for a while. I try to time it where they deliver in the spring or fall, but it doesn't always work out that way."

"Can you tell if she's pregnant?" Matt bent down beside Becky.

She took her thumb and first finger and clamped down on either side of the goat's tail. "When a doe gets to the end of her pregnancy, her tailbone elevates, and the ligaments that connect it to her pelvis stretch." She reached for his hand. "Feel here."

She helped him position his fingers. Becky's hands were soft, and Matt breathed in her aroma, wishing he could bottle it to keep with him all the time. "Her ligaments are firm," she said. "When she gets close to kidding, they'll get really soft, and she'll also hollow out on either side of her tail."

Becky stood up. "She's either not with kid, or she has a long way to go," she said.

"*Danki.* That will help me know."

Becky giggled. "They're tricky, though. One time I showed up to give them feed during the winter, and someone had kidded overnight. I had no idea that she was pregnant, much less that far along."

"*Mamm* is happy with the milk. She won't pet Chester, but I've seen her out here with the does. And of course all *mei* sisters think they're great."

"How are plans coming for Marie's wedding?"

Matt shook his head, grinning. "I don't know. You tell me. You probably know more about it than I do." He laughed. "I'll be glad when this wedding is over and life gets back to normal. Until the next sister gets engaged."

"You men think all Amish weddings are the same. But every bride fusses over it, just like the *Englisch*. It's our special day."

At that moment Matt pictured himself and Becky standing before their congregation, exchanging vows. It was a premature daydream, but it happened just the same.

"Do you want to have supper with me Saturday night?"

Becky swallowed hard as her heart pounded, and she felt a rush of pink stain her cheeks. She'd always hoped this moment would come, and now that it was here, she wanted to appear cool and relaxed. Instead, her voice squeaked when she said, "*Ya*, I'd like that."

"*Gut.*" Matt shifted his weight. "I guess I'll take you home before *mei* family gets here. They would wear you out with questions, wondering what we're doing here together. And then *Mamm* would want you to have supper at the house Saturday night instead of us going out."

Becky's heart hammered against her ribs, and when Matt reached for her hand, his touch upset her balance and she almost tripped.

"You okay?" He squeezed her hand tighter.

"*Ya.*" She swallowed hard and tried to steady her breathing as Matt helped her into the buggy.

On the way to Becky's house they talked mostly about goats, and she was thankful for the casual conversation. Her heart had eventually stopped thudding in her chest. When they pulled in the driveway, Matt got out and walked her to the front porch.

"See you Saturday. Five o'clock okay?"

Becky nodded. She had never felt so unsteady on her feet, and a knot rose in her throat. When Matt leaned over and kissed her on the cheek, she felt the blood surge from her fingertips to her toes.

She waved as he pulled out. Becky couldn't move as her mind swirled with anticipation and wonderment about what it would be like to share a real kiss with Matt.

It was going to be a long six days.

She walked into the living room, and her mother was sitting on the couch. "Where is everyone?"

Mamm looked over the rim of her gold reading glasses. "Your *daed* is napping. Ruben and Lena stayed at the Bowmans' *haus*. Some of the *kinner* were getting a volleyball game together." She pulled her reading glasses off. "We couldn't find you anywhere, but someone said they saw you leave with Matt King." She smiled as she crossed her legs. "Is that true?"

Becky sat down on the couch beside her mother. She tucked one leg underneath her and took a deep breath. "*Ya*, it's true." She covered her face with her hands for a few moments, chuckling, then she looked back at her mother. "And I just can't believe it. He asked me out for next Saturday."

Mamm set her glasses on the end table. "I don't know why you're so surprised. You're a beautiful girl with a kind, loving heart. I've noticed lots of young men giving you attention over the years, but you always ignored them."

Becky sat taller, frowning. "I was fat. No one wanted to go out with me. And you know how cruel some of the kids were when I was young."

Mamm shook her head. "Becky, you have always worried too much about your weight. You've always imagined yourself bigger than you really were." She frowned. "And I don't want you losing any more weight."

"Ten more pounds and I'll be at my goal weight."

Mamm sighed as she picked up her glasses. She opened up the Bible and was starting to read again, but there was something else Becky needed to talk about. It had been weighing on her, and she hadn't exactly promised Lena she wouldn't tell. It was time to discuss it with *Mamm*. "Lena told me awhile back that she doesn't plan to get baptized. Do you know anything about that?" Becky twirled the string of her *kapp*.

"Your sister wakes up in a new world every day," *Mamm* said, then grinned. "Right now she doesn't understand why a woman can't be the bishop, so she's decided not to join the church. She questions everything about our faith, the *Ordnung*, and the Lord."

"And you're not worried about it?"

"*Nee*, not really. I think it's healthy. But I don't think that she'll choose to leave us. She's young. She still has her *rumschpringe* to experience."

Becky smiled. "I guess you're right. I just wanted to mention it." She stood up. "I'm going to go take a little nap myself, I think."

Upstairs, she lay back on her bed, closed her eyes, and tried to picture her and Matt at supper Saturday night. Where would they go?

She opened her eyes when Elam showed up at the forefront of her mind. It saddened her every time she recalled the look on his face when she told him she didn't love him the same way he loved her.

She missed her friend. Under different circumstances, she would want to share her news about Matt. But there was no way now.

What she needed was a girlfriend.

But Becky had spent her entire life isolating herself from girls in the community, afraid of being mocked or hurt, never getting too close to any of them. Now she wished she had a good friend to share with.

She closed her eyes again. What a lonely soul she had been when she was fat. Being thin changed everything. Matt King had asked her out. What were the chances of that happening six months ago?

She felt called to pray for Elam, for him to find the right person who would love him and be good to him. *Dear Lord . . .*

Elam ran Leader hard out in the pasture until they were both dripping with sweat. He dismounted, walked his horse to the water trough, and then led him to the barn.

"That was a *gut* run, boy." Elam rubbed the horse's damp snout, then got a brush and ran it the length of his wet coat. He had hoped to burn off some of the resentment he felt toward Becky.

It hadn't worked.

He supposed it wasn't her fault that she didn't love him the way he loved her, but the sting was still fresh. He'd also gotten word from four different people that Matt King was taking Becky out on Saturday. Gossip might be discouraged in the community, but when it came to relationships, rumor was plentiful.

Elam was pretty sure Matt never would have asked Becky out

before, back in the days when she was much larger. He didn't know the real Becky, the person inside, the way Elam did.

Elam had been praying for Becky, hoping she wouldn't get too thin, and also hoping that Matt wouldn't hurt her. He didn't know Matt well, but he'd seen several girls get their hearts broken by him. He would date them for a little while, and then, for whatever reason, the relationship ended.

He was almost through brushing Leader when his mother walked into the barn with a glass of iced tea. "Thought you could use this."

"*Ach, danki, Mamm.*" Elam took the tea and chugged from the glass until it was almost all gone.

"Elam, I want to talk to you about something." *Mamm* sat down on a hay bale in the corner of the barn.

"What is it?" He took another drink before he set the glass on his workbench.

"I think we need to hire some help. This is just too much for you to do." *Mamm* crossed her legs and nervously kicked her foot. "There are a lot of things we've let go." She took a deep breath. "The house needs a fresh coat of paint, the fence needs repairs, and the chicken coop could stand an overhaul. I could go on and on, and we just don't have time to get to all these things. And I'm worried the roof might leak again."

Elam scratched his forehead, sighing. "I know." The last thing he wanted was to hire help, but he knew his mother was right.

"Anyway, I spoke to Anne King, and she said that Matt has been taking on side jobs, trying to build up his savings account, so she is going to talk to him about doing some work around here on Saturdays and in the evenings."

Elam grunted as he folded his arms across his chest. *"Nee, Mamm.* Not Matt."

"He's a *gut* boy, and he would be a lot of help. I thought you liked Matt."

"I don't know him that well." He avoided his mother's eyes. The thought of having to be around Matt in the evenings and all day on Saturday made his stomach churn. "What about James? Can't you talk to Hope and see if James can help us out?"

His mother smiled. "I already did, but James mows lawns, and he's been spending time with a girl." She shrugged. "He's not interested in taking on anything else."

She stood up from the hay bale and brushed the wrinkles from her maroon dress. "So, you either find someone else, or I'm going to offer the job to Matt. We have got to get some repairs done around here before the place falls down around us."

She walked out of the barn, leaving Elam to stew. He could barely stand to think about Matt. Being around him daily would be a nightmare. He went back to brushing Leader, searching his mind for who else might be available to help them.

Chapter Nine

Saturday afternoon Becky changed her dress four times. Each one was identical, just a different color, but she couldn't choose between the dark blue, green, brown, or maroon. In the end, she wore the pine green dress with a black apron. She shined her black leather shoes as best she could and slipped a tube of lip gloss in her apron pocket. Even though makeup was forbidden, most of the girls her age wore lip gloss. Unless they were baptized or married.

Becky hadn't really had much of a *rumschpringe*, so she figured a little lip gloss was okay. She'd found some at the market in Bird-In-Hand last week. She'd also splurged on a bottle of perfume, and as she sprayed herself, she hoped her parents wouldn't notice. *Mamm* probably wouldn't say anything, but her father might. *Daed* already seemed a little uptight about her going out with Matt.

Her mother said that was normal for a first date. "*Daed* will lighten up," she'd said. "He just knows that you'll be leaving us someday, and he wants you to choose wisely."

There was no doubt in Becky's mind that Matt was the right man for her. She'd known it for years, but the dream of being with him had seemed so far out of reach until lately. She pulled her mirror from the drawer of the nightstand, gave herself a final look, and decided to wait to put on the lip gloss. No need to get her father all worked up.

But he'd be plenty worked up if he knew the truth—that all she'd been able to think about was Matt kissing her tonight.

She hoped.

"You look very nice," *Mamm* said when Becky walked into the living room.

Her father sat up and sniffed the air. "What's that smell?"

"It's all right, dear. She's in her *rumschpringe*," her mother said before Becky had a chance to answer.

Daed shook his head but went back to working his crossword puzzle.

Becky sat down in the rocking chair opposite the couch so she could see Matt pull in. She pushed against the wooden floor with her shoes and rocked nervously.

Her pulse quickened when she spotted a buggy coming up the driveway.

"Sounds like your date is pulling in," *Mamm* said.

Becky swallowed hard and stood up. "Do you want him to come to the door, *Daed*, or is it okay for me to go meet him at the buggy?"

"I know Matt well enough." He sighed. "You go ahead, but be home by nine."

"*Ya*, I will." Becky darted out the door, then forced herself into a slow stroll across the yard, holding her head high. She was a different person now. Thinner. More confident. It was time she started acting like it.

She wished she'd put the lip gloss on, but as she fondled it in her apron pocket, she knew she could find a time later.

Matt got out and walked around to the passenger side. He offered her his hand and helped her into the open buggy.

Courting buggy, she thought. Just the idea filled her with warmth.

"You look pretty," he said, smiling.

"*Danki.*"

"Where would you like to eat?" Matt flicked the reins as they went down the driveway toward Lincoln Highway. "Somewhere in Paradise? Or we can go to Bird-In-Hand. I'm *gut* with anything."

Becky turned to face him. "You pick." Visions of her supper with Elam danced through her head again. She didn't feel the same way about Elam as she did about Matt. But she did miss him.

"Does pizza sound *gut?*"

She wanted to tell him no, that the pizzeria had been hers and Elam's special place, but she nodded. "That sounds fine."

Matt crinkled his nose. "You, uh . . . you smell different."

It was not the reaction she'd been hoping for.

～

Matt waited for Becky to sit down before he eased into a chair across from her. He had wanted to go out with her for a long time. She intrigued him, and the fact that she'd never seemed interested in him made her all the more alluring.

He'd dated other girls, but it never lasted. They were all worried about how they looked on the outside, and Matt usually didn't find them nearly as pretty on the inside—or they just ended up not being compatible with each other.

He had spent enough time with Becky recently to have high hopes that maybe she was the one for him. Her kind spirit and gentle ways had always appealed to him. But until she lost weight, she wouldn't even talk to him. Maybe she'd been self-conscious about her size.

Well, she had nothing to be self-conscious about now. She was, he had to admit, absolutely stunning sitting across from him, and he struggled to keep his eyes from her full lips. He'd been counting down the hours until today, and dreaming about the possibility of kissing her.

I hope I'm her first kiss.

"What kind of pizza do you like?" Matt stared at his menu as he spoke. "I'm starving."

Becky thought about Elam again, and the large pizza they always ordered, with everything except mushrooms and onions. She wasn't planning to eat much anyway. "I'm fine with anything."

Matt closed his menu. When the waitress came back, he ordered a supreme pizza, and they both asked for iced tea. Becky wished she'd brought a sweater. It was cooling down in the evenings, and it was cold inside the restaurant. She briefly glanced at the booth where she and Elam always used to sit.

"You're shivering." Matt turned to the waitress and asked if she might be able to adjust the thermostat.

"Sure." The *Englisch* girl had long blond hair pulled back in a ponytail, big blue eyes, tight blue jeans, and a white blouse that revealed ample cleavage. *And . . . did she just bat her eyes at Matt?*

Becky had never tried on a pair of blue jeans in her life, but since she was in her *rumschpringe*, maybe she needed to start acting like it. She knew plenty of Amish girls who went to movies, out to eat, and other places wearing *Englisch* clothes. Most parents knew their teenagers were enjoying privileges that went along with the running around period, but Becky was pretty sure her father would have a fit if he ever saw her wearing *Englisch* clothes.

"Have you ever been to a movie at the theater?" Becky pulled a slice of hot pizza onto a plate the pretty blond had given her. She tried to choose the one with the least amount of onions and mushrooms.

"*Ya*, twice." Matt took a large bite. "But it was a long time ago. Have you?"

"*Nee.*"

"Do you want to?" Matt finished off his first piece and reached for another one.

"*Ya*. I would. After I'm baptized, I won't be able to, so it seems like I should experience it at least once." She paused, holding her slice of pizza but still not taking a bite. "I haven't really done much in my *rumschpringe*."

"How about next Saturday? We could get an earlier start than we did today and go eat and to a movie." Matt didn't look up as he took another bite. *He meant it when he said he was starving.*

Becky closed her eyes, took a breath, and prayed that if she was dreaming, she'd never wake up. She was getting everything she'd hoped for. Matt was already asking her on a second date, and they'd hardly begun the first one. "I would love that," she finally said.

Matt wiped his mouth with his napkin. "*Ach*, I wanted to let you know that Elam's mother asked if I would be interested in working on their farm some evenings and on Saturdays."

Becky put the slice of pizza down and twisted a corner of her napkin.

"Don't worry. I'm not going to do it. I mean, I'd like to help them out, but I don't think I'm Elam's favorite person right now." He took a sip of tea and helped himself to more pizza. "Thanks to *mei* sisters, word got out pretty fast that we were going out tonight. And since Elam seems to want more than friendship from you— well, I thought it would be best not to take the job."

Becky breathed a sigh of relief, but she hoped that Elam and his mother could find someone to help them. She knew they struggled, and members of the community helped them as much as they could, but the last time she was at the Miller farm, she had noticed that the fence needed repairing and the house could use painting.

She looked around the nearly empty restaurant. A wave of regret filled her heart. "You're probably right about Elam. But it's a shame because I know they could use the help."

"I wouldn't have a problem with it, but now that we're dating, I think Elam would."

Now that we're dating. The words sent a thrill through Becky's veins. She finally took a small bite of her pizza.

Matt scowled at her plate. "You're not eating much."

"*Ach*, I am." She took another bite, then a sip of tea. "I just don't eat near as much as I used to." She paused. "For obvious reasons."

"I love to eat." He chuckled, then turned serious. "Becky, I want you to know that I like the person you are. I always have. Heavy or thin."

"You don't mean that." She didn't want to have this conversation, but the words came out before Becky could stop them, and then she felt the need to explain. "I mean, I don't think you would have asked me out when I was so big before."

"You don't have a very *gut* memory," Matt said. "I asked you if you wanted to go to the singing with me before you lost any weight."

"*Nee*, you just asked if I was going." Becky avoided his eyes and desperately tried to think of a way to change the subject. She didn't like to think about how things were before.

Matt chuckled. "I kind of botched it up, I guess. I was *trying* to ask you to go with me, but I'd been wanting to get to know you for a long time, and you just wouldn't have any part of it." He paused, frowning. "Why'd you change your mind?"

Becky swallowed a small bite of pizza, trying to avoid a small mushroom. "I didn't think . . . you know . . . that you were interested back then." She smiled, hoping to change the subject. "I love black olives. I could put them on everything."

"Well, I *was* interested, back then." Matt reached across the table to still her fidgety fingers. "But we're here together now, and that's all that counts. And next weekend we'll go see a movie."

They both asked for another glass of tea, and after the waitress removed the empty pizza pan and both their plates, they settled into a conversation about Marie and John's wedding. The subject changed to the goats, and then Matt started talking about his favorite foods. Becky wished she had eaten more pizza.

"Elizabeth is only seventeen, but she is the best cook at our *haus*." Matt laughed. "But I'd never tell *Mamm* that. Lizzie just took to it at an early age. She makes the best *yummasetti* I've ever tasted."

Becky used to love to make *yummasetti*. But now that she thought about it, she realized she hadn't been cooking as much lately— something she used to enjoy almost as much as eating. She helped her mother out in the kitchen, but *Mamm* had been making the main meals, and Becky had settled into a routine of setting the table and handling cleanup with Lena. Even when she was at the bakery, she would find other things to do that didn't involve the actual baking.

"What's different about the way Elizabeth makes *yummasetti*?"

Matt shrugged. "I have no idea, but I hope that when I get married she'll show *mei fraa* exactly how she does it." He picked up the bill from the table. "Whoever I marry is going to have to love to cook and eat."

Becky swallowed hard. *Eating would mean getting fat again.* As soon as she had the thought she realized that she was placing herself in the role of Matt's wife, and no matter how blessed she'd been, having such a thought on their first real date seemed far-fetched. Would their relationship really get that far?

"So, what's your favorite food?" Matt said. "When you eat, that is."

"I *do* eat." Becky tapped her finger to her chin as she recalled all the specialties she used to cook for her family. "I had lots of favorites."

"You say that like you don't anymore." Matt raised an eyebrow.

"I stay away from some foods that I used to love because—well, I wanted to lose weight." She paused. "But I do miss the cinnamon rolls we make at the bakery. I miss pancakes, snickerdoodles, buttered noodles, Shoofly pie, *Mamm's* brownies, spaghetti, meat loaf, meat pies, potato salad, chicken and dumplings. Oh, and a dessert called church windows that I used to love to make—" She realized what she was doing and clamped her mouth shut.

Matt's mouth hung open. "What *do* you eat?"

Becky shrugged. "Lots of stuff." A tiny lie.

"Butter bread?"

Becky shook her head. "*Nee.* And I think I miss that most of all."

Matt stared at her long and hard. "So why do it?"

"Because I don't want to be fat."

"You were never that big, and I thought you looked great."

Becky sighed, wondering how they got back into this conversation again. "That's sweet of you to say, but I was miserable. When we were young, you must have heard people talking about the fat girl."

Matt looked down for a moment, then back up at her. "*Ya*, I did. But I never paid attention to it. I always thought you were pretty, and I wanted to ask you out way before this dieting you started."

"It's hard for me to believe that," she said. "Anyway, it doesn't matter. I really enjoyed the pizza and the conversation."

Except for the parts about weight and food.

~

Becky was the first girl Matt had ever really connected with. And that made him hopeful about his future. But this obsession she had with food was worrisome. She was giving up a lot to make herself look good, and that was a reflection of vanity and pride. He had broken up with several girls over this very issue.

The truth was he wanted to be around someone who enjoyed food as much as he did, not a girl who just picked at whatever was on her plate because she didn't want to gain weight. Maybe it was

just hard for him to understand because he had always eaten anything he wanted without having to worry about it. He knew girls
didn't like to be fat, but Becky had so much more going for her than
she realized. He wondered if this new physical transformation had
changed what was inside as well. He hoped not.

On the way back, Becky was shivering. He motioned for her to
scoot closer to him, and when she did, he put his arm around her.
She didn't smell the same—that fragrance of her *mamm's* homemade
lavender soap she had told him about. Instead, she had an unnatu-
ral, perfumed scent. Like . . .

Like an *Englischer.*

They were mostly quiet on the way home. Matt tried to ignore
the perfume and concentrate on one thing: kissing Becky good night.

Chapter Ten

Becky held her breath as Matt's arms encircled her, one hand in the small of her back. She hoped her father wasn't watching out the window, but she was willing to chance it. Her first kiss was moments away, and she'd waited a long time. *I hope I do it right.*

"I had a really *gut* time," he whispered. His lips came down to press against her forehead. He towered over her, but she could feel his uneven breathing as he pulled her closer, and she buried her face against the muscles of his chest.

"I had a *gut* time too," she managed to whisper.

He eased her away, and his large hands gently cupped her face as he leaned closer to her. He moved his mouth over hers, and as she parted her lips, her stomach flew into a wild swirl. A heady sensation filled her from head to toe, but there was an awkwardness she was willing to blame on her inexperience. Matt's mouth slowly left hers, and he brushed a soft kiss against her cheek.

"I'll try to stop by the bakery this week, but if I'm not able, I'll see you next Saturday." He smiled and touched a tendril of hair that had escaped onto her cheek. "One o'clock okay?"

She nodded, afraid to speak, afraid of what she might say. Instead, she watched him drive away, touched her lips with her hand, and wondered what she had done to deserve such a miracle.

Thank You, God.

~

Matt stopped in at the bakery every day the following week. Sometimes he came in the morning to get muffins for him and his father. Other days he came late in the afternoon and drove Becky home from work. Every time he kissed her before he pulled away. She felt like she was getting better at it.

And today they were going to the movies. She continued to thank God every day for His blessings but tried not to think about her life before she lost her weight. Things were so different then.

She sat on her bed and retrieved the stash she kept hidden in her nightstand drawer. She lacquered her nails with a clear coat of shiny polish, and once they were dry, she plucked a few stray eyebrows. She held the mirror close and inspected, pleased with the way they made her eyes look larger.

She pulled out the makeup she had bought earlier in the week and brushed on a light rose-colored blush, then dabbed her lips with a soft pink color. A tiny bit of mascara, a splash of perfume, and she was done. She'd never felt so pretty before, and the man of her dreams was coming to pick her up soon.

Without warning, her bedroom door flew open.

"Ruben! I've told you to knock." She tossed everything back into the bag and slammed it into the drawer. Her brother sidled closer and peered at her.

"What's on your face?" he said. "Makeup? *Mamm* and *Daed* are never going to let you out of the *haus* like that."

Becky sat taller on the bed. "I'm in my *rumschpringe*, you know that. You'll be there in a couple of years."

Ruben folded his arms across his chest. "You're doing all this for your new boyfriend." He rolled his eyes.

Becky sighed. "Ruben, what do you want?"

"Guess that's why you lost all that weight—so you could get a boyfriend." He cocked his head to one side. "I hope he's worth it."

"*Ach*, he is. Now, what do you want?" She stood up, walked to her dresser, and pulled out a thin silver bracelet she'd bought several months ago but never worn. As she slipped it on her wrist, she looked up at Ruben and raised an eyebrow.

"Matt's here. In a car."

Becky thought for a moment. "We're going to the movies and to eat," she said. "Too far to take the buggy." She glanced down at her dark blue dress and black apron, wishing she was wearing blue jeans and a nice shirt. Maybe next time.

She brushed past her brother and hurried down the stairs. Matt was talking with her parents when she hit the landing. Her father scowled the moment he saw her, and Becky knew it was because of the makeup, even though she'd been careful to only apply a little bit.

"Ready?" Matt said. He turned to her father. "I'll have Becky back before dark."

Daed stroked his beard as he looked at the clock above the mantel. "That's a long day. What do you have planned?"

Becky held her breath. "To a movie, and then to eat," Matt said.

Daed frowned but nodded. "Choose the movie wisely," he told Matt as he shook his hand.

When they got to the black car, Matt opened the back door so Becky could get in, then he walked around the other side and slid in beside her.

"This is Mr. Hensley," he said as he nodded to the driver.

An older man with gray hair and a matching beard smiled at her from the driver's seat. "And where are you two kids off to today?"

"Lancaster," Matt said. He reached for Becky's hand and squeezed. "To the theater."

"Okay then. Off we go."

Becky had seen Mr. Hensley before. He offered rides to members of their district, and he didn't charge very much. His wife had died a few years ago, and he said he enjoyed the company. He did most of the talking on the way to the movie theater, and Becky was thankful for that.

"I'm going to do some shopping, then I'll be parked over there by the time the movie is done." Mr. Hensley pointed to his left.

~

Matt paid for the movie tickets and murmured a quick prayer that there wouldn't be anything on the big screen that would embarrass either of them. He had let Becky choose the movie—a romantic comedy that looked like it should be okay.

They walked straight to the concession stand. "This is the best part of going to the movies—the buttered popcorn and soda."

He tried to concentrate on the menu board, but other thoughts kept getting in the way. How could he find a way to tell her that she didn't need that makeup? Sure, she looked really pretty, in an *Englisch* sort of way, but he thought she was even more beautiful without it. And that perfume! He couldn't stand it. What he wanted to smell was the scent of *her*—lavender soap and fresh air and grass.

He pushed the thought away. "What do you want?"

"*Ach*, I just ate before we came. I don't need anything but a diet soda."

Matt forced a smile. Movie popcorn wasn't nearly as much fun if you didn't share it. But he wasn't about to argue with her. "Okay." He ordered her drink and a buttered popcorn and large Coke for himself.

"Everyone must want to see this movie," he whispered as they searched for a seat in the full theater. He was excited for Becky to get to see her first movie. "How about here?" They slid past two *Englisch* girls and sat down. It was a little too close to the screen for Matt, but there weren't many seats available.

As much as he wanted to put his arm around Becky, public affection was frowned upon, so he just reached for her hand instead.

They both laughed through much of the movie, and Matt loved watching her reactions. He could have done without some of the language the characters used, but overall it was a funny movie without anything too embarrassing.

"Well?" he asked as they walked to where Mr. Hensley was parked after the movie.

Becky's face lit up with a smile. "I loved it! *Danki* so much for taking me. My favorite part was when she walked into the *haus* and he'd filled the living room with yellow roses."

"*Ach*, a romantic, *ya*?" He opened the car door for her.

"I guess so." She blushed as she reached down and fumbled with the silver bracelet she was wearing.

Mr. Hensley backed the car out of the parking space. "Where to now?"

Matt turned to Becky. "What are you in the mood for?" Inside, he silently begged, *Please don't tell me you're not hungry.*

"Anything is fine with me."

Matt took off his hat and put it in his lap, scratched the top of his head. "How about a burger?"

"Sure." She gave him a dazzling smile.

But when they got to the restaurant Mr. Hensley suggested, all Becky ordered was a small dinner salad.

"That's all? Mr. Hensley said they have great burgers here."

The waitress tapped her pen to the pad, waiting, but Becky nodded. "*Ya*, I'm sure. That's plenty for me."

Matt glanced at the clock on the wall. "By the time we get done here, there will still be lots of daylight left. I could have Mr. Hensley drop us at my *haus*, then we could take the buggy to the creek. I could still have you home by dark." He paused. "Unless you think it will be too cold."

"It's not too cold," she said, "but it's really windy."

A pretty noncommittal answer, he thought. He tried again. "We can take the covered buggy."

She nodded and took a bite of her salad. Matt couldn't tell if she really wanted to go or not, but he figured they could at least give it a try.

~

Becky hadn't been to the creek since the day she'd asked God for a miracle almost three months ago. As Matt slowed the buggy near a poplar tree where everyone tethered their horses, she thought about how much her life had changed. She was no longer the fat girl that people made fun of. Matt liked her. Everything was perfect.

Everything except Elam.

She hadn't seen or heard from him in ages. She hoped he was okay.

She walked with Matt to the water's edge and came at last to the spot where she had stood that day. Her stomach clenched with anxiety as she looked down at the creek. The water level was low, not rushing and wild as it had been before. She had been so desperate that day, desperate enough to consider—

She pushed the memory away. "Do you know if the Millers found someone to help out on their farm?" she asked Matt.

"*Ya*, I heard that Bennie Stoltzfus was helping them out."

"Mary's *bruder*?"

"*Ya.*" Matt picked up a rock and skimmed it across the creek.

"Elam thought you and Mary were dating." Becky held her breath, fearful of the answer. Mary was so pretty, and Becky felt like she had to work so hard at it.

Matt shook his head. "*Nee.* She's not my type." He tossed another rock out into the current, although this one didn't skim the top like the other one.

Becky pulled her sweater tighter and sat down on a fallen log. He sat down next to her and put his arm around her. "Cold?"

"*Nee.* Not too much."

"This is my favorite spot at the creek." Matt leaned over and kissed her gently. "And I'm glad to be here with you."

"I'm glad to be with you too," Becky said. But the truth was, she wished she were somewhere else. Anywhere else.

What on earth was the matter with her? Here she was, on a date with the handsomest man in the district. He had his arm around her. He was kissing her.

God had answered her prayer. Made her thin. Given her the miracle she'd always wanted.

So why did everything feel so wrong?

Chapter Eleven

Becky arrived at Marie King's Tupperware party with her mother the Saturday before Marie and John's wedding. The groom's mother, Esther, was hosting the party. As was customary, the attendees would purchase items, and the hostess would earn points, all of which would be given to the bride-to-be to make selections.

Becky was standing in a corner in the living room when the guest of honor walked in. She made a beeline across the room. "So, will there be another wedding in our future?" Marie said. She grinned and raised an eyebrow.

"Rosa and Adam's in a few weeks." Becky paused. "That's all I know of."

Marie inched closer. "*Nee*, I meant you and *mei bruder*. Are you and Matt moving in that direction?"

Becky lowered her eyes. "We've only been dating a couple of . . . a little while."

"Matt seems very happy. I wouldn't be surprised if we end up sisters-in-law."

Becky couldn't think of anything in the world she wanted more.

"Guess we'll see." Marie winked at her before she eased away to mingle with her guests, and Becky felt warm all over. If things should move in that direction, apparently she would have Matt's family's blessing. She went to join her *mamm* and Hope Bowman.

"There's lots of delicious food in the kitchen." Hope was carrying a small plate filled with appetizers. "You have to try Rosa's pineapple pecan cake." She pointed to a square on her plate. "I could probably eat the entire cake, it's so *gut*."

For the first time in a very long time, Becky's mouth watered as she eyed Hope's plate.

She took a deep breath and lifted her chin a bit higher. She could beat these temptations. "I don't eat things like that anymore," she said.

Hope stopped chewing for a moment and glanced at Becky's mother.

"She's taken this diet thing too far," *Mamm* said with a shrug. She scowled at Becky.

Becky stiffened and glared at her mother. "I've worked very hard to look like this."

The moment the words slipped out of her mouth, she regretted them. She sounded vain and snobby and condescending. And she was pretty sure her comment to Hope about the pineapple cake came across that way as well. Neither Hope nor her mother responded, but her mother's expression was one of pure disgust.

"I—I'm going to browse the items displayed on the table. *Gut* to see you, Becky." Hope eased away toward the long table on the far side of the living room where the Tupperware items were available for viewing.

"This is not how I raised you, Becky." *Mamm* spoke in a loud whisper as she folded her arms across her chest. "I'm glad you feel better about yourself. I really am. But enough is enough. You've lost plenty of weight, but pride and vanity have slipped in under your skin. Remember where beauty lies, *mei dochder*—in the eye of the beholder. And we have but one real Beholder, so keep that in mind."

Becky felt the sting of her mother's words. "I didn't mean it like it sounded."

Mamm sighed. "Just don't let outer beauty interfere with the inner beauty that has always made you special." She gave Becky a pat on the arm and moved toward the table.

Becky glanced around the room. Small groups of girls were clustered in different areas. She wasn't part of any of the cliques that had naturally formed over the years, and it occurred to her that rather than isolating herself, perhaps she should have made more of an attempt to fit in.

But now things were different. She was no longer the outcast. She was thin. She had Matt. She belonged.

She made her way across the room to where Mary Stoltzfus and two other girls were gathered. As soon as she entered their circle, everyone went quiet.

"It's a great turnout for the party." She forced a smile.

Two of the girls nodded, but Mary avoided eye contact with Becky. "Excuse me. I'm going to go help Esther in the kitchen." She ducked out of the circle and hurried off.

Maybe she had waited too long to try to be better friends with some of the girls. Or maybe Mary was just jealous because of her relationship with Matt. Either way, she wasn't about to give up.

She stuffed her hands in the pockets of her apron, since she was the only one not toting a plate of food. "Hannah, how are things going with James?"

Hannah was a year younger than Becky, but the rumor was circulating that she and Hope's son, James, were sweet on each other. And while gossip was frowned upon, Becky was determined to do whatever was necessary to be a part of the inner circle.

Hannah swallowed, then blushed. *"Gut."*

"I'm dating Matt King," Becky said.

"Uh, *ya* . . . we heard." Hannah glanced at Naomi, then both girls were quiet as they snacked on appetizers.

"We went to see a really *gut* movie recently." Becky took her hands from her pockets and folded them in front of her. "Matt hired a driver, and we went to Lancaster."

Hannah nodded. "I'm going to go get some more food." She eased away, leaving just Becky and Naomi, but Naomi said she needed a refill and followed Hannah.

Becky searched the room for her mother. In the past, being separated from the groups hadn't bothered her. But now she was one of them—thin, dating, and with common interests. She expected them to be more accepting.

She finally located *Mamm*, but she was deep in conversation with several other women, so Becky made her way to the table of displayed items. Hannah and Naomi had returned with plates of food, and they were browsing as well, slightly ahead of Becky and with their backs to her.

"The only reason Matt is dating Becky is because she's thin now," Naomi said, still loud enough that Becky heard.

"I liked the old Becky better," Hannah said. "She was kind of quiet, but she wasn't so prideful. Now that she's lost all this weight, she seems to think she's better than the rest of us."

Becky felt a knot form in her throat. *That's not true. I just want to be like the rest of you.*

She wanted to defend herself, to tell Hannah and Naomi that God had granted her a miracle, and that they were going against the Lord by condemning her weight loss, but she just stood there listening.

"I used to think she was dating Elam, but obviously that's not the case." Hannah still had her back to Becky as she picked up a yellow Tupperware bowl. "Or if they were dating, he must have dumped her."

"Too bad for her," Naomi said. "He's a catch, that Elam."

⁓

Elam got Bennie started on the back fence, then went to the barn to repair the door that was about to fall off its hinges. He whistled as he worked, feeling better than he had felt in a long time. He missed Becky, and he prayed for her every day. He kept hearing how much she'd changed, and that saddened him. Becky had always had the spirit of an angel, and he wondered if Matt King had stripped her of that. But Elam was missing her less and less each day as other things occupied his mind.

He finished installing a new hinge on the door just as his mother came out of the house. "I brought you a jacket." She handed him his black coat. "I can feel the cold front blowing in, and I thought you might want this."

"*Danki.*" Elam slipped the coat on as the cool October air rushed through the barn windows and door. "It is getting colder."

"I hope Bennie is warm enough out there." *Mamm* nodded to where he was working on the fence.

Elam held a hand up and squinted into the setting sun. "*Ya,* I think he's okay. He's got a coat on."

"All right, then." *Mamm* inspected the barn door and nodded in approval. "Be sure to round up Bennie at five, and you boys get cleaned up. Don't be late. We're having company for supper."

Bennie's work on the farm had been a blessing over the past few weeks, and Elam could see things coming together around the place. But the best part of Bennie working for them had nothing to do with home improvements.

Becky lay in bed awake, glancing at her clock every half hour. Sleep wasn't going to come easily tonight. She rolled onto her left side, then the right, then back again. Finally, she kicked the covers off and sat up.

Her mind was swirling with the events of the day, and her hurt feelings weren't improving. To make matters worse, she hadn't heard from or seen Matt in three days.

She lit the lantern beside her bed, pulled the drawer of her nightstand open, and pulled out her cell phone. Her parents knew she had it, even though she rarely used it. One more leniency that would be lost when she completed her *rumschpringe.*

Most people her age had a mobile phone, and many of the older folks did too. It was something the bishop didn't encourage, but he tended to overlook it. She turned the phone on and waited, thinking about who she would call.

Part of her wanted to call Matt, but it was eleven o'clock, and he'd mentioned more than once how he went to bed at nine. She recalled the late-night phone calls she used to have with Elam. He always kept his phone on.

What would she say to him? *I'm sorry we haven't seen each other. I'm sorry that we can't still be friends now that I'm with Matt.*

He answered in a whisper on the first ring. "Becky, it's late. Are you okay?"

She fought back the urge to cry. It was so good to hear Elam's voice. "*Ya.* Are you okay?"

"I'm fine. Something must be wrong if you're calling this late."

"I—I miss you. I miss talking to you."

Several seconds went by before Elam answered. "I miss you too."

They were both quiet again, then Becky asked, "Do you think I've changed?"

"I don't know." Elam sighed. "I haven't been around you recently, or even talked to you. Do you think you've changed?"

"*Nee.* I don't think so." She lay back down on the bed and covered her eyes with one hand. "I don't know. I shouldn't have called."

She heard another sigh on the other end of the line.

"Did I wake you up?"

"*Ya,* but that's okay." He cleared his throat. "Shouldn't you be calling Matt if you want to talk this late at night?" There was an edge to his voice that Becky should have foreseen.

"I guess so. I'll let you go." She sat up and swiped a tear from her face.

"*Nee*, wait. I'm sorry, Becky. I shouldn't have said that. I'll always be glad to hear from you, no matter what you're doing or who you're seeing. We were friends a long time before things got weird."

"I'm just—" She sniffled. "Just feeling badly. About myself."

"And why is that?"

She waited a few moments before she answered. "I asked God for a miracle, Elam. I asked Him to make me thin. And He did. He truly granted me a miracle. But now I'm wondering if I have acted the right way about it all. I'm just confused."

"I'm not sure what to tell you, Becky. Like I said, I haven't really heard from you, and we've barely said hello after worship services. If you feel like you've changed, maybe you need to do something about it."

She flinched at the harsh comment. "You don't seem the same, Elam."

"What do you mean?"

She paused. "I don't know. You just sound different." She was expecting more excitement from him. She'd figured he would be elated that she called. That didn't seem to be the case.

"You're with Matt now. I don't know if *you're* different, but things between us are." He sighed. "I hope you feel better, Becky. I'm glad you got what you wanted. I'll always wish you well. You know that."

"That sounds like good-bye forever." Another tear slid down her cheek.

"Take care, Becky. Good night."

Becky hung up and tossed the phone back into the drawer. Elam was the one person she thought would always love her, the one person she could be honest with. But he was different now. He didn't grovel or beg her for a visit. He didn't ask when he'd see her or talk to her again. Nothing.

She wished she could talk to Matt, be honest with him about how she was hurting. She wanted to tell him about the girls at the party and how they had hurt her feelings. She wanted to tell him how she missed Elam. But she didn't want him to think less of her.

She picked up the lantern and put her slippers on, then tiptoed downstairs to the kitchen. The cookie jar was filled to the rim with snickerdoodles, Ruben's favorite. She hesitated. Once she dove in, there would be no turning back. She'd get fat again. God would be disappointed in her. And she wouldn't have Elam's friendship or Matt's love.

She pried open the lid of the jar and stuffed an entire cookie into her mouth.

Then ate the rest.

Chapter Twelve

Matt got out of the house as fast as he could Saturday morning. With only a week left until Marie and John's wedding, everyone and everything was in chaos. He'd only seen Becky once in the past week, when he'd stopped in at the bakery. His parents had been keeping him busy in preparation for the wedding. There was a crazy amount of cleaning going on inside and outside the house, and Marie was so wound up that she was giving Matt a nervous stomach and a headache.

He couldn't wait to see Becky.

They'd made plans to spend the day together, and as he pulled into her driveway, he was thinking of things she might want to do. He picked up the bouquet of yellow roses and walked to the door. Becky's mother answered. "Those are lovely, Matt." Sarah smiled and motioned for Matt to come in. "I'll go get Becky."

Even with her baggy dress on, Matt could tell that she'd gained weight. *Thank goodness.* He worried she might be getting too thin, but her face was filling out again, the way it used to be when she had cute round cheeks and great dimples.

"*Danki.*" She took the roses, barely smiling.

Hmm . . . He had expected more of a reaction, since this was the first time he'd given her flowers.

"Yellow roses," he prodded. "Remember? You said that was your favorite part of the movie—when the guy filled the girl's living room with yellow roses."

"Right," she said.

They drove up the road a ways. "So," Matt said, "what would you like to do?"

"It's up to you."

They were quiet for a while. "Are you okay?"

"*Ya*, I'm fine."

Matt slowed the buggy and pulled to one side of the road as a car passed them much too close. Dark clouds hovering overhead were threatening rain.

"*Danki* again for the roses," she said once more after a while.

"You're welcome." He paused, turned toward her. "Are you sure you're okay?"

She nodded. "*Ya.*"

"It's too cold to go to the creek. Do you want to go to the diner and get some *kaffi*?" Matt figured he could at least get a cinnamon roll or something.

"Okay. That sounds *gut.*"

Matt pulled into a diner off one of the back roads, a place the *Englisch* tourists didn't visit much. There was only one elderly Amish couple in the back, and he and Becky picked a booth on the other side. They'd barely gotten seated next to a window when it started to pour.

"I thought that might be coming." Matt ordered a cinnamon roll and a cup of coffee, and much to his surprise, Becky ordered the same thing.

"I'm glad to see you eating again." Matt leaned back and put his hat on the seat beside him.

Becky shrugged. "I'll probably get fat again."

"I doubt one cinnamon roll will do that. And besides, I told you . . . I like you no matter your size."

I like you. Puny words for what he had been feeling, but he hadn't had the nerve to say anything more. He knew that once he said *I love you*, he was locked in. He needed to be sure.

Her eating habits bothered him, but maybe this was a good sign, the cinnamon roll. She was still wearing a little makeup and that awful perfume. He could live with the makeup if he had to but wished she'd go back to her homemade soaps and get rid of the perfume.

He waited until they had both finished their rolls and were sipping coffee, then reached over and grabbed her hand. He took a quick peek at the elderly couple, but they were busy eating and not paying any attention to Becky and Matt.

"Becky, there's something I've been wanting to tell you." Matt swallowed hard. He'd come close to telling a girl he loved her twice before, but the relationships hadn't worked out, so it was just as well.

Maybe he fell in love too easily. Maybe he should take more time. Maybe—

"I love you," he blurted out.

Becky stared across the table. The man of her dreams. The one person she'd always wanted to love her. The catch of the town. Matt King. Handsome and kind, loving and sincere.

"I love you," he said. This was her moment, the one she'd wished for, longed for, prayed for. She waited for the warm and tingly feeling to consume her, for her heart to start pounding so hard she wouldn't be able to breathe.

Matt was waiting too. Waiting for her to respond.

"Becky?" he said softly.

Tell him how much you love him. Open your mouth. Tell him. But she couldn't move or speak. The only person on her mind was Elam, and she couldn't figure out why. She'd always loved Elam—like a brother. But hearing his voice last night, and looking at Matt right now—

She hadn't just been missing Elam. She'd been missing *them*, the way things used to be between them. Maybe she'd always thought Elam would be there waiting for her. As unfair as it might seem, maybe she'd held on to him as a backup in case things didn't work out with Matt.

But last night she had dreamed of what it would be like with Elam. Not Matt.

What it would be like to kiss Elam . . .

"Becky?" Matt let go of her hand. "Do you have anything to say?"

She swallowed hard. She had hurt Elam, and now she was going to hurt Matt as well. "I'm sorry."

Matt's expression shifted. "Are you kidding me? Really?"

"I—I said I'm sorry. I just . . . it's just not the right time. I'm confused, and I—"

"You don't have to tell me. I think I've already figured it out." Matt lowered his head, then looked back up at her. "Just forget I said anything."

Becky gazed across the table at this wonderful, handsome man whom she'd dreamed of being with for years.

Then she told him the truth.

It was raining and almost dark when Becky ran up the porch steps at Elam's house. She felt awful about Matt. He hadn't taken her news very well, but the more pressing issue was telling Elam that she loved him. That she'd always loved him, and that she wanted to spend the rest of her life with him. Fat or thin, good times or bad, better or worse. It was Elam she wanted.

Maybe it took a romantic interest in someone else to show her what true love was. It was all very confusing, but she knew—beyond any doubts—that Elam was the one for her.

Elam's mother opened the door. "Goodness, Becky. What in the world are you doing out in this weather?" She latched onto Becky's arm and gently eased her into the house. "Let me get you a towel, you're soaking wet."

Becky stood dripping on the hardwood floors in the living room until Eve came back with a towel and draped it around Becky's shoulders.

Eve motioned for Becky to move near the fireplace. "Warm yourself, child. You're shivering." She laid another log on the fire, and red sparks shimmied upward. "I'm guessing you're here to see Elam. I'll go get him."

A minute later Elam came downstairs alone. "What are you doing here?"

Becky hung back for only a moment. Then she flung the towel aside and ran to his arms. "I love you, Elam. I've always loved you." She leaned back and swiped at her tears. "I don't know what has been going on with me. I feel like a crazy person." She looked up at him. "But I know I love you. You're the one."

Elam gently guided her away and held her at arm's length. "Becky, did you and Matt have a fight or something?"

She shook her head. "*Nee*. But I broke up with him."

Elam was still holding her at arm's length, his eyes wide. "When?"

"Today. Just a little while ago. He told me he loved me, and—" She tried to move closer, but Elam was still holding her at a distance. "And I realized that Matt is great. He really is. But it's you, Elam. You're the one. I miss you so much it hurts. You're the one I want to hold me, to kiss me. I want to be with you, and I'm so sorry that I needed to test the waters before I realized this. I love you, Elam. I love you so much."

She broke free of his hold, wrapped her arms around him, and buried her head in his chest. "I want us to love each other for the rest of our lives."

"Becky . . ."

She held on, waiting. Waiting for him to say *I love you too.* Waiting for him to lean down and kiss her.

"I'm seeing Mary Stoltzfus, and I have been for a while."

Chapter Thirteen

Becky dressed for Marie and John's wedding and wished more than ever that she didn't have to go. She wasn't sure what was going to be worse—having to face Matt or having to see Elam with Mary.

"Time to go!" Lena burst through Becky's bedroom door. Why couldn't anyone ever knock?

"I'm coming. I'll be there in a minute." She waved an arm toward Lena. "Go. I just have to get my *kapp* on."

Lena had decided she wanted to be Amish again. Becky was happy about that, of course. Sometimes she wished she could be young and carefree like Lena. Waking up in a new world every day, as *Mamm* put it, free to make decisions based on a whim. But reality had knocked on Becky's door, and there was no going back.

As Lena scurried out, Becky pulled her hair into a tight bun and put on her prayer *kapp*. She'd missed breakfast this morning, and her stomach growled. Well, let it. Ever since the breakup with Matt and Elam's rejection, she had been using food as a crutch. She had let everyone down. Matt. Elam. Even God.

Regret settled over her like a thick fog. She should have held on to Elam, and now she'd lost him to Mary. And Matt was so handsome and so kind, yet she couldn't return his love the way he deserved.

Ach, Elam. I messed everything up.

"Becky." *Mamm* walked into the room and put her hands on her hips. "What are you doing? We need to leave. Didn't Lena tell you?"

Becky hung her head and fought the tears building in the corners of her eyes. Her mother sat down on the bed beside her. "What is it, dear? What's wrong?"

She gazed up at her mother for a while before she spoke. "I asked God for a miracle, *Mamm*. I asked Him to make me pretty and thin." She paused, swallowed hard. "And He did." She swiped at her eyes. "Then He put Matt in my life, and everything should have been perfect."

"And it's not?"

Becky shook her head. "*Nee.* I've made a mess of things."

Mamm reached for Becky's hand and clutched it in her own. "Maybe the miracle you're referring to has nothing to do with dieting or food or weight. Sometimes when we pray, the Lord sees fit to answer our prayers in a way we can't foresee."

"I don't care about being thin anymore. I worked so hard to lose weight, to be pretty . . . and now I've lost the one person I've always loved. I pushed Elam aside because I thought I wanted Matt. And now Elam is no longer available." She pulled her hand from her mother's and covered her face.

"Now, now." *Mamm* put an arm around her shoulders. "There's your miracle, Becky. God answered your prayer, just not the way you expected Him to. He's given you the wisdom to know that it's what's inside that counts."

Becky raised her head and blinked her eyes a few times. "But now I have no one."

"It's a hard lesson to learn, I'm sure. Most of the really important lessons are. But there is someone for you. You'll see."

There is no one for me but Elam. How could I have not seen that?

~

Matt helped his father and the other men set up chairs in the living room. Since before daybreak there had been a bustle of activity in preparation for the wedding. The aroma of roast turkey filled the air. Propane heaters were warming the house, and late yesterday afternoon Matt and his father had moved the living room furniture to the barn to make room for benches and chairs. They were fortunate to have a large living room, but there were still chairs set up in the dining room, downstairs bedroom, and mud room.

Matt kept his mind occupied and tried not to think about Becky. Surprisingly, it didn't take as much effort as he'd thought it would. His ego was more bruised than his heart, he supposed. But it was the first time anyone had ever rejected him, and it stung.

They'd just finished getting everything set up when a line of buggies began coming up the road and turning into the driveway. Marie was still upstairs getting ready; she and John would be staying the night here, as was expected of the newly married couple. Tomorrow they would help with cleanup before going to their new home. In some cases the bride and groom stayed with the bride's family for weeks, but John had already built them a fine home not far from here.

Hope Bowman emerged from the crowded kitchen. "Your *mamm* said she'd like you to carry more firewood inside." Matt nodded and went to carry in more logs.

When he got back, he saw Becky across the room. She'd gained some weight back. He thought of how she was before and wondered if it was likely she'd get that fat again. He had always found her intriguing, but that might have been because she paid so little attention to him. Now that he had dated her, she didn't seem quite so interesting. Or at least that was what he kept telling himself, so that her rejection wouldn't bother him so much.

"Wie bischt?" Mary Stoltzfus strolled by with her parents, smiling. "It smells *gut* in here."

Matt had never been out with Mary, which now seemed odd, since most of the community seemed to think they were a perfect match. She'd flirted with him plenty over the years, and she was beautiful—on the outside. But what about on the inside? Too late for him to find out now. He'd been told just yesterday that Mary was seeing Elam Miller.

Becky had confessed that she loved Elam, but apparently the feeling wasn't mutual. Although he wasn't proud of it, he had to admit that the idea pleased him a little. At least she couldn't just reject him and then run into Elam's waiting arms.

As the wedding came to a close, Elam realized that he'd missed much of what the bishop had said, and he'd barely been tuned in for Marie and John's vows. He kept thinking about Becky, and he found himself glancing back and forth between Becky and Mary throughout the ceremony.

He hated the way weddings affected him. He always felt like he was going to cry, so maybe it was best that he hadn't been one hundred percent focused on the exchange of vows. The last thing he needed at the moment was to draw attention to himself with an emotional outburst.

The women were cleaning up after the meal when he finally found Becky sitting by herself on a bench near the garden. Even from a distance he could see that she was shivering. He pulled off his jacket and walked over to her. "Here." Elam draped his coat around her shoulders and sat down beside her.

"Danki," she said in a shaky voice.

"It was a nice ceremony."

Becky nodded. *"Ya,* it was very nice."

She still wouldn't look at him. "And you look very nice," he said.

"I guess you and Mary will be the next ones to get published."

Elam took a deep breath and blew it out slowly. *"Nee."*

Becky nodded. "I guess maybe it is still too soon." She paused. "Rosa and Adam's wedding is in a couple of weeks. I'm so happy for Rosa." Then she finally looked up at him. "Elam. Your eyes."

He smiled and focused both eyes on her beautiful face. "I had the surgery Tuesday."

She leaned closer and looked into his face. "I'm so happy for you. I know how much your eyes bothered you."

Elam glanced around. Everyone had moved inside or gathered in the barn where it was warmer. "Becky—"

"*Ya?*"

"I love you with all my heart. I always have. I always will. There is no one else for me either."

Becky couldn't speak. She could barely believe what she had just heard. "But—but what about Mary?"

"I broke up with her. She always would have been second to you, and I think that deep down she knew that."

"She's so pretty. And nice." Becky couldn't believe that Elam would break up with someone like Mary to be with her. "And thin."

She glanced down. She had been trying hard to eat healthy and not obsess about it, but she had put some of the weight back on. She would never be as naturally thin and beautiful as someone like Mary Stoltzfus.

The left side of Elam's mouth curved up slightly. "*Ya.* Mary is all of those things."

Becky hung her head.

"But she isn't you. And you are the one I want to be with." Elam pushed his new glasses up on his nose. "I'm not as good-looking as Matt, but no one could love you any more than I do."

Becky gazed into Elam's beautiful, sincere eyes, and she didn't think she'd ever seen a handsomer man. "I told you that you have always been the one for me." She paused as a tear rolled down her cheek. "I messed everything up."

"Then let's fix it." Elam reached for her hand, pulled it to his lips, and kissed it. "I love you, Becky Byler."

"I love you too."

Elam leaned over and kissed her on the mouth. The kiss was tender, gentle, and loving, nothing like the way Matt had kissed her. No hesitation. No anxiety. No awkwardness.

As she eased away from the kiss, she nodded toward the porch, where Matt and Mary stood, both laughing and smiling. "I think maybe everyone will be okay," she said.

"God has a way of working things out." Elam tucked an errant strand of hair back into Becky's *kapp*, then kissed her on the lips again. "Becky, my sweet Becky. I love you so much. You have always been beautiful to me, inside and out." He cupped her cheek in the palm of his hand. "*You* are my miracle."

Becky closed her eyes and silently thanked God. "And you," she whispered, "are mine as well."

Reading Group Guide

Always in My Heart

1. Why does Hope still harbor resentment for her father? What kind of difficulties does this create for her mother?
2. James is initially reluctant to feel a part of Hope's family on any level. What are some of the contributing factors to his emotional isolation?
3. Stephen Bowman would consider himself a happy man. Why would he so readily welcome a fifteen-year-old *Englischer* into his life?
4. This story is about forgiveness as much as it is about God working miracles in our lives. Describe the four types of forgiveness illustrated in *Always in My Heart*.

Always His Provision

1. Rosa prays about her finances but continues to fret about what might happen. How is this taking it out of God's hands? Has there been a time when you've continued to stress over a situation you've already prayed about?

2. How did the neighbor's attitude about Rosa's chickens influence her actions? Have you ever thought God might be waiting for your heart to change over a matter so that He can pour out His blessing on you?

3. Even though Rosa had given throughout the years to her district's widows' fund, she didn't want to ask for help when she was in a time of need. Why do you think her pride stood in her way?

Always Beautiful

1. Becky asks God for a miracle, to make her thin and beautiful. So often God answers our prayers, but not in a way that we could have foreseen. Becky got her wish, but what is the real miracle in the story?

2. Elam and Matt are both great guys. Who were you rooting for to win Becky's heart? Did you change your mind throughout the story? What was the turning point for Becky when she finally realized that Elam was the one for her?

3. Exactly how big do you think Becky was—a little overweight, quite heavy, or obese? How did the different characters see Becky? How did she see herself?

4. Do you believe in miracles? If so, have you ever personally experienced one?

Amish Recipes

Snickerdoodles

> 1 cup butter, softened (do not use margarine)
>
> 2 cups sugar
>
> 2 eggs
>
> 1/4 cup milk
>
> 1 tsp. vanilla
>
> 3 3/4 cups flour
>
> 3/4 tsp. baking powder
>
> Cinnamon sugar

Cream together butter and sugar. Add eggs, one at a time, beating well after each addition. Stir in milk and vanilla. Sift together flour and baking powder; then add to creamed mixture.

Roll dough into one-inch balls and roll in cinnamon sugar mixture. Place on ungreased cookie sheet and flatten slightly. Bake at 375 degrees for 10–12 minutes.

WALNUT CHOCOLATE CHIP COOKIES

2 cups butter

2 cups sugar

2 cups brown sugar

4 eggs

4 cups flour

5 cups oatmeal

1 tsp. salt

2 tsp. baking powder

2 tsp. baking soda

Approx. 40 ounces chocolate chips (Can use 2 different varieties, such as milk, dark, mint, or white.)

3 cups chopped walnuts

In mixing bowl, cream together butter, sugar, and brown sugar. Add eggs, one at a time, beating well. In separate bowl, combine flour, oatmeal, salt, baking powder, and baking soda. Mix flour mixture into sugar mixture. Add chocolate chips and nuts.

Roll into one-inch balls. Place on ungreased cookie sheets 2 inches apart. Bake at 375 degrees for 10 minutes.

Makes approximately 9 dozen cookies.

Acknowledgments

Mary Ellis

Thanks to Natalie Hanemann and Becky Philpott at HarperCollins Christian Publishing for helping to bring my story to life. Thanks to my proofreader, Joycelyn Sullivan; my agent, Mary Sue Seymour, for her faith in me; and my husband for his continued patience with very late dinners.

Ruth Reid

I praise God for His provisions! God has blessed me with a wonderful supportive family. Dan, Lexie, Danny, and Sarah, I love you all so very much. God has also blessed me with many prayer warriors who lift me up in prayer and with trustful friends who help critique my books. I especially appreciate Kathy Droste, who bravely reads and red-inks my first drafts. I'll forever be thankful for my outstanding editorial team: Becky Philpott, Natalie Hanemann, and line editor, Penny Stokes.

May God bless the reader in miraculous ways!

Beth Wiseman

It was an honor to be able to work with Ruth Reid and Mary Ellis on this collaboration. You girls rock! ☺

Special thanks to my editors, Natalie Hanemann and Penny Stokes, and to all the great folks at Thomas Nelson.

To my agent, Natasha Kern . . . you continue to amaze me! Glad to have you on board. ☺

Barbie Beiler, I hope to see you soon. Thank you for always being available to answer my questions at a moment's notice.

Thanks to my fabulous assistant, Janet Murphy. I know I can be a handful sometimes, lol.

And to my husband Patrick, friends, and family—thank you all for everything.

God gets all the credit. He lays these stories upon my heart, and for that I am grateful and blessed.

About the Authors

Photo by Christopher Norris

Mary Ellis grew up close to the eastern Ohio Amish community, Geauga County. Before "retiring" to write full-time, Mary taught middle school and worked as a sales rep for Hershey Chocolate. Mary is a CBA and ECPA best-selling author as well as an ACFW Carol Award finalist and runner-up for the 2010 Holt Medallion Award.

Photo by Lexie Reid

Ruth Reid is the CBA and ECPA best-selling author of Heaven on Earth series. She's a full-time pharmacist who lives in Florida with her husband and three children.

Photo by Saxton Creations

Beth Wiseman is hailed as a top voice in Amish fiction. She is a Carol Award winner and author of numerous bestsellers, including the Daughters of the Promise and the Land of Canaan series. She and her family live in Texas.

The garden plays a pivotal role in every Amish
household. Explore the different ways the
garden provides for four different women
in this new collection of Amish novellas
from Beth Wiseman, Kathleen Fuller,
Tricia Goyer, and Vanetta Chapman.

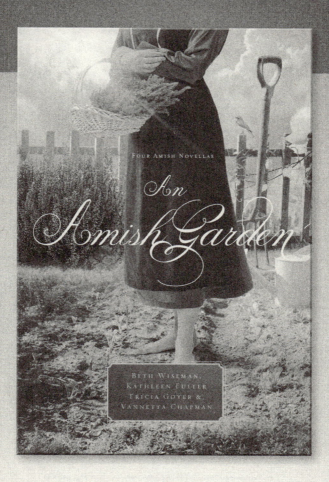

FOUR AMISH NOVELLAS

An Amish Garden

BETH WISEMAN,
KATHLEEN FULLER
TRICIA GOYER &
VANNETTA CHAPMAN

AVAILABLE MARCH 2014